MODERN CONSTRUCTION CASE STUDIES

Emerging Innovation in Building Techniques

Second Edition

ANDREW WATTS

Birkhäuser
Basel

MODERN CONSTRUCTION CASE STUDIES

Since the turn of the 21st century, the linear relationship between architecture/engineering/ construction has been slowly dissolving and interweaving into an entirely new workflow, requiring a new kind of relationship between architect, engineer and construction teams in order to achieve the great built works of our age.

Building design has evolved from hand-drawings, hand-calculations and construction-in-the-field to a new process of digital design, engineering analysis/simulation and digital (BIM) construction models. This is not merely a change in medium from paper to computer. It is an entirely new paradigm.

Building envelopes are no longer the exterior wall of the building. The line between facade, structure, lighting, climate-response and mechanical systems begins to blur and suggest new evolutions. The exterior envelope can evolve to also be the structure – it can be an intelligent membrane that not only separates inside from outside but can also engage it.

DESIGN TO PROTOTYPE

END · 220

COMPLEX GEOMETRY

CONTENTS

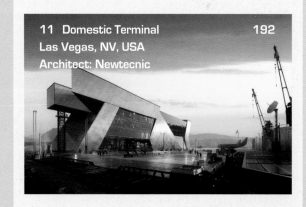

I am writing this introduction as the new edition of 'Modern Construction Case Studies' is about to go to print in April 2019, nearly 20 years into the 21st century. It arrives during a moment of tremendous change in the history of architecture, engineering and construction.

During the 20th century, architecture, engineering and construction were seen as distinct professions – divided into 3 linear steps in the process of making a building:
(20th c.) – Architectural design and documentation.
(20th c.) – Engineering design and documentation.
(20th c.) – Construction.

Since the turn of the 21st century, this linear relationship between architecture/engineering/construction has been slowly dissolving and interweaving into an entirely new workflow, requiring a new kind of relationship between architect, engineer and construction teams in order to achieve the great built works of our age. Building design has evolved from hand-drawings, hand-calculations and construction-in-the-field to a new process of digital design, engineering analysis/simulation and digital (BIM) construction models. This is not merely a change in medium from paper to computer. It is an entirely new paradigm:
(21st c.) – Design/engineering/building a digital version of the building simultaneously.
(21st c.) – Integrated, multi-disciplinary documents for construction.
(21st c.) – Construction.

In this age of digital design and construction, new minds and new mind-sets are emerging. Our new digital tools allow us to explore design forms of greater complexity and simultaneously be informed of the technical issues involved. The result is that as designers, we are able to be more creative, ambitious and intelligent.

Buildings made this way allow for a fully-integrated design that thoroughly considers the architecture, engineering and construction equally from the conceptual stage through construction completion. This holistic, multi-disciplinary approach to design is the engine under the hood of the book that you are holding.

Andrew Watts, as a practicing engineer and architect, has been operating at this high level of design for numerous internationally acclaimed, iconic buildings. With the help of his team at Newtecnic, he is generously sharing his experience and integrated design methods for 12 projects in order for us to better understand this new design workflow for architecture of the 21st century.

Prepare to be immersed in a visually rich and intelligent conversation about state-of-the-art skyscrapers and groundscrapers, ambitious transportation buildings, office buildings, cultural buildings and multi-family housing. The building envelope for each project is the primary focus of the book, as this is where the technical meat of the conversation lies.

Andrew Watts shows us that building envelopes are no longer the exterior wall of the building. The line between facade, structure, lighting, climate-response and mechanical systems begins to blur and suggest new evolutions. The exterior envelope can evolve to also be the structure - it can be an intelligent membrane that not only separates inside from outside but can also engage it.

For the past 20 years I have been leading university-level design courses in the U.S. and the U.K. - teaching design to architecture and architectural-engineering students. It is a rare gift to find a technical book that can communicate content not only clearly but in a manner that is visually compelling and intuitively understandable to both students and experienced designers. 'Modern Construction Case Studies' - in particular, this new edition, is indeed one of these rare gifts to us as designers and helps pave the way deep into the 21st century.

Gregory Brooks
The University of Texas at Austin
Faculty Director, Emerging Technologies program
Associate Professor of Practice, Architectural Engineering program

Modern Construction Case Studies focuses on the interface between the design of facades, structures and environments of 12 building projects. In all cases, Newtecnic have developed innovative aspects of the facade design as architects and engineers.

The primary aim of the book is to compare facade technologies, particularly in the way they interface with structure and MEP (mechanical, electrical, plumbing services) in complex projects, and to provide insights into the design process for building envelopes, by exploring specific themes through case studies of live projects.

Each envelope technology is described with a particular emphasis on one of three aspects:
- Complex geometry
- Innovative construction
- Enhanced performance

For each case study presented in the book, only one aspect is investigated in more detail, although all 12 case studies show strong components of all three aspects of facade technology. The comparative analysis, which follows this introduction, links the 12 case studies by comparing their structural and environmental performance through tables and graphs. These comparisons are used to illustrate trends across complex projects, for which each design is significantly different. This aim is achieved by analysing typical bays which are representative of each project and which illustrate the implications of using different building envelope technologies.

The design methodology, developed by Newtecnic, and used to design each of the case studies, is explained through the introductory essays. These texts explore core themes.

The principles described in this book are presented as a palette of design tools which are applicable to the design process for building projects with external envelopes of complex geometry. The application of this approach to each new design is project-specific and inherently dependent upon the specific function and spatial organisation of each building, and consequently cannot be generalised to a simple set of steps. Newtecnic hopes that the reader will find the content of use in their own engineering design work, as well as benefiting from the project comparisons which are also set out in this book.

Steps to build a working prototype
The purpose of this section is to show the reader how to engage with a fabricator in order to build a working prototype of a facade assembly. This prototype could be used for performance testing in order to obtain certification for its use on a specific building project. The procedures for the fabrication and testing of a working prototype are set out as a series of sequential steps. Such a prototype will typically be made when the contract has been awarded for the construction of the facades, but the prototype can be used during the design development stage in order to eliminate risk of exceeding the budget.

The method of 'steps' described later in this chapter is essential for ambitious or cutting-edge projects in order to remove the uncertainties inherent in the use of current technologies which are combined to form an emerging technology for a building project. At Newtecnic, warranties provided by contractors for pre-tested current technology systems are not relied upon for their combination in an emerging technology.

Cross-referencing MCE3
Specific references to materials in this book are to be found in the companion volume Modern Construction Envelopes, 3rd Edition (MCE3). Since it is good practice to not duplicate information across multiple sources, technical information for the specific materials shown on inventory model pages is contained in MCE3 only. As a result, this case studies book is linked directly to MCE3: The case studies featured here are a development of the current technologies set out in MCE3. The prototypes shown in this book are larger in scope than those in MCE3 as the examples here are more suited for performance testing. The prototypes in MCE3 are visual mock-ups that assist the design process. The steps to achieve a small-scale mock-up are set out in MCE3 and those steps should be followed prior to the steps shown in this book.

A development in this new edition is the addition of examples of both structural and environmental engineering analysis that allows the advancement of the systems, shown as prototypes and typical bays, to go beyond the architecture-led approach of MCE3.

A primary objective of the Modern Construction Case Studies is to provide a comparative analysis of different facade technologies used for complex geometry building envelopes, in relation to the climate and environment where they have been implemented on each project. The 12 case studies illustrated in the book have been compared in the tables and graphs below in terms of the environmental and structural performance of their building envelope.

	Project	Facade system	Facade zone	Panel thickness
1	HQ Building	Opaque composite rainscreen with glazing insets	200mm	38mm
2	Transport Hub	Metal rainscreen with full height stick glazing	500mm	4mm
3	Workshop Tower	Opaque and glazing unitized panels	450mm	35mm with 120mm ribs
4	Conference Center	Unitized glazing with UHPC cladding	1000mm	25mm with 100mm ribs
5	Technology Center	Monolithic open-joined GRC rainscreen	425mm	20mm with 90mm ribs
6	Innovation Campus	Metal rainscreen with unitized glazing units	500mm	6mm
7	Entertainment Complex	UHPC open-joint rainscreen with full height stick glazing	Up to 1350mm	40mm
8.a	International Terminal	GRC rainscreen with full height cable-glass facade	300mm	25mm
8.b	International Terminal	UHPC rainscreen with glazing unitized panels	Up to 3000mm	50mm
9	Laboratory Tower	FRP open-joint rainscreen with double skin facade	850mm	25mm
10	Multi-use Design District	Timber boards with stick glazing	270mm	65mm
11	Domestic Terminal	Sprayed GRC used as permanent formwork	375mm	40mm
12	Baku Airport	Precast GRC rainscreen with stick glazing	535mm	50mm with 120mm ribs

Weight of facade vs. facade zone

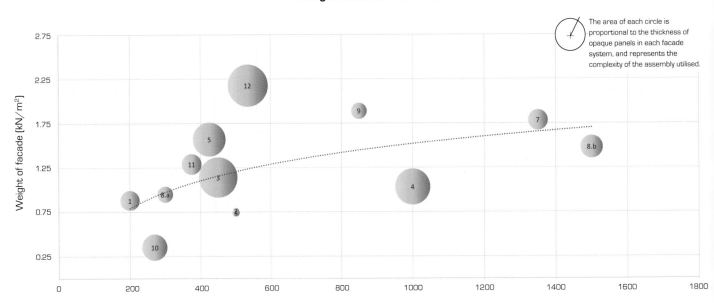

The area of each circle is proportional to the thickness of opaque panels in each facade system, and represents the complexity of the assembly utilised.

The numerical result used for the comparison have been obtained from the analysis performed on each project. Each facade technology, designed to suit all project conditions, has been assessed on a representative typical bay in order to compare facade systems across projects. The numerical values provided in this book are for comparison only and are not directly applicable to other projects.

Number of opaque panels	Number of glazing unit	Number of non-flat panels	Total area of panels requiring unique moulds	Total weight of facade, including secondary structure (kN/m²)	
2076	1026	620	2356	0.88 kN/m²	1
9631	1157	5631	13582	0.76 kN/m²	2
15120	9249	0	0	1.14 kN/m²	3
4488	1527	3141	4909	1.03 kN/m²	4
2208	730	1543	7547	1.57 kN/m²	5
589	222	89	214	0.74 kN/m²	6
3858	402	340	973	1.78 kN/m²	7
3844	720	700	467	0.95 kN/m²	8.a
1920	290	200	1091	1.48 kN/m²	8.b
11885	363	1285	5730	1.89 kN/m²	9
1680	240	672	518	0.35 kN/m²	10
1470	424	0	44	1.29 kN/m²	11
3443	260	344	1032	2.18 kN/m²	12

Panel Types Distribution

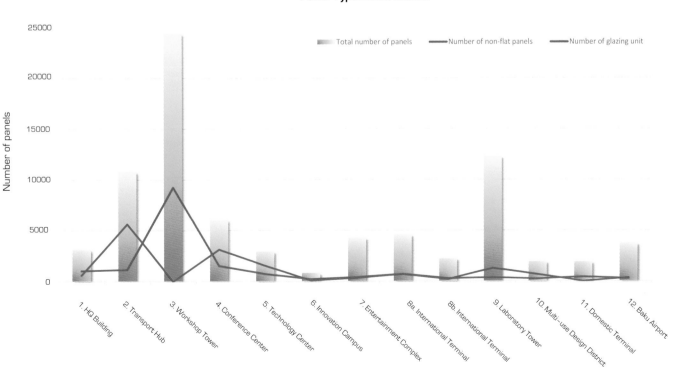

A primary objective of the Modern Construction Case Studies is to provide a comparative analysis of different facade technologies used for complex geometry building envelopes, in relation to the climate and environment where they have been implemented on each project. The 12 case studies illustrated in the book have been compared in the tables and graphs below in terms of the environmental and structural performance of their building envelope.

	Project	Primary structure type	Span of primary structure	Secondary structure type
1	HQ Building	Steel gridshell	8800 mm	RHS steel sections
2	Transport Hub	Concrete slab and column	10500 mm	CHS steel sections
3	Workshop Tower	Steel frame	12000 mm	RHS steel sections
4	Conference Center	Steel tensegrity core	-	Steel T profiles
5	Technology Center	Steel shell	-	-
6	Innovation Campus	Steel moment frame	7500 mm	Cold formed steel sections
7	Entertainment Complex	Concrete frame	5000 mm	Extruded aluminium profiles
8.a	International Terminal	Steel arches and cables	Up to 102000 mm	Cable
8.b	International Terminal	Steel arches and cables	Up to 102000 mm	RHS steel sections
9	Laboratory Tower	Bundled tube	3750 mm	RHS steel sections
10	Multi-use Design District	Structural timber frame	1325 mm	Timber battens
11	Domestic Terminal	Steel diagrid	10000 mm	Extruded aluminium profiles
12	Baku Airport	Steel space frame	3500 mm	Extruded aluminium profiles

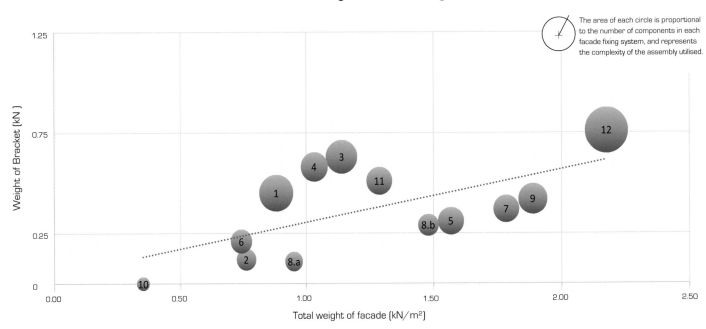

Facade weight VS bracket weight

The numerical result used for the comparison have been obtained from the analysis performed on each project. Each facade technology, designed to suit all project conditions, has been assessed on a representative typical bay in order to compare facade systems across projects. The numerical values provided in this book are for comparison only and are not directly applicable to other projects.

Weight of secondary structure	Facade bracket type	Number of components in fixing systems	Weight of bracket	
0.18 kN/m²	Spider bracket with four adjustable arms	14	0.45 kN	1
0.4 kN/m²	Spider bracket with two adjustable arms	5	0.12 kN	2
0.28 kN/m²	Serrated plates; welded and bolted	12	0.63 kN	3
0.14 kN/m²	Standard bolted pieces	9	0.58 kN	4
–	Spider bracket with four adjustable arms	8	0.31 kN	5
0.13 kN/m²	Cast aluminium brackets, bolted through unitised joints	6	0.21 kN	6
0.08 kN/m²	Serrated plates; post drilled anchorages	8	0.37 kN	7
0.07 kN/m²	Spider bracket with four adjustable arms	4	0.11 kN	8.a
0.35 kN/m²	Serrated plates; welded and bolted	5	0.29 kN	8.b
0.35 kN/m²	Spider bracket with two adjustable arms	10	0.42 kN	9
0.04 kN/m²	Serrated plates	2	0	10
0.08 kN/m²	Spider bracket with four adjustable arms	8	0.51 kN	11
0.11kN/m²	Spider bracket with two adjustable arms	22	0.76 kN	12

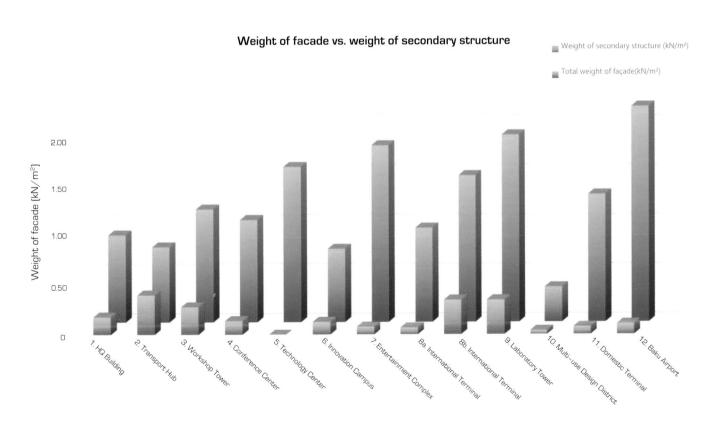

Weight of facade vs. weight of secondary structure

Weight of secondary structure (kN/m²)

Total weight of façade(kN/m²)

	Project	U–value of system envelope (W/m²K)	Linear thermal bridging effect for system typical detail (W/mK)	Insulation thickness (mm)	Total glazed area (m²)
1	HQ Building	0.69	0.12	125	2727
2	Transport Hub	0.67	0.11	75	15043
3	Workshop Tower	0.93	0.25	50	55860
4	Conference Center	0.44	0.32	125	5705
5	Technology Center	0.39	0.18	145	1010
6	Innovation Campus	0.48	0.11	150	674
7	Entertainment Complex	0.22	0.09	180	961
8	International Terminal	0.20	0.23	140	5613
9	Laboratory Tower	0.32	0.15	100	1545
10	Multi–use Design District	0.38	0.06	120	585
11	Domestic Terminal	0.53	0.28	105	7479
12	Baku Airport	0.57	0.18	80	2671

U–value of system envelope vs thickness of insulation layer

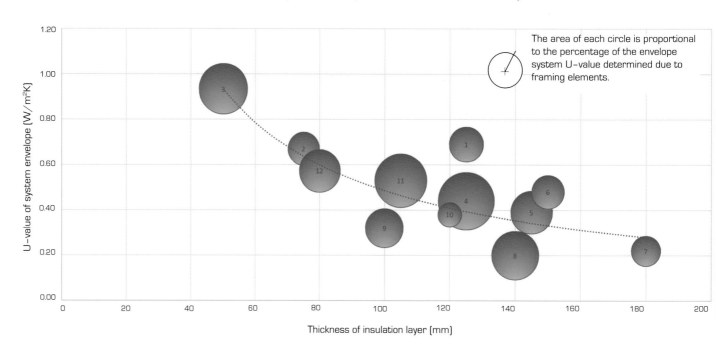

The area of each circle is proportional to the percentage of the envelope system U–value determined due to framing elements.

The relationship of inverse proportionality between U–value of each envelope system and thickness of the main insulating layer is illustrated in the graph, which also shows the potential effects of thermal bridging within more complex system assemblies.

Annual cumulative radiation – Total on glazed area (MWh)	Annual cumulative radiation – Average on glazed area (MWh/m²)	Geometry of external shading (l/L)		Reduction in annual solar gain by shading system [%]	
1909	0.7	0.29	–	58	1
16548	1.1	0.16	–	13	2
55860	1	0.17	–	20	3
5135	0.9	–	0.23	39	4
1313	1.3	0.16	–	31	5
539	0.8	–	0.23	43	6
1346	1.4	–	0.27	51	7
4491	0.8	–	0.34	44	8
2009	1.3	0.66	–	40	9
351	0.6	0.08	–	12	10
9723	1.3	–	0.42	34	11
1335	0.5	0.15	–	21	12

Effectiveness of external solar shading systems

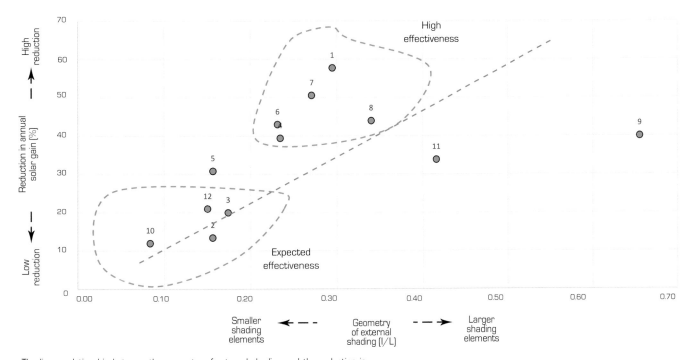

The linear relationship between the geometry of external shading and the reduction in annual solar gain illustrates the expected effectiveness of external shading systems and allows to identify areas on the graph that represent shading systems with high effectiveness.

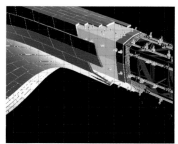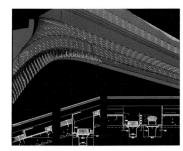

Current design methodology

The application of current and emerging technologies for the design engineering of facades is linked to the information available in established technical publications. These sources focus on providing an understanding of the main components within a given building assembly and illustrate the different choices available for the construction of assemblies for the building envelope, as well as construction methods used for the interior of the building. Specific technologies or materials can be selected by the architect or designer as a point of departure in order to select a construction system based on visual, performance or cost criteria. The details contained in these publications are often used by the facade engineer as a point of departure for facade system drawings. These publications typically require an experienced facade engineer to be able to extract relevant knowledge for use on real projects. The information available from these primary sources is also used by architects as a library of visual references and precedent built projects.

Beyond these primary sources, a mix of standards, codes and design handbooks are used for the specific design of components and assemblies, such as those used for connections in steel frames or concrete frames, for example. These design handbooks do not provide guidance for the reader to evaluate the appropriateness of the technology nor do these publications provide a means of validating the choice of a specific technology for a design application. Technical sheets and informal advice from fabricators are also a source of information for current technologies, which are often used as the basis for calculations during the design stage. The design is also often informed by information provided by a specialist contractor and is specific to the project.

Limitations of current methodology

These primary sources of information present information which is focused on the application of current and emerging technologies to specific materials or to specific projects. From the project-specific application of each technology, it is often impossible to extract information about the first principles driving its behaviour. Technical sheets from manufacturers rarely provide sufficient data with the given technology to design from first principles and to verify their suitability for a specific application. Often technical information is presented to satisfy commercial objectives and there is no method in place for the facade engineer to ensure the correctness or completeness of the information utilised.

Direct contact with specialist fabricators, manufacturers or contractors does not often result in the designer developing an understanding of the general principles and common methods used, as manufacturers tend to guard such technical information as being key to the commercial value of their specific product. Fabricators are also often not willing to provide design advice as a result of similar commercial considerations.

These various sources of information cannot be used directly in the design of complex building envelopes, which require an in-depth understanding of the first principles behind each technology; principles which form the basis of the design with its accompanying cost certainty.

Newtecnic's methodology

In order to develop an understanding of the first principles underpinning the design of current and particularly emerging technologies, a primary source of information is scientific papers published in journals and proceedings from specialist conferences, which are peer reviewed by the engineering community. Peer-reviewed publications are concerned with methods of analysis using a given technology, not on the relative merits of one technology against another. The objective of these publications is to fill in the current gaps in knowledge of the members of the engineering community in the application of current and emerging technologies.

This technical information is combined with project-specific research, in order to assess the appropriateness of each technology and to develop an understanding of constraints related to their fabrication. For emerging technologies, this typically requires physical prototyping and testing to validate their project-specific application, which cannot be validated through desktop analysis only.

For the case studies in this book, the design methodology applied is focused on ensuring the appropriateness of the technology in relation to a series of parameters that go beyond its technical application. In the approach used for the case studies, the technology deployed is linked to the values and culture determined by the geographic location of the project and the common aspirations of that culture; linked to sustainability, justification of the use of resources, local skills in fabrication, but with the global reach of these shared values taken into account. The technology utilised meets the expectations of the client and increases the value of the product delivered. A detailed understanding of local markets and associated fabrication methods builds confidence in the project and ensures its realisation. As part of project-specific research, Newtecnic ensures that for each given project there are always at least two companies that are both capable and interested in realising the project. An important aspect is to generate interest in the design through the construction of proof-of-concept mock-ups and by providing a high level of design resolution, which shows direct engagement with the fabrication process. Part of this approach is to ensure that smaller local companies are able to realise and are willing to construct the design. The technical publications which are used at the primary sources of information on building technology do not typically seek to engage with specific issues of resolution of any completed building but instead make comparisons with other specific design solutions which are based on the adaptation

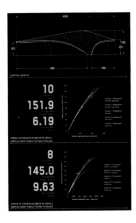

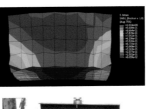

of available industrial processes to building construction. Emerging technologies are often based on new methods of fabrication. For the case studies presented in this book, the applied technology aims to increase the value of both product and process. New processes for fabrication can only be developed by linking design from first principles, academic research, physical testing and prototyping.

The facade assemblies shown in this book were conceived as a 'product'; a specific design solution with a high degree of resolution. For most projects, the facade assemblies were documented to provide a 'set of instructions' for the construction of those facades, which include a proposed sequence for assembly and installation. As a set of instructions to be followed by a contractor, these designs required validation of the method and outputs that underpin the design for each project.

This essay sets out the key issues in the use of current and emerging construction technologies as applied to building envelopes of complex geometry. Designs of this type require a high level of integration between structure, facade and MEP (mechanical, electrical, plumbing services), which often comprises an external envelope with an integrated self-supporting structure that is independent of the building structure that supports floors and service areas, combined with high thermal performance. The design of complex building envelopes with a high level of integration requires a careful selection of suitable technology and its adaptation to project specific facade assemblies, in order to meet a set of different performance requirements for structure, facades and environmental systems.

In the context of this book, technologies are tools for generating facade assemblies. In turn, the assemblies generated for a specific facade design determine the components and the connections within each assembly, and therefore affect the assumptions for 3D modelling and associated engineering analysis tasks, such as hand calculations and computational simulations. A facade assembly is made from a set of materials, the fabrication of which will be based on either current or emerging technology, or a mix of the two, as the term 'technology' can apply to both an assembly and the materials used in that assembly. At Newtecnic, complex building envelopes are designed from the point of view of the technology for the assembly, with the specific material used being chosen at a later stage of design development, once the required performance and physical properties of a material have been determined. The choice of a specific material for a facade assembly, such as that used for a solar shading device, is determined later in the design process. The material that will meet the performance criteria of this specific function will often have its own material technology. Consequently, the technology used or developed for the assembly should be interdependent with the materials used in the assembly as well as the technology used for their fabrication. This approach allows 'material selection' to be finalised later in the design process, with the possibility

of introducing significant value engineering possibilities without fundamental design changes at that later stage of the project. The alternative approach of using assemblies that are material-specific introduces higher interdependence in the design at an early stage of design development, which would limit the ability of the design to respond to later changes in the design of the external envelope. Consequently, the selection of facade materials is made at a later stage of design development.

Current technologies in facade assemblies

Current technologies are used in facade assemblies where the project design criteria are typically well-understood, and where alternatives can be provided to the solution proposed by the design team, while still meeting the same project-specific requirements. This approach can lead to facade designs which are more 'generic' in their level of resolution; an approach that allows contractors to propose alternative facade solutions at a very late stage in the design development of the project. Typically, a contractor's alternative solution will be adopted if proven to be substantially cheaper than that proposed by the architect's design team, while still providing the same overall performance as defined in the performance specification for the project. A potential hazard introduced by late design changes from a contractor is the unexpected effects on coordination with other trades or construction packages.

Current technologies require only project-specific performance testing for final validation. Consequently, the expected performance of a well understood technology is validated through physical testing for the specific configuration proposed for the project. Typically, current technologies are optimised for one specific function or a narrow range of functions. For facades, current technologies are typically offered by specialist fabricators and manufacturers as proprietary products which suit the fabricators' own fabrication capabilities. The use of different current technologies across a single project typically leads to a high number of interfaces between each of the facade systems. This approach often leads to a laborious construction methodology which is both difficult to achieve on site and time-consuming to design. Current technologies are typically unable to respond to widely varying conditions of geometry on a single project, making it difficult to enclose the complete external envelope with a single facade system. Current technologies offer fewer opportunities for optimisation and associated cost reductions from reducing the number of interfaces. This makes current technologies less suitable for novel building forms. Typically, current technologies for facades are suited to a 'loose fit' design approach, where a more generic solution is used to provide support to the architect rather than serving to help drive the design forward with innovation. The alternative approach of using emerging technologies allows a project-specific

technology to be brought to the facade design, where it is adapted in a process which resembles that of 'product development'.

Emerging technologies in facade assemblies

Typically, an emerging technology used in facade design is formed by the relationship between a set of novel components within an innovative assembly. Despite associations with the word 'emerging', the engineering basis of an emerging technology must already be demonstrated successfully on previous similar built applications when applied to large-scale projects. Therefore, as part of the design development process, project-specific prototyping and physical testing is required for any facade assembly where an emerging technology is used. This is because an emerging technology requires both proof-of-concept performance testing and final compliance testing, which follows standard procedures. Consequently, emerging technologies are not experimental technologies, but cutting edge applications of proven facade technology. Experimental technologies are considered to be technologies linked to a high degree of uncertainty in their performance and which require further research and development in order to become emerging.

Emerging technologies offer opportunities for significant cost reductions through project-specific design development, while maintaining the high value of the specific technology utilised. These technologies also provide opportunities to innovate for a specific building project, in order to reduce costs of the construction of that project. This approach allows an external envelope to be delivered with both high value and high performance at a cost lower than that of an older technology. However, an emerging technology for a facade system requires a higher level of design development at an earlier stage than a current technology, and consequently is developed as a 'product', for which the emerging technology is tailored to the specific requirements of the project. This approach is key to the design methodology developed by Newtecnic.

Use of current and emerging technologies in facade design

Both current and emerging technologies require a similar level of documentation when applied to facades for a specific project. For emerging technologies, documentation and supporting outputs is provided earlier in the design process as a tool for problem-solving rather than 'recording choices' in order to provide the same level of cost-certainty as would be expected for an equivalent current technology.

The use of a current technology often leads to project-specific design requirements being set out in a performance specification. The use of an emerging technology usually leads to a specification which sets out a project-specific solution as well as determining the required performance. The use of emerging technology in facade design directs the designer to achieve a set of clear design and performance objec-

tives at an earlier stage of a project, while allowing the choice of key materials within the facade assemblies to be determined at a later stage in design development. This approach allows assemblies that respond directly to project-specific design priorities to be identified, resolved and costed at a much earlier stage of design.

For current technologies used in facade assemblies, a key consideration in the process is the design of interfaces and movement joints between adjacent facade systems. For emerging technologies used in envelope designs, a key consideration is the selection and project-specific development of a single facade system that is optimised to suit all conditions of geometry in the facades. The design of interfaces in facades, which are associated with the junction of current technologies, are slower to implement during the site installation phase than a single system that uses an emerging technology. The design of interfaces between facade systems is also slower to resolve as a result of design changes during design development, as current technologies are not usually optimised for connectivity with other technologies. Consequently, the design development of facades which use a current technology is generally confined to the later stages of a design process when the final design, and associated performance criteria, are determined. The experience of Newtecnic is that the use of current technologies in facade design results in a low level of facade system development for the first 75% of the design time. The remaining 25% of the design time requires an accelerated approach in order to provide the required documentation, but only after the design has been largely determined by the architect. In addition, the documentation of the facade design will be 'generic', almost entirely based on stating the performance requirements of the system, in order to allow for proprietary products to be proposed by contractors to meet the stated performance criteria.

The implementation of both current and emerging technologies in facade design are required to follow a disciplined process of documentation during the early stages of the design process. At the concept design stage, examples of existing assemblies (or existing technologies) are proposed with the purpose of demonstrating the feasibility of each assembly independently. In this process of 'differentiation' of assemblies, options are identified for different technologies that may be applicable to the facade design. At the schematic design stage, precedents of current and emerging technologies applicable to the proposed facade design are brought together as a synthesis, and compared again with the precedents proposed at the concept design stage. The purpose of this process is to clearly distinguish the aspects of the facade design that involve current technology from those that use emerging technology. This method allows the design priorities for the following stage of design development to be determined for necessary prototyping and physical testing.

Current design methodology

For large-scale building envelopes of complex geometry, the design method is often driven by the design of the facade assembly, and with the current or emerging technologies that are associated with that facade assembly. The design method for a building envelope includes all the steps and iterations required to deliver the final design from concept to delivery of a tested and validated physical prototype. The current method for the engineering design of facades for buildings is based on a sequence of steps which attempt to integrate design and manufacturing to ensure continuity from design to construction. This approach attempts to implement an effective project management method in order to control the process in terms of people, time and resources. The project management method facilitates the application of known solutions to supporting tasks in the design process. The current project management method for the design of buildings is based on a linear approach which makes use of Gantt charts to regulate the progress of both tasks and deliverables, as well as to define specific interdependencies between tasks. The assumption of this method is that the time required for each task is well understood from experience of previous projects, and that tasks can be prioritised in terms of amount of time assigned to each task.

The regulation of the design process through a linear project management method is applicable to projects where the design focus is the optimisation of current knowledge, where most of the design aspects are known and where design components which require optimisation can be pre-established. The standard design method for buildings is generally led by an architect, following procedures set out in the work stages of internationally oriented organisations such as the AIA (American Institute of Architects) and the RIBA (Royal Institute of British Architects). On many design projects the role of the building engineer or facade engineer is typically one of providing technical support to the architect rather than one of partnership in the generation of the building design. This approach is based on the building engineer providing a 'service' to support the architect's outputs with knowledge of structural and MEP engineering (mechanical, electrical and plumbing), which is well-established and is provided throughout the duration of the project on a day-to-day basis.

Limitations of current methodology

The current approach focuses on the time taken to develop and document a design solution which uses current technology. The current method assumes that current technologies are validated, and attempts to identify, at the outset of the project, the aspects that require a greater effort to be validated. The limitation of using the current method for both design and project management is that only current technologies

can be implemented for well-understood applications. This design approach does not apply to complex building projects where the relationship between the parts is not determined. The limitation of the linear approach applied to project management can be a reduction in the ability of the building engineer or facade engineer to provide innovative designs which match the innovation suggested by the architect. This comes as a result of the limited time available to inform the architect's concept with a project-specific facade technology. An innovation by an architect may be based on a novel spatial arrangement in relation to the required function of that space, or may be a visually-driven concept for the form of the building. The engineering design, at the interface of structure, facade and MEP, will not necessarily reach the level of accomplishment anticipated by the architect, as the time scale expected for an innovative architectural design is less than that required for innovation in the corresponding facade engineering design, which typically requires research and development through testing. Consequently, the level of technical ambition in the facade engineering design of a project is reduced to suit the critical path of technical development of the architectural design. This leads to the current trend in facade engineering design of using proprietary systems selected through competitive tender, a process supported by a performance specification and associated drawn or 3D modelled outputs, such as a BIM (building information model).

Newtecnic's methodology

The method applied for the case studies in this book is driven by problem-solving, an approach which is applied at each step of the design process. No step in the design sequence is allowed to produce only 'documentation'; the primary output must be a working design which is quantified and costed through 3D models and physical prototypes.

This design approach is non-hierarchical as there are no priorities set on the design criteria or on specific aspects of the design to be innovated or optimised. This method is based on a design engineering approach as applied across other engineering disciplines which are based on the design, fabrication and manufacture of 'products' and is applied to tasks involving the structural, facade and environmental engineering of buildings. This design approach suits engineers who are trained across several building engineering disciplines or, alternatively, have a global understanding of building design beyond their speciality.

This design method assumes that the parts of the design that require innovation emerge as the design develops, the innovation ranging from that of individual components, to creating novel relationships between components that lead to innovative assemblies and a corresponding enhanced performance. This approach to building design is strongly based on first principles and is open from the start of the project to the innovation of any

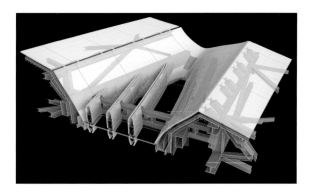

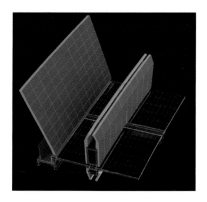

of the constituent parts of the design. As the design develops, it becomes clear which aspects drive the design and which aspects require innovation to achieve the required enhanced performance. The approach also allows a clear assessment of which parts of a design will most benefit from the application of either a current technology or an emerging technology. This design method focuses on generating quantified, comparable outputs within a short time-frame which will allow the design to progress through a sequence of steps, where the immediate consequences of each step are clearly understood before the next step is taken.

This method is founded on three key principles, which aim at overcoming any restrictions in delivering innovative design solutions:

- Research: University-based research of technologies which integrate facade, structures and MEP, conducted in-house and through academic partnerships. This process is independent of project-specific time scales and is aimed at both gathering knowledge on emerging technologies and developing new knowledge on experimental technologies. This aspect is discussed in the essay 'Design implementation and research method'.
- Digital tools for design and analysis: The use of high performing and calibrated digital tools to perform complex analysis at the early design stages, which is aimed at understanding behaviour. The capabilities of the commercially-available tools are often developed with the software provider as the design progresses. This aspect is discussed in the essay 'Analysis method and scientific foundations'.
- 'Agile' management: 'Agile' techniques provide a method of delivering successful innovation in building design if projects are developed as a 'product' rather than being a process with drawn and written outputs only. This aspect is discussed in the following paragraphs.

On any project, these three aspects enable a set of working facade prototypes to be developed, physically tested and approved through consecutive steps and completed before the stage of competitive tender. These three aspects also allow the design engineering process to generate new knowledge and innovation, which can be applied to subsequent projects.

'Agile' management applied to facade projects

In the delivery of facades of complex geometry for large-scale projects, the design methodology usually drives the management method used by the facade design team. Newtecnic has found 'agile' management techniques to be highly effective in achieving a high level of design resolution within the time constraints typically expected of a building design that would otherwise produce more generic outputs. Agile management techniques have recently spread outwards from the software development industry and are now widely applied across several fields in engineering that require innovation for both design and manufac-

ture. 'Agile' management is highly suited to facade design work on high profile-projects, as the method supports four key aspects of facade design for large-scale projects of complex geometry:

- A multi-disciplinary engineering design approach.
- Short, intense iterations for a team of 8 to 10 engineers with different specialisations.
- Continuous innovation through all stages of design development.
- The creation of new knowledge at all stages of design development.

This 'Agile' approach allows facade design outputs to be communicated and delivered to customers as a highly evolved design 'product', rather than by providing a design 'service' with more generic outputs. This approach allows the focus of a facade engineering team to deliver, quickly, an innovative product which is cheaper, better or easier to construct than an existing product, rather than that team providing a design 'service'. Agile management in facade design provides a method for delivering high quality, innovative 'products', in which the ability to adapt to evolving customer requirements during the course of the design development stages is an essential requirement.

The design engineering of facades of complex geometry is output-oriented and is based on producing design proposals as quickly as possible; increasing the scope and quality of the design with succeeding iterations. The design process is typically 'kick-started' through linear iterations where engineers may be required to work in isolation or in small teams on explorative tasks. These tasks are typically analytical with the aim of identifying the driving design parameters for each discipline. As soon as key design objectives are identified, a large team is tasked with focusing on one specific issue at a time, which ensures that each task benefits from an effective team dynamic.

A tangible longer-term outcome of the application of this method is the production of the following outputs:

- Templates for reports.
- Technical notes for procedures and new knowledge.
- Example outputs of innovative solutions for facade engineering.

Templates and procedures provide the basis for the planning of future tasks of a similar nature. Agile management for facade engineering is based on the following core values:

- Collaboration and self-organisation of an engineering design team.
- Empowerment and continuous improvement of an engineering design team.

The principle of continuous improvement is essential for improving design outputs with each new iteration. An essential aspect of the design methodology for complex facades is ensuring that engineers are able to explain, at any given point, the design process to others within the team and to the customer. Every member of the facade engi-

neering team should be responsible for the content of their outputs, ensure the success of the task, and improve the quality of outputs for the next iteration in a process of continuous improvement.

Generating innovation

Innovation is at the heart of this design method for the facade engineering of complex forms. The method aims at generating new knowledge which adds value to the product delivered to the customer, and is usable by facade engineers on other projects. This is achieved through:

- Technical notes: processes developed in-house for projects are documented through technical notes, which are peer-reviewed by external research partners.
- Visible outputs: making outputs visible at every iteration and making the work visible at every stage of the process. This allows gaps in knowledge that require further research to be identified.

Knowledge creation, which is specific to the project, is part of the value the customer gains from this design approach. The customer is able to take ownership of the project-specific part of the technology if they so wish, together with the knowledge and innovation embedded in the design and documented in the project-specific outputs. This means that the client can at any time use the design documentation produced up to that point and continue independently with the design development. This design methodology generates new knowledge through prototyping and physical testing; activities which have seen a greater development in other industries but are not yet conceived as part of the mainstream of design processes for building construction. The creation of key links between building engineers and contractors is an essential step towards collaborating directly with leading fabricators in the construction field and acting as a bridge between design research and project-specific applications.

The approach to optimisation in innovative facade projects is driven primarily by the need to bring facade, structure and MEP together into an integrated solution. Optimisation of specific components cannot be done in isolation, as this can result in the sub-optimisation of other parts of the facade assembly. Components within facade assemblies are not optimised in isolation, but are instead evaluated as part of a matrix of optimisation. Optimisation is not specifically an 'agile' process; it is an iterative process of searching for the removal of unwanted complexity, with the benefit of reducing costs and improving quality for a building project. Optimisation is the 'calibration for economy' of any given facade design. In order to avoid sub-optimisation, an understanding of the cost of individual components is required. For example, the cost of glass in a given assembly can be lowered by reducing glass thickness as a result of decreasing the span of its supporting frame, but the increase in cost of the frame should be no greater than the cost saving achieved from the glass. Innovation in facade engineering

design, as distinct from optimisation, is generated through establishing new links between components and facade assemblies.

Application of design method and project management

The aim of this design method for large-scale projects of complex geometry is to bring ambitious concepts to life without basing the design on specific solutions supplied by specialist contractors. This method of project management allows the delivery of facade engineering packages with a high level of technical resolution. These packages are able to be optimised for value and installation time, and would already have received approval for their fabrication and installation. The level of design resolution permits a high level of cost certainty. As part of this approach, each facade assembly deployed on a given project can be conceived as a facade 'system', which can be described in two parts:

- System architecture: The arrangement of functions at the small scale or large scale of a single facade assembly type.
- System engineering: The analysis and performance of a single facade assembly type.

Both 'system architecture' and 'system engineering' are developed through two phases:

1. 'Differentiation', where each system component is firstly analysed and designed in isolation.
2. 'Integration', where all components are finally made to converge into one design solution.

At the schematic design stage, robust concepts and strategies are established and deployed across the scope of the facade design project by exploring in full their applicability to project-specific conditions. The primary objective of outputs at this stage – beyond the design itself – is to obtain preliminary costs based on providing initial quantities, preliminary structural weights and number of components, expected performance criteria and preliminary MEP loads.

At the detailed design stage, or design development stage, analysis is undertaken in order to inform an understanding of each building technology proposed for the project. Outputs are derived from analysis at this stage, rather than from the general considerations of assembly investigated in the schematic design stage. During this stage the facade technology being proposed is developed to suit the visual language of the design as generated from the architect's concept. The following specific analysis tasks are undertaken at this stage:

- Understanding of secondary effects.
- Dimensioning of secondary elements.
- Refining of sizes of primary elements.
- Design of connections.

At the construction documentation stage, drawing outputs are finalised and coordinated with coordination and dimensioning of drawings.

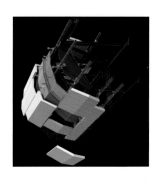

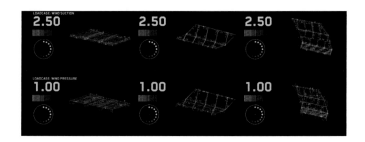

Current design methodology

Analysis is the tool used to demonstrate the validity of a given design concept and is based on the application of a given set of scientific foundations. The current approach to analysis in facade engineering design is to conceive the analysis as a numerical quantification of a proposed design, which is generally conceived by the architect. This approach is based on keeping the scope of the design within codes and standards which provide the scientific foundation for the analysis. Generally, both national and international codes and standards integrate mathematical engineering foundations with empirical data, calculation formulae and procedures. The approach taken aims to ensure an agreed level of design safety for any given facade assembly. The engineer using codes and standards does not have direct access to experimental results or raw empirical data, which are already interpreted in the calculation formulae provided. Codes and standards provide calculation templates for the numerical quantification of current technologies, and ensure that the performance expectations for a current technology are met for a specific design. Calculation procedures from codes and standards are often integrated within design tools provided by specialist manufacturers in order to size specific components for their proprietary products. These tools include tables, software packages and design guides; these are typically provided for commercial purposes and allow the facade engineer to safely integrate proprietary products within the facade design. With the current approach, analysis is based on independent studies that take separate aspects of the design into consideration.

Limitations of current methodology

When using codes and standards, it is difficult to interrogate the first principles behind the calculation formulae utilised. The physical behaviour synthesised through the formulae is often not apparent. The derivations of the empirical factors describing the relative importance of different aspects affecting the behaviour described by the formula are also not apparent. In the current approach, the design process is not informed by digital finite element (FE) tools, which are instead used to provide final numerical validation or as a labour–saving tool. These tools are not in general use for the exploration of design options. This approach suits buildings of rectilinear geometry, for which the analytical basis of the design is well understood.

The consequence of the current approach is the generation of separate calculation packages, where the assumptions considered for the analysis are not required to be coordinated in order to ensure a 'loose–fit' design outcome.

Newtecnic's methodology

In the method used for this book, the design approach aims to understand the first principles behind the analysis, following the academic approach taught at universities with leading engineering departments. In addition, the approach followed is applied by academic research teams attached to these engineering departments, who provide technical support to design engineers. The combination of first principles and physical testing becomes the basis of the scientific foundations when standards are not directly applicable to a design concept, as in the case of emerging technologies. The results are compared with standards and codes which are used to set expectations to verify experimental outputs. The analyses for a complex facade design are of two kinds: geometric and numerical. Geometrical analysis is performed at the beginning and throughout the evolution of the design. This analysis engages with the geometry of the complete building to establish the required complexity of the models required for the numerical analysis. Geometry analysis also ensures that all aspects of the design are tested and integrated into a final design solution following the numerical analysis which splits the design into parts that are calculated following different rules (the 'integration' phase of the design following the 'differentiation' phase).

For complex building designs, the use of first principles through finite element analysis tools is calibrated by physical testing. This approach requires a high level of engagement with institutions that are specialised in the application of first principles to testing of materials, components and assemblies to generate empirical data, which are shared and reviewed by peers. Physical testing is performed in order to calibrate digital models as well as to integrate safety factors into the design. As part of the approach proposed, openness and the sharing of technical knowledge for peer review and evaluation is critical to ensure best practice in the design methods applied, which are validated by the engineering community. In order to be able to effectively share information for peer review, an infrastructure is needed for facade engineering specialist advice, physical testing and peer review of outputs. In order to develop a design, a partnership between the building engineer, or facade engineer, and the architect is required, which is enabled though multidisciplinary team members who also have architectural training. The building engineer should draw a clear boundary around the engineering design, intended as the assistance provided to the technical development of the design concept. This is about realising the design rather than conceiving it: the nature and motivations behind the design concepts are not questioned, and the focus is on finding solutions to a technical problem. The design process allows changes to be absorbed quickly and is used as a tool to develop a deeper understanding of the design and its behaviour.

The design of complex geometry buildings typically requires emerging technology to be deployed in order to construct high performance envelope systems. A complex geometry envelope typically involves an interde-

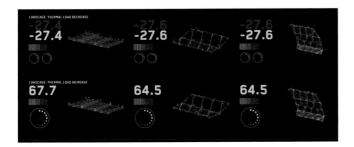

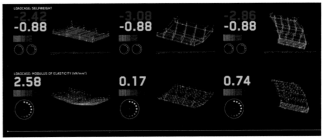

pendency between supporting structure, enclosing layer and environmental control. These building forms are often conceived as 'wraps' for the internal spaces through a changing relationship between the facade and the floors and voids behind the external wall. Such envelopes are typically self-supporting, as the form of the facades is often independent of the arrangement of floor slabs behind the facade and often forms the external wall of large-scale spaces within the building. The complex geometry facades shown in the case studies within this book are supported either by a self-supporting frame or by load-bearing panels. Where the facade is load-bearing, the structure takes the form of shell structures which are realised with a mix of beam, plate and shell modules, and are distinct from braced frames or load-bearing boxes, as the geometry drives their behaviour. The specific nature of these structures is set out in the Modern Construction Handbook, which forms part of this book series.

The envelope regulates directly the flow of heat energy through the building skin, a factor which determines both peak heating/cooling values used to size mechanical equipment, and the total energy consumptions, which drive the running costs of the heating/cooling installation. Complex facade forms often make use of doubly-curved geometry, which can be exploited to achieve thinner envelope build-ups through shell action.

Analysis method and scientific foundations

The analysis method described here was used to generate early stage engineering designs for the case studies described in this book for the interface of structure, facade and MEP (mechanical, electrical and plumbing services). Through a process of integration of the constituent parts of the facade design, coordination between these components provides an opportunity for optimisation of the facade design. This process of 'integration' aims to achieve material savings, minimise the depth of the facade, and reduce the time required for fabrication of facade components and assemblies.

A current facade engineering approach, based on providing a design 'service' within a strict time-frame, requires the building engineer or facade engineer to apply well-understood technology to specific project conditions and to provide numerical validation of the appropriateness of their use through analysis.

An alternative method of analysis for facades of complex geometry, as used in the case studies in this book, is based around the design of the 'assembly', which is developed like a design 'product' that meets project-specific requirements. The 'assembly' is conceived as the fabric of the building envelope where structure, facade and MEP are integrated. Assemblies respond to specific performance requirements which vary across the building envelope. The numerical analysis involved is a function of the design of the assemblies, which must respond to both structural and environmental performance requirements. This approach results in, for example, varying structural strength and stiffness in adjacent structural members, varying air permeability and solar transmittance, and varying acoustic mass and thermal transmittance. The facade assembly is analysed at different scales by examining local effects at the scale of a typical structural bay, together with global effects at the scale of the entire building. The design of each component in an assembly can be equally driven by local or global effects, and requires a 'multi-scale', 'multi-physics' analysis to identify a global optimum solution. The analyses are typically undertaken in parallel using specialised software packages and the results are compared on the basis of their effect on the design. Sensitivity analyses are conducted on each relevant parameter in order to identify the factors that drive the design.

The scientific foundations for the engineering analysis of complex geometry envelopes are mostly grounded in the finite element, finite volume or finite difference methods, for both structural and environmental design. This approach is implemented in a range of digital tools which allows complex shapes or components to be discretised and analysed. Finite element digital analysis looks primarily at the equilibrium of forces in structural analysis and the flow of energy in environmental analysis and analysis of HVAC (heating, ventilation, and air conditioning). These are investigated through 3D models in both wireframe and surface format, as a method of capturing the geometry of the building form or components. From these models, meshes are generated in order to interface with finite element software platforms. Numerical accuracy in finite element analysis is linked to mesh density and mesh density is linked to computational time. The objective of numerical analysis at the early design stages is to understand behaviour through a simplified but thorough approach. This ensures that robust design concepts are generated which do not depend on a very high level of accuracy of analytical models, which is not achievable within limited project time-scales.

For facade envelopes that integrate structure and skin, optimisation is mainly achieved by reducing the time required for installation on-site, rather than specifically reducing the weight of each assembly. This aim is achieved typically by reducing the complexity of the assembly and the number of components, which attracts a longer installation time and higher costs associated with more time on site. This approach requires a higher level of design input than would be expected for a less ambitious facade design, in order to develop components which are multi-functional rather than having a single function in a facade assembly. The optimisation for weight reduction of each assembly, undertaken in isolation, is of secondary importance in the process of optimisation.

Finite element methods are well-established but, being dependent on the computational power available, have only recently been fully integrated within powerful analytical tools. This has allowed analysis to become a tool for exploring behaviour rather than simply a tool for the numerical quantification of a given design. Numerical analysis during the early stages of the design of facades of complex geometry should be robust

and ensure that the design is functional across a sufficiently wide range of input values. Finite element tools are primarily used to assess behaviour and establish which components can be analysed independently and which cannot be dissociated and must therefore be analysed together. The first iterations of analysis aim at establishing relationships between individual components as well as the magnitude of combined effects.

Finite element analysis (FEA) is based on static equations that resolve the equilibrium of forces, fluxes of fluids or energy in 1D, 2D or 3D. The basic implementation of these equations makes use of the mathematical balance present in an equilibrium steady-state condition. Differential equations are required when analysis is time-dependent and quantities vary over time. The use of FE tools represents an inherent mathematical approximation, which implies a trade-off between accuracy and time in any given analysis. The objective of the analysis is to identify a set of calculation models which are representative of real world behaviour to a sufficient degree of accuracy. The different level of resolution of each design parameter, particularly during early design stages, inherently limits the accuracy of the analysis. Considerations of constructability, construction tolerances and material safety factors are equally important in establishing a design concept. Seen in isolation, the analysis results are not sufficient to ensure the robustness of a design concept. The compatibility between the degree of geometric approximation, the accuracy of input values and the specific use of the analysis outputs, sets the level of accuracy required for numerical analysis. Hand calculations are performed on simpler models in order to set order-of-magnitude values which typically include lower and upper boundaries for the analysis.

A comparison of strategies of analysis is an essential basis of early stage facade design. Comparison between two results is only meaningful if the two terms show the same the level of accuracy. During the concept design stage, a broad range of studies is undertaken and the implications of the design concept for each set of results are assessed against one other. Requirements for design are prioritised on this basis and are directed towards 'convergence' as a single design concept. The prioritisation of requirements is an exercise of judgment by the designer, a judgment which is reviewed in the light of associated costs of fabrication and installation.

A basic implementation of the finite element method is in computational fluid dynamic (CFD) software and structural analysis software packages. CFD is used primarily to explore global behaviour of external and internal flow, in order to understand key relationships between 'parts' and 'quantities' (e.g. between temperature and velocity distributions). CFD is also used to design specific 'parts' of an assembly in order to enhance its global behaviour (modify a diffuser design or external louvres to facilitate air flow). This use of finite element tools during concept design suits 'agile' thinking as applied to project management: the relationship between components may change as a result of decisions made

by the customer, resulting in a high level of adaptability required in the process of design. Consequently, the tools must be in place to allow for quick analysis iterations, and the design should be sufficiently robust to have an adequate degree of interdependency between individual components. This allows changes by the customer to be absorbed in the design without impacting the whole concept.

The aim of the design method used in the case studies of this book is to reach a level of 80% cost certainty for the facades and their resolution at the interface with structure and MEP design by the end of the schematic design stage; a level of certainty which would be expected for facade designs that use current technologies rather than the emerging technologies used in innovative facade designs. This approach requires robust design concepts to be in place which integrate the requirements of structural stability, energy consumption and thermal comfort. These concepts inform directly the architectural design; they do not provide only numerical validation. At the concept design stage, a matrix of design recommendations is provided for the customer. This matrix allows different configurations of structure, facade and environmental control system to be assessed against each other. The matrix is used as a decision-making tool to establish the strategies to be developed in the following schematic design stage.

Method for structural analysis of complex facades

The method described here is for the design of structures for facades of complex geometry, which typically follow the structural primitive of a shell. These structural forms typically create large scale enclosures around a more standardised internal structure, made from reinforced concrete or steel, whose purpose is to support floor slabs. The internal structure typically follows the structural primitive of a braced frame or a load-bearing box. The analysis of braced frames and load-bearing boxes is well understood and progresses from the structural design of a typical bay that establishes preliminary sizing, to a final global structural model that allows member sizes to be adjusted and which can account for global static or dynamic effects. The relationship between the internal structure and the external enclosure can vary, primarily as follows:

- The two structures are completely independent, or
- The external enclosure is partially restrained or propped at intermediate locations against the internal structure which requires a high level of coordination between the two, and usually implies a combined analytical/numerical model of the two structures, or
- The external enclosure supports directly the internal structure: the two structures are effectively one and must be considered together.

The first step in the design of a complex geometry structure is to establish a strategy that responds to the architectural programme. The strategy is subsequently deployed across different parts of the building

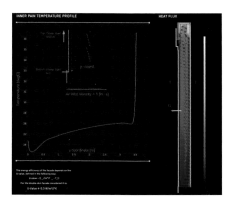

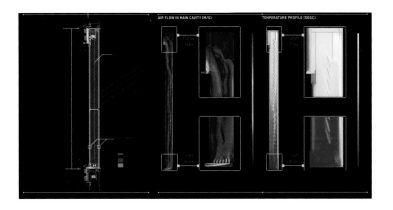

and is the starting point for the generation of structural concepts. The behaviour of each part of the facade, or building, structure is controlled by a distinct structural primitive. Each structural primitive is combined with the general strategy for the envelope that responds to the architectural programme, in order for a structural concept to be generated. A structural concept for a facade of complex geometry addresses the following primary aspects:

• Structural stability at global and local building scale.
• Robustness of the design proposed.
• Integration of primary, secondary and facade structure.

The structural design of a complex geometry structure follows a process of 'differentiation' and 'integration': all components (connections, constitutive components, modules, etc.) are designed and analysed in isolation but are ultimately assessed in their global behaviour by establishing the load path through the structural elements. For complex geometry structures the 'integration' usually reveals the final structural behaviour, which is driven by the overall geometry. The step of differentiation is nonetheless required in order to integrate the technology required at the level of an assembly.

The general strategy established at the outset of the design is driven by the technology of the proposed facade assembly. To this aim, current and emerging technologies are assessed to establish the strategy for the envelope by examining existing built precedents. These precedents are used to demonstrate the suitability of the technology proposed in relation to either a specific building type, or the project location, climate, etc. During 'differentiation', each assembly is examined independently through simplified calculation models, which range from hand calculations to a finite element assessment of a typical structural bay, whose size is representative of local effects. This is aimed at assessing the robustness of the assembly and its local stability. During 'integration', the structural concept for the load-bearing envelope is analysed through a global finite element model. This is aimed at assessing global stability and support reactions. The stiffness of the building is assessed primarily by estimating natural frequencies and global displacements. Stiffness is typically the driving parameter for the structural design of large-scale enclosures for facades of complex geometry. Global displacements are required to be linked back to local effects in order to obtain preliminary estimates of movement that will have to be accommodated within envelope assemblies, whilst still ensuring weather tightness. The interaction of the structure with the surrounding structures is investigated through support reactions, which are the basis of establishing load paths. The global model allows to assess areas of stress concentrations in order to establish strategies to redistribute internal forces and stresses.

'Integration' and 'differentiation' are developed through iterative loops, where strategies for the technology of the assembly are tested by examining their impact on a global finite element model. This approach captures the geometry-driven behaviour of the envelope. Typically, the behaviour of large steel enclosures is expected to be driven by its global displacements at serviceability. Large concrete shells are likely to be driven by maximum stresses at ultimate limit states. Analytical/numerical models are simplified in order to represent the essence of the object analysed. This is valid from small-scale components to large-scale structures. This ensures that analytical models are robust and do not produce misleading results, in which potential analytical errors are of the same order of magnitude of the results.

Following this design approach, the envelope fabric is optimised in terms of structural stiffness and strengths to match the performance required by the geometry at different locations. The structural optimisation is done through digital analysis, where the global effect of changing the stiffness of one part of the envelope is examined in real time. In this way the assembly is conceived as a flexible set of sub-assemblies and components, so that a single facade system can be used across the project to match the performance required by the envelope geometry. This approach is driven by a thorough understanding of current and emerging technologies used for facades of complex geometry, which inform both materials and assemblies. Assembly technologies are brought into the design process when establishing the general strategy for the load-bearing envelope. The approach in designing complex geometry structures is assembly-driven.

Method for MEP/environmental analysis of complex facades

The approach used to analyse the case studies in this book is based on establishing a balanced set of environmental performance criteria. A commonly used approach sets environmental criteria based on 'best practice'. However, this approach, where each criterion is derived independently, does not allow for an assessment of combined effects, nor for any subsequent optimisation.

The objective of this design method is to produce a balanced set of studies that are coordinated and that document a robust design concept by demonstrating a global understanding of all the implications when choosing a given environmental strategy. This method aims at gaining a basic understanding of the order of magnitude of all the environmental phenomena and their relative importance in the design within a very short time-frame. It departs from a more typical approach where one specific aspect of the design is optimised on the basis of an intuitive 'fit' with the proposed architectural concept. Environmental design covers a wide range of variables. Embedding interdependency between variables is necessary to ensure design robustness, which is achieved by establishing an equilibrium between all the design criteria rather than allowing one criterion to dominate.

The case studies shown in this book have been examined primarily by looking at eight aspects of environmental design (listed below) which affect the performance of both the external and internal environment. Each aspect of an environmental design can be divided into three essential components:

- Natural phenomena. The natural phenomena linked to the specific project climate.
- Analysis type. The effect of natural phenomena can be assessed by means of digital tools and hand calculations, which evaluate specific quantities.
- Design solution. The objective of the analysis is the selection of an assembly or material technology. Different design solutions are able to meet the same performance requirements.

These three categories can be divided further into the following primary categories of environmental study:

Natural phenomena

1. Thermal transmission and condensation.
2. Solar gain.
3. Daylighting.
4. Movement of air inside and outside the building.
5. Heating and cooling loads in relation to external heat gains.
6. Acoustic transmission.
7. Rainwater evacuation.
8. Material design life/fire resistance/corrosion resistance.

Analysis type

1. U-value calculation and calculation of condensation risk internally/interstitially/externally.
2. Calculation of peak solar gain across the year. Calculation of peak radiation, annual cumulative and solar exposure across the year.
3. Calculation of daylight levels (lux) and risk of glare across the year.
4. For the main wind directions, external CFD for cladding pressures (wind speed from codes for structural design) and pedestrian comfort (wind speed from wind rose for a typical year).
5. Estimation of each thermal load (solar gain/losses, conduction gain/losses, internal gain/losses, ventilation gains/losses). Environmental performance simulation tools (e.g. IES-VE) can be utilised for final assessment of the interaction of the thermal loads for the entire building across the whole year.
6. Sound attenuation index calculation for each assembly, by using digital analysis where each material and component can be modelled to assess the overall assembly performance.
7. Water flow digital analysis tracking the direction of water under gravity on curved surfaces. Preliminary 3D drainage layout including gutters and outlets. Preliminary gutter sizing.
8. Material research and selection. Proof-of-concept fire testing if required.

Design solution

1. Selection of insulation material, thickness and position of waterproofing. Design of framing and interfaces to meet requirements on linear thermal bridges.
2. Selection of glass type and external shading strategy in order to meet level of solar control required for peak solar gain.
3. Selection of glass light transmission levels and internal shading

strategy to meet internal daylight levels for internal visual comfort.
4. Preliminary cladding pressures for structural and facade design. Velocities around the building at pedestrian level for main wind directions. Internal velocities and temperature profiles for thermal comfort assessment.
5. Breakdown of component values of cooling/heating loads in order to assess the relative importance of each component. Establish environmental zones. Duct and AHU layout and sizes.
6. Amount of acoustic mass required from each assembly to provide the required sound attenuation, establish how mass is distributed across the assembly and which layers provide sound attenuation.
7. Design of drainage system (selection between gravity or siphonic types). Sizing and integration of drainage within facade build-up.
8. Material selection. Material specification. Testing specification.

The undertaking of environmental analysis in a facade design project is essential in order to establish a close relationship between envelope performance and requirements of mechanical ventilation (HVAC). The envelope performance regulates the main thermal gains or losses which require heating or cooling: solar, conduction and ventilation. The following design process is aimed at linking the two together:

a. Thermal loads assessment for a typical bay. Before undertaking any environmental analysis, a basic understanding of HVAC requirements is obtained by means of an estimation of thermal loads for each representative typical bay of the building. This initial assessment uses benchmark values which are based on best practice.
b. Preliminary duct sizes for a typical bay. The thermal loads computed for a typical bay are used to estimate the amount of air and the duct sizes required. As ventilation ducts typically occupy a significant volume of space within a building, this estimate allows zones for both facade and ceiling to be established.
c. Preliminary assessment of global loads. The global loads for the whole building are assessed by scaling-up the loads obtained from the representative typical bays proportionally to surface area.
d. Preliminary estimate of number of air handling units (AHUs). By using the global loads, the amount of air to be provided can be estimated, together with the required number, capacity and size of the AHUs, incorporating the required level of redundancy/back-up.
e. Specialist environmental studies. These studies are aimed at understanding the implications on user comfort of varying envelope performance parameters in relation to HVAC requirements.
f. Final environmental/envelope/HVAC strategy. This is based on a matrix of recommendations where different design solutions are combined to form options. The matrix is used as a decision-making tool.
g. Refinement of calculations. Calculations are refined for thermal loads, energy consumption costs for the building, for determining both the sizes of AHUs and the sizes of ducts for air supply and return.

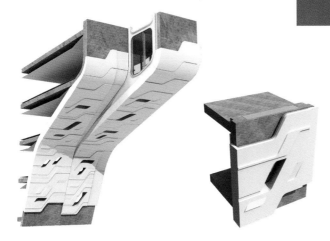

Current design methodology

The outputs generated through analysis and design require a method of design implementation in order to be transformed into a set of instructions, which is how the design is delivered for construction. Following the current approach in building construction, the building envelope design is delivered through a set of drawings, which represent the design intent, and a performance specification, which contains the performance requirements for the facade systems illustrated in the drawing set. These two outputs can be disengaged from one other.

The use of performance specifications originally comes from other industries where the project requirements are set out at the outset of the project, with limited change expected during the design process. In building construction, this approach assumes that contractors will complete all the detailing of systems and interfaces using the tender drawings as a visual guideline, in order to optimise for cost and ease of construction. The building engineer will check tender returns from bidding contractors based on compliance with what was issued at tender. Since aspects of the design are not described in the tender documentation, the contractor is allowed to propose design changes on the basis of their technical appropriateness. Different tender returns are compared on the basis of their 'quality'. After tender, the engineer is involved primarily in the assessment of visual benchmark mock-ups as well as maintaining a limited involvement during fabrication and construction phases. The role of the 'site inspection' for a building designer is usually limited to checking the visual quality of the construction only.

Project specific research allows the facade engineer to gather all the necessary information to ensure the design can be implemented. Research for most facade design projects is focused on project-specific procedures, mainly in order to unlock approvals and avoid delays in the programme. This approach is structured through a Gantt chart that sets out a series of sequential steps. The research is aimed specifically at understanding the full implications of building regulations, local standards and approval procedures. Research into design topics is limited to the understanding of all the technical requirements for the project. Regarding facade assemblies, the approach is based on obtaining, from specialist contractors, specific information about their products which is understood to be common to all competing manufacturers. This information is added to the performance specification as a way of determining a set of 'benchmark' criteria for assessment at the time of competitive tender. This usually leads to products or specific contractors mentioned in the specification, with the mention of 'or equivalent', in order to define that benchmark.

Limitations of current methodology

The limitations of the current method are that the performance specification does not capture how the various parts of the design are coordinated across the various disciplines. Consequently, there is no method to ensure that all design requirements are both compatible and coordinated. In the drawings, the specific method of assembly is not described. The drawings are organised as a hierarchy of general arrangement drawings, general assembly drawings and typical details, which describe only general design requirements at different scales. These do not engage with interfaces and illustrate only representative parts of the envelope. Similar to specifications, drawings do not validate coordination and compatibility between envelope systems or between different trades. Often, this specific information is thought to be unnecessary, as contractors are considered to possess the required experience in implementing well-known solutions. This approach suits projects where known solutions are implemented and is based on the fact that embedding coordination in the design documentation would increase cost as it would mean being overly prescriptive for certain parts of the design.

With the current approach there is no real mechanism to compare specific parts of the design with alternative proposals, made by contractors, which are not described in the tender package. For these parts, the assessment is limited to a visual comparison with the design intent. The technical aspect of the design does not need to be scrutinised, as the final engineering design is the contractor's responsibility in most construction contracts.

In this context, any project specific research is aimed at defining the scope of the design problem and limiting the opportunities for competing contractors to provide alternatives which do not meet the agreed design criteria. The process is one of collating technical information which is readily available and which is deemed to be relevant to 'define' the requirements of a design solution rather than provide a specific solution to these requirements. The lack of the availability of a specific solution can lead to unexpected consequences for the design if no specific alternatives are available.

Newtecnic's methodology

When the consequences of the proposed design are required to be fully understood at an early stage of project development, the emphasis turns to achieving a high level of design resolution. Early stage design documentation allows costs to be obtained from contractors as the design progresses. In the following design phases that lead to tender, value is added to the design process by undertaking detailed analysis of specific design aspects. The following additional outputs are provided at tender for design implementation:

- A full 3D model of the building envelope, which provides a full description of the detailed design, coordination between the envelope and the other trades and a tool for a direct take-off of quantities. The 3D model is developed at an early stage for cost certainty and then developed as the design evolves.
- Results for proof-of-concept physical tests and documented testing procedures to be used by the contractor to validate specific design aspects.
- Procedures for contractors to respond to the design at tender. These procedures include the documentation of any non-standard analysis process which is part of the proof-of-concept calculations, and is also provided as part of the design documentation.

This high level of design resolution can be achieved whilst avoiding the increased costs associated with being more prescriptive, as high cost certainty is already achieved at early stages through cost estimates obtained from contractors rather than by a cost consultant, who does not usually provide specialist knowledge for non-standard projects.

Factory visits, and the construction of performance mock-ups to validate fabrication, construction sequence and assembly performance, are an integral part of the design implementation method. This method includes the background research which is required to gather a set of project-specific information in order to define the most effective way to implement the facade design concept, generated by the facade engineer in response to the architectural brief. In order for the design to be implemented, a series of steps is required to validate the design proposed in in relation to the specific fabrication constraints of the appointed contractor.

Newtecnic's method of research is focused on generating new knowledge which is used to design material systems and assembly technology. The method of research serves as the basis for project implementation. The research required for an innovative facade design is driven by specific gaps in knowledge which are required in order to implement the facade design. These gaps in knowledge are typically:

- Physical properties of a primary material (material selection).
- Selection of a technology for a primary facade assembly (assembly technology).

The objective of the research method is to transform useful knowledge into design constraints/drivers for a given facade design project.

Material selection

Research associated with material selection considers how the facade engineer can design with a given material, in order to establish design constraints and analysis methods. Research is often focused on establishing the need for physical testing in order to calibrate finite element (FE) models or to provide validation for the use of a given material

system. Research identifies the limits of analysis and need for testing.

A second part of the research into material selection looks at constraints of manufacturing or fabrication, in order to set constraints on their use in a facade design. For example, the maximum size of a sheet material, the minimum thickness of an aluminium extrusion, the minimum radius of curvature for hot bending process of steel sections, can be determined. Visits to factories to identify the fabrication processes, and associated production costs, contribute significantly in the selection of materials. This is because the limiting factor in a material is often the ability of an individual fabricator or manufacturer to achieve the desired level of quality, complexity or precision, often as a result of the production cost of those processes.

Assembly technology

Research associated with assembly technology is concerned primarily with the identification of design constraints which are determined by the combination of components and materials within a facade assembly. The research may lead to physical testing to assess the performance of the assembly in terms of structural stability or weatherproofing.
The main topics of investigation are:

- Durability. The durability of the assembly is linked to the design life of the project and the frequency of cleaning and maintenance cycles planned for the completed installation.
- Fire and corrosion resistance. Fire resistance typically requires bespoke testing of a 1:1 scale mock-up in order to be able to meet the overall performance requirements of the full facade build-up.
- Maintenance and repair. The ability to repair local damage to a material is particularly appealing for heavyweight assemblies, which avoids replacing entire facade modules by mobilising equipment or causing disruption to the building occupants.

One of the primary purposes of the research conducted at an early stage is to compare examples of the application of the assembly technology with other built projects, in order to demonstrate the feasibility of specific aspects of the design.

Design validation

The first set of steps for design implementation after tender is aimed at validating the design concept proposed. The following steps are applicable to different degrees depending on the specific project:

1. Geometry definition. The coordination between facade, structure and HVAC (heating, ventilation, air conditioning) requires a strategy for the dimensional setting-out of each facade system. This setting-out is documented through drawings and through a fully coordinated digital 3D model, from which fabrication drawings can be extracted through a partially automated process.

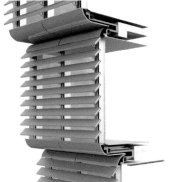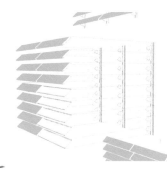

2. Material properties and testing. In order to validate the design of each assembly, the mechanical properties of each material are confirmed by each fabricator. For non-standard materials, such as advanced composites which are fabricator-specific, material testing is required. Material testing for non-standard materials is undertaken during the design phase in order to set minimum performance requirements to be met by the proposed fabricator. This preliminary testing provides both a proof-of-concept design, and a validated set of mechanical properties to be used as inputs for the structural analysis. This process significantly reduces uncertainty in the properties of the materials utilised and sets clear boundaries for contractor-specific variations on the materials, by imposing lower boundary values for the mechanical properties that drive structural sizes. Each specialist fabricator re-runs the same material tests after tender award in order to confirm compliance with the minimum requirements set during the preliminary testing.

3. Structural design and safety factors. The mechanical properties of a given material are the basis of the structural design of a facade system. Structural calculations are also based on the structural loads, including the weights of facade assemblies, wind loads obtained from wind tunnel testing, thermal loads, seismic loads, maintenance loads, impact loads, etc.

Material and load safety factors assumed during the design stage are based on minimum values imposed by structural standards. In order to confirm these assumptions, safety factors include - at this stage - considerations of the expected precision of workmanship during both fabrication and installation. When standards and codes do not directly apply to the design due to its innovative nature, these considerations assume even more importance in confirming the safety factors.

4. Project-specific testing. As part of the implementation of the design, critical items that require validation through physical testing are identified. Physical testing is required when designing outside standards and codes. It is conducted alongside calculations, which are based on first principles and generate the hypothesis that is tested. The purpose of physical testing is typically to establish the design capacity of a structural component, assembly or connection between components used in a facade assembly. The design capacity is typically compared against the most unfavourable design scenario in order to verify compliance with design safety factors, which must be appropriate for the application and are determined prior to testing. Similar proof-of-concept tests can include impact tests or water tightness tests, and are used to validate specific parts of the assembly rather than verify the general compliance of the system (which is covered in 'performance testing'). These tests are not covered by standards and codes, and are required to be designed from first principles. These are usually small-scale tests which are representative of the real project conditions. Typically, digital finite element analysis is used to establish the size and shape of representative samples, by comparing the performance of the sample with the real component through numerical simulation. Numerical simulations are only used for general comparison, as physical testing is required in order to ensure the safe behaviour of the assembly or component, which cannot be determined by numerical analysis. These bespoke tests are typically undertaken during the design stage as a proof-of-concept in order to establish the viability of both design outputs and process.

Project-bespoke testing typically requires the laboratory performing the testing to validate through peer reviews the procedure devised for the specific test as part of their own research activities. In order to carry out ambitious design tasks, a network of expertise is required in which methodologies are peer-reviewed. Consequently, design activities that lead to physical testing cannot be carried out in isolation.

5. Prototyping. A final validation of the assembly design may be required through a 1:1 physical mock-up or a scaled mock-up, where all the critical components are fabricated and installed according to the final design. This typically demonstrates the feasibility of critical design aspects and their visual appearance and is constructed before the performance mock-ups. The prototype is also typically used for informal structural testing, where the structural stability of the prototype is tested under project loads. This provides an effective method of validating complex assemblies before final compliance testing, described in the following paragraph.

6. Performance mock-up and testing.

The final validation of the assembly design is required through a 1:1 physical mock-up, where all the components are fabricated and installed according to the final design. This mock-up validates the following aspects:

a. Fabrication time. This is used to test the fabrication process and time required to fabricate each component.

b. Assembly performance. Sufficient adjustment is provided, ease of fabrication of components, ease and sequence of assembly of components.

c. Installation sequence. The proposed installation is tested and timed.

d. Testing of structural and environmental performance. The performance mock-up must withstand a series of tests which are performed following standard procedures set by codes, such as air and water tightness and impact resistance. The failure of any of these tests may require changes in the original design or in the fabrication techniques. After successful testing, fabrication can begin.

This section sets out preliminary specification information for the prototypes described on the third angle projection pages described in this book. The standards and norms can be used in early stage design work only, with a view to deriving preliminary costs for project-specific use of the facade and roof systems set out in this book.

STEP 1.0	Naming of facade systems as prototypes
STEP 1.1	Scope of the prototyping task

1.1.1 The scope of the prototypes is subject to this document which defines the nature of the works, their procurement and their installation, In addition to the requirements of other documents in tender documents,

1.1.2 The Contractor shall provide implicitly all services described or necessary for the full execution of the works and its completion.

1.1.3 The Contractor should be informed of all the requirements of other trades.

1.1.4 The prototypes are to be installed at a location to be agreed with the Project Architect.

1.1.5 The Contractor for this package of prototypes is responsible for the fabrication and installation of the following [example] prototype assemblies:
- ES.01 [External System]
- ES.02 [External System]
- ED.01 [External Door]
- ED.02 [External Door]
- FS.01 [Facade Structure]
- FS.02 [Facade Structure]
- RS.01 [Roof Structure]
- RS.02 [Roof Structure]

STEP 2.0	Definitions

2.1 Contractor's outputs include drawings, method statements, risk assessment, calculations and any other relevant information, maintaining the design and visual intent, functional, performance criteria and technical requirements as stated in the documentation provided by the Project Architect.

2.2 Design should be interpreted as an understanding of the visual intent as represented by the Design Drawings and Specifications.

2.3 Working Drawings of the Project Architect are detailed drawings provided by Project Architect.

2.4 The Project Architect's Drawings are the drawings and documents produced by the project architect, which include coordination between The Project architect and consultants in structural, electrical and MEP.

2.5 Tender Return is the submission by the Contractor to the Client for the completion of design, fabrication and installation of the prototypes at the end of the period of tender, for evaluation.

2.6 Detailed Design is that prepared by the Contractor represented by the Working Drawings and the contractors Written Documents.

2.7 Working Drawings of the contractor include all the graphical outputs produced by the Contractor after winning the bid for the fabrication and installation of the prototypes. These drawings are prepared by the Contractor based upon the Design Drawings of the Project Architect and which are included in this bid. The contractor must produce plans, elevations, sections and full size details of fabrication, assembly, installation and fixings of the prototypes. The Working Drawings are submitted in their entirety to the Project Architect for approval as mentioned above for checking before fabrication and installation.

2.8 As-built Drawing Prototypes are drawings produced by the Contractor, which show the Works as finally constructed on completion of the works. These as-build Drawings documents are to be submitted in 2 printed copies before acceptance of completed work.

2.9 Contract Documents are drawings listed in the Contract, comprising Design Drawings, written documents, and Contractor's Proposals as approved by the Project Architect.

2.10 Evaluation refers to the reviews carried out by the Project Architect The project architect will study the Tender Returns for the prototypes and to discuss options, materials, typical details and critical interfaces to ensure that the proposal is consistent with what is expected from the Design.

2.11 Inspection is the action carried out by the Project Architect, in the evaluation of materials, components, equipment and installation of the prototypes produced by the Contractor. Such inspection shall be limited to an inspection of the visual appearance only and not to the selection of materials or the Detailed Design or construction of components and equipment, which shall remain the sole responsibility of the Contractor. Such inspections by the Project Architect shall not relieve the Contractor from compliance with the drawings and written documents set in the Tender Documents.

2.12 An Inspecting Authority is a competent independent body or association, which verifies compliance with the Design. A testing authority is a qualified independent organization or association employed by the Contractor, accredited in testing, that provides equipment and facilities for the performance of appropriate tests, and issues results of independent tests in relation to graphical and written parts of this document. The choice of the testing authority is subject to acceptance by the Project Architect.

2.13 A testing authority is an organization employed by the Contractor, qualified independent accredited testing or association that provides equipment and facilities for the performance of appropriate tests, and issues results of independent tests in relation to graphics and written elements of this document. The choice of the supervisory authority is subject to acceptance by the Project Architect.

2.14 The Works is the scope of work covered by the graphical and written elements of this document.

2.15 Fabrication and Installation Program: Produced by the Contractor during the process of submission, indicating the dates of submission of Working Drawings of the Company designs, submission dates samples, prototypes and testing procedures before fabrication conforming to the Design.

2.16 Detailed Fabrication and Installation Program: the detailed planning of implementation of the Project, established by the Contractor during the preparation period following the order to start construction, and validated by the Project Architect and Client. This program is contractual after validation by the Project Architect.

2.17 Drawings to be read in conjunction with the prototype geometry models to be issued by Project Architect and panelisation 3D models are issued for information only.

2.18 Contract Documents include Design Drawings and written documents of the Design Team, as well as the Contractor's Proposals as submitted for approval by the Design Team, and the Approval Authority. The Design drawings of the Design Team are provided in a PDF version and in a digital version. Refer to the Drawing Register for the list of drawings and documents.

STEP 3.0   Reference documents

STEP 3.1   Scope of this document

3.1.1 These documents must be considered carefully by the Contractor during the development of its shop drawings, in order to ensure compliance with the design and required visual appearance. However, the Contractor may present alternative solutions to limit costs in line with Step 5.0 of this document. When the Contractor has alternatives and solutions that are considered not to be traditional then the Contractor must provide a strategy for certification.

3.1.2 The Contractor shall retain full responsibility for the production drawings of the Contractor and works in accordance with the performance criteria specified in this document.

3.1.3 The Contractor should never have a lesser standard of material or manufacturing process as specified in the articles of this document. Performance criteria when specified must be considered as minimum standards that the Contractor will necessarily achieve. All requirements in this document have to be taken into account in the submission of the Contractor.

3.1.4 The submittals that are required from the contractor and the process for their review and validation are set out in Step 7.0 of this document.

STEP 4.0   Methodologies during fabrication

4.1 Supporting Concrete and Steel Structure is expected to deflect under self-weight and will deflect further under load of prototype assemblies.

4.2 Facade Contractor to take into account weight already occurring and to calculate and submit conditions to the Project Architect for approval.

4.3 Facade Contractor's method statement to include a survey on how to create adjustment to what is constructed and to supporting structure to accommodate the installation of the prototypes.

STEP 5.0	Alternatives proposals and substitutions

5.1 The contractor is responsible for the production of all documentation including drawings and written documents relating to alternative proposals and substitutions.

5.2 All alternatives proposed by the contractor must be validated by the Project Architect

5.3 At Tender the Contractor may present alternative solutions for all systems, including: fixing systems for panels, support systems for panels, fixing systems for balustrades, and handrails. In the Contractor's submission, a report must be produced on this subject.

5.4 Any alternative proposals should be made during the tender stage.

5.5 Substitutions are admissible after contract signature for the prototypes.

STEP 6.0	Contractor-generated 3D BIM model

6.1.1 The Contractor is required to build an accurate 3D model to enable effective 3D coordination geometry of the prototypes. The 3D BIM model will integrate structural and facade components.

6.1.2 The Contractor will fully produce a 3D BIM model as described below. The Project Architect shall provide a copy of the model for information only. The 3D BIM model produced by the Contractor is to use same origin point as that of the Project Architect. This requirement allows the import and export of 2D and 3D data to the required location of the prototypes through the different platforms. The contractor must establish and implement the basic 3D data points, 3D reference points, the name of the model and distribution protocols, and a common site origin point as an insertion point for all data related to the site.

6.1.3 The 3D BIM model will be part of the implementation record of the Contractor and will be submitted to the Project Architect for review. The Contractor shall present the 3D BIM model, as well as 2D working drawings and shop drawings. The obligation to provide a 3D model does not remove / does not diminish the other requirements concerning the content of the construction documents as indicated in this document.

6.1.4 The Contractor and other sub-contractors appointed shall provide updates to the 3D BIM model weekly and shall perform overall coordination and 3D collision detection with other packages and with the Project Architect.

6.1.5 The Contractor shall demonstrate the skills of its team in 3D BIM modelling by presenting document geometrically complex projects previously undertaken. In addition, the Contractor shall employ 3D consultants who can prove by documents their experiences with projects with complex geometry.

6.1.6 The Contractor shall establish the basis of 3D data points for 3D reference, and the name of the model.

6.1.7 The naming convention is also described in Section 8 of the "AEC BIM Protocol v2.0" available for download on http://aecuk. wordpress.com/ documents/ and a common origin site as an entry point to all data relating to the site.

6.1.8 The Contractor of the Facade package will be responsible for the receipt, management and assimilation of all 3D project information in the central database.

6.1.9 A comprehensive strategy will be subject to the approval of the Prime Contractor and the Owner prior to commencement of work.

6.1.10 The Contractor will be responsible for related equipment (including all fees), responsible for the project team and sub-contractors (approved by the Project Architect and the Client) and staff to assist the Project Architect in the use of the 3D BIM model.

6.1.11 The Contractor of the prototypes package is responsible for all other costs associated with the provision of a 3D model manager system, license fees, hardware, software, installation, maintenance, operation, training, coordination and technical support.

STEP 6.2	Licences, authorship rights

6.2.1 All plans, drawings or figures containing copyright information shall display the appropriate authorization for the use of data.

6.2.2 The model shall be returned to the Project Architect at the end of the task.

STEP 6.3	Production of working drawings and shop drawings

6.3.1 The Project Architect will not approve shop drawings and other documents submitted by the Contractor of the prototypes package if they are not integrated in the 3D BIM model maintained by the Contractor. To avoid confusion, the Contractor is solely responsible for the accuracy of the model. The Project Architect will approve only 2D shop drawings in conjunction with 3D information.

6.3.2 The BIM model to be completed ahead of fabrication of the prototypes in order to avoid any delays to program for fabrication and installation.

STEP 6.4 Coordination drawings: 2D plans and 3D model

6.4.1 The Contractor shall provide the coordinated outputs in 2D and 3D based on the Project Architect's drawings and those of associated primary structure.

6.4.2 The Contractor shall ensure that all outputs in 2D and 3D, that form the basis of submittals, are generated from the BIM model and all changes resulting from the 3D BIM coordination model are incorporated into the shop drawings 2D and 3D are not automatically generated by the 3D BIM process.

6.4.3 Additional plans are not created from the 3D model shall be designated as such by the Contractor.

STEP 6.5 Level of detail of the 3D model

6.5.1 The Contractor will be responsible for the preparation, coordination, management and update of the 3D BIM model.

6.5.2 The Contractor shall construct a BIM model on the basis of 2D DWG formatted information for primary structure files and facade. This DWG information will be provided in a compatible format. The complexity of primary structure and of the facades shall be taken into account by the Contractor when creating its own 3D model.

6.5.3 The Contractor shall create native 3D BIM model elements size greater than 50 mm in any direction. Items smaller than this size shall be imported from 3D software used for manufacturing of facade components, thereby adequately describing the geometry part at small scale.

STEP 6.6 Digital databases

6.6.1 The computer database includes 2D digital computer files that describe graphically or by listing or location of work parties.

6.6.2 These files may include plans, sections and details. These files are produced by geometrical extractions / derivatives 3D database and as such will follow the principles of the geometrically 3D database.

6.6.3 2D computer files for this project are produced with a suitable 2D CAD drawing package. If the Project Architect decides to change the common 2D CAD drawing package platform, the Contractor shall allow two weeks preparation time. The Contractor and Project Architect will conduct the change of software at the same time.

6.6.4 The 3D computer data consists of the 3D model and contract documents, showing the design, location and dimensional position of key point's 3D descriptive lines and surfaces of the structure. The 3D database for this project will be incorporated into the 3D model.

6.6.5 As most 3D modelling software is not compatible with other earlier versions, this requires that all design team works with the same version.

6.6.6 Database files and 2D drawings are created from information taken from 3D data files, and as such are subject to the geometrically and dimensionally files 3D database that have a role of control of dimensions and of geometric verification.

6.6.7 For these items, the setting out, information for geometry and dimensions contained in the 3D database takes precedence over the information contained in the other contract documents. All 2D information should be linked dynamically to 3D information directly and not form a separate set of information.

6.6.8 Files of digital electronic data that form the basis of two-dimensional and three-dimensional data shall be updated weekly and distributed through a secure file sharing site implemented by the Contractor and approved by the Project Architect.

STEP 6.7 Coordination requirements for geometry data

6.7.1 The Contractor shall coordinate files 2D data and plans for 3D data files. In case of conflict between the 3D data files, plans and specifications or other documents, the anomalies identified will be reported to the Project Architect, who will assist in resolving the conflicting requirements.

6.7.2 The Contractor shall also verify the dimensions and construction conditions on the site, and report to the Project Architect, in writing, of the differences between the actual conditions, plans and 3D models to make possible decisions and receive the instructions of the Project Architect prior to overcome these differences.

6.7.3 In case of discrepancies or conflicts between plans, 3D models, specifications or errors on existing plans, 3D models, prescriptions, the situation shall be reported to the Project Architect in writing and it will issue a clarification.

6.7.4 The Contractor shall report any discrepancies between the dimensions shown on the drawings on paper and dimensions shown on the drawings in electronic format to the Project Architect for resolution format. The Contractor will be held liable if it fails to coordinate, verify dimensions and report anomalies to the Project Architect for resolution.

STEP 6.8 Use of 3D database

STEP 6.9 Data ownership

6.9.1 The 3D model, 3D databases, electronic media, electronic forms and other similar terms are subject to the terms and conditions of use documents provided by the Project Architect.

STEP 6.10 Using 3D Models

6.10.1 The Project Architect has developed a 3D model and can distribute data using computer database and dimensional inspection. Its use by the Contractor is limited by the Project Architect as follows:

6.10.1.1 To establish certain elements of work, as described by the 3D BIM model and the geometry of the project according to plan.

6.10.1.2 To make use of the dimensional control elements recognized as needing dimensional inspection and / or having a geometric authority.

6.10.1.3 For use as a basis for the development of the arrangement, coordination and production, plans and databases of these elements represented. The Contractor shall use all the technology available and applicable methods to monitor, locate and identify the elements of on-site construction, check tolerances and quality of surface and geometric continuity, execute plans workshop three-dimensional and two-dimensional with the approval of the Project Architect and the Client.

6.10.1.4 The Contractor shall use all the technology and methods available and applicable to continuously monitor the conditions requiring adjustment on site, check tolerances of surfaces and geometric continuity, execute shop drawings in three dimensions and in two dimensions with the approval of the Project Architect and the Client.

STEP 6.11 Conditions of use

6.11.1 Using these databases 3D model, the Contractor agrees to the following provisions:

6.11.2 Authorized use of 3D data: The Project Architect grants to the Contractor the non-exclusive right to use the 3D database for the prototypes in accordance with the terms and conditions of this document. The 3D database should be used to establish the geometry of three-dimensional surfaces and elements represented and their relationship with the digital 3D setting information, as (x, y, z) coordinates set out in the tender documents.

6.11.3 The Contractor and their respective sub-contractors, agents or representatives are not entitled to rely on the details or specifications contained in the 3D database for other purposes.

6.11.4 The Contractor acknowledges the limited completeness of data in the 3D database and these data are intended to complement other contract documents, and understands that the model is not transmitted produced for the construction or manufacturing purposes.

6.11.5 Unauthorized use of 3D data: 3D data should not be used by the Contractor, or transferred to another party, for use in other projects, or for any other purpose not provided for Project Architects, without the express written permission of Project Architects. Unauthorized modification or reuse shall be at the sole risk of the Contractor and the Contractor shall accept sub-contractors these conditions for access to 3D databases shall take the Project Architect out of all claims for injuries, damages, losses, costs and legal fees resulting from modification or unauthorized use of such information. The 3D database developed by the Project Architect is provided only to provide a service to the Contractor and is protected by copyright laws and conventions. In providing the 3D database, the Project Architect and the Contractor shall not change the scope of their service to which each was assigned under its contractual arrangements with the Client, and shall not modify the division of responsibilities between the Project Architect, the Contractor and the Client as defined in their respective agreements.

6.11.6 Compatibility and Interoperability: The Project Architect acknowledges that the good compatibility of the 3D database to other programs may be necessary to use some or sub-contractors. Compatibility is the responsibility of the Contractor, unless otherwise agreed.

6.11.7 The Architect and the Contractor will review the software compatibility tests before the planned issue of the 3D model to the sub-contractor for use. The Contractor is responsible for ensuring that all Master 3D models are perfectly coordinated with each other and their sub-contractors, use common point settings, they are in the correct units and scales. To clarify, all models shall operate fully as if they were created as native elements in the 3D software.

6.11.8 If problems are encountered with 3D models provided by the Contractor or any of their sub-contractors, the Project Architect or the Client has the right to ask the Contractors to rebuild their models, within a two week period.

STEP 6.12   Control of geometry

6.12.1 The objectives of the design of the outer surface of the prototypes are shown in 3D model provided by the Project Architect.

6.12.2 The Architect's 3D model represents the basis for determining the size, shape and configuration of the surfaces of the prototypes and / or related elements, and for the definition of the geometry for dimensional control of the finished shape surface location, common axis and of setting out points.

6.12.3 Changes in the 3D database: configuration, sizes and profiles of the prototype geometry cannot be changed after it has been fully documented in the files and plans developed with the express written permission of the Project Architect. Changes and adjustments details may be made to the design of the Project Architect for the structure, materials, attachment and seals, provided that the general design and intent of performance described in this document are maintained or exceeded, in the judgment of the Project Architect only. Such changes and modifications are to be shown and identified on 3D files developed and described in the proposal and submission to the Project Architect for approval.

6.12.4. Maintain the design concept and elements of the assemblies shown as base profiles, joint design, and alignment of the elements and distance from the finished surface meeting at the surface of the primary structure. Do not change without the express written consent of the Project Architect. All these changes require modification by the Contractor related 3D files. Dimensions, sizes and spatial relationships of components or assemblies that are not exposed to the view can be modified by the Contractor, but will always be subject to 3D files linked by the Contractor and submitted to the Project Architect for approval. All 3D electronic files submitted to the Project Architect shall be formats to match the version of the original files of the Project Architect.

STEP 6.13   Requirements for coordination by the Contractor

6.13.1 Before using the information contained in the dimensional control 3D database for the development of working drawings and shop drawings, the Contractor shall:

6.13.2 Review and verify the conditions, dimensions and data from 3D data prior to the development plans of manufacture, control management plans, equipment manufacturing CNC, or other applications that define and / or regulates the manufacture and assembly of a prototype element;

6.13.3 Take all reasonable measures to prevent unauthorized access or loss of the 3D database;

6.13.4 Keep an independent record of all changes to the database of 3D data that can be processed by the Contractor, sub-contractors and their employees and agents;

6.13.5 Ensure that its sub-contractors are solely and exclusively responsible for the accuracy and relevance of all subsequent 3D data models or other electronic media developed by these sub-contractors. The Project Architect is not a party and has no control over the use of media generated by other parties;

6.13.6 Take appropriate measures, through training or otherwise, with its sub-contractors, employees and agents who have access to this 3D database to ensure compliance with these conditions;

6.13.7 Send copies of 3D data models or other electronic media generated by the Contractor or sub-contractor to the Project Architect for review prior to commencement of manufacturing operations. Project Architect may review and comment on these media at its discretion. This information is added to the submission of shop drawings.

STEP 6.14   Additional requirements

6.14.1 In using the 3D database, the Contractor also agrees to the following conditions:

6.14.2 To check the location of critical elements during and after installation, such as points of connection between the various materials and systems. Notify the Project Architect items that range from 3D database. Update the database with location data corrected.

6.14.3 To import and overlay data for points, surfaces and field lines manufactured and installed in the 3D database, and place them in separate files, as agreed with the Project Architect. If translations of software are required, verify the data after the translation process and certify the accuracy in writing to the Project Architect and consultant architect.

6.14.4 Transmit copies of data files to the Project Architect to partial completion. Coordinate with documents and statements of the prototypes.

6.14.5 At the request of the Project Architect, make the basis of original 3D data and all other paper documents, materials and other property of the Architect held by the Contractor, sub-contractors, employees and agents in the project.

6.14.6 Data ownership of the Project Architect. Because the information stored in the database of 3D data can be modified by other parties, intentionally or otherwise, without prior notice or indication of the said amendment, the Project Architect reserves the right to remove all indications of ownership and / or participation in the 3D database from each electronic medium that is not in its possession. The Project Architect does not provide, and the Contractor does have receive, rights or recognition in ownership of the 3D database from computer programs, the specifications or information provided or developed by the Project Architect.

STEP 6.15   Data integrity and deterioration

6.15.1 The Contractor recognizes that the design, plans and data stored on electronic media such as CD, DVD may be subject to undetectable alterations or uncontrollable deterioration. The Contractor therefore agrees that the Project Architect will not be responsible for the completeness or accuracy of any materials provided electronically. The database in three dimensions and other contract documents are intended to be complementary to each other, and do not necessarily supersede the information contained in the other contract documents. Paper documents with electronic data files form the basis of the scope of work.

STEP 6.16   Submission of 3D coordination plans

6.16.1 The Contractor shall prepare coordination plans if the limited availability of space requires maximum utilization of space for efficient installation of different components, or if coordination is required for installation of products and materials fabricated by separate entities.

6.16.2 The Contractor shall also indicate the sequences necessary for the installation.

STEP 6.17   Quality of geometry

6.17.1 The 3D database describes the geometric relationships between the different prototypes. It also contains the geometric definitions of these elements which form the geometric continuity of the surface between the individual elements of the prototype panels. The Contractor shall ensure that the geometric definitions surface quality and continuity are implemented as described below:

6.17.2 Surfaces: The 3D database defines the geometric shape of each element of the prototype panels. Some elements are geometrically either flat, singly curved or doubly curved. Each area is defined as a smooth continuous geometry, without bumps, blocks or folds, with the exception of the edge panels. The Contractor shall ensure that the shape of the surface of each panel follows the overall geometric form as defined in the 3D database.

6.17.3 Continuity of the geometric surface: The 3D database describes the geometric continuity between the panels at each joint and edge. The continuity of the surface is described mathematically by the geometry of the model itself. The Contractor shall ensure the production of panels and the assembly on site ensures the geometric continuity between the panels at each point where the tangent or curvature continuity is described in the 3D database between panels.

6.17.4 Quality Control Process: The Contractor shall provide a set of quality control / quality assurance procedures for the 3D design, engineering, manufacturing, and corresponding geometric alignment of the installation on site. This methodological note shall be submitted to the Project Architect for approval.

6.17.5 Checking the implementation of the Master 3D model geometry of the surface: The Contractor shall verify the geometric quality of each panel of the Facade in the shop fabrication and the correct geometric continuity between the panels on the site. The Contractor shall assist the Project Architect in inspecting the geometrical conformity of the work performed to the geometry defined in the 3D database.

STEP 6.18   Tolerances

6.18.1 In addition to the dimensional tolerances specified for manufacture and installation described elsewhere in this document, the Contractor shall comply with the following tolerances:

6.18.2 Geometric continuity: Where the continuity of tangency between the panels is defined in the 3D database, the angle between the planes tangent to a common joint between two panels executed tangent continuous shall not exceed ± 0.1 degrees

6.18.3 Deviation from the geometry of 3D database: The deviation of the geometry of 3D database should not exceed + / –10 mm panel and the geometric positioning of the location (dot) provided.

6.18.4 The alignment of the joints: The angle between two adjacent edges of the panels to any joint shall not exceed ± 0.1 degrees or + / –10mm. The deviation from the geometric database, the alignment direction of the 3D edge shall not exceed ± 0.1 degrees or + / –10mm compared to the given point and anywhere given geometry.

STEP 7.0   Contractor's responsibilities

STEP 7.1   General procedures

7.1.1 The contractor is responsible for the shop drawings, the manufacture work in factory or on site, the supply of all elements, the supervision of installation, prototypes of the works whilst complying with the visual intent indicated on the Design Drawings and criteria stated in this document.

7.1.2 Where no material, product or supplier is indicated in this document, propose suitable materials and systems prior to Contract award which comply with the visual intent and performance criteria stated and remain fully responsible for the Detailed Design of the prototypes.

7.1.3 Where a particular material, product or supplier is indicated in this document, such material, product or supplier shall be deemed indicative representing the project architect's design intent only. The Contractor may complete the installation using that product, or such other confirmed as acceptable by the project architect in writing, but shall remain fully responsible for the Detailed Design and performance of the works.

7.1.4 Coordination Register. In the absence of coordination being undertaken between prototype package documentation and the documentation of other packages, due to information not being available, a coordination register is provided in this document. The Contractor is to undertake and complete all the coordination tasks set out in the Coordination Register. Following coordination with the contractors of the other packages, the Prototype Contractor shall be responsible for implementing the works in accordance with the written and graphic parts of this document, together with the documents listed in this document.

STEP 7.2   General responsibilities

7.2.1 The Contractor is to take responsibility for the Contractor Design Works as identified within this document as follows:

7.2.2 Undertake the Detailed Design maintaining the function, visual requirements, and performance of the Design.

7.2.3 Provide detailed proposals, demonstrating compliance with the visual intent and confirm the provision of fully warranted systems in accordance with the Contract conditions.

7.2.4 The Contractor's proposals shall include drawings, calculations, methods, technical specifications and risk assessment detailing the proposed materials and systems in order that a technical appraisal can be made by Project Architect.

7.2.5 A Tender based on the Contractor's own preferred design solution may be offered for acceptance by the Project Architect provided the performance and visual requirements are fully satisfied. Any alternative solutions shall not alter the performance requirements, appearance or design intent of the Design Drawings and this document. An associated risk assessment shall be submitted as part of the proposed design solution documentation.

7.2.6 This document and Design Drawings may be modified and amended prior to Contract award to reflect the agreed final scope of the Works, materials and systems selected to reflect the visual intent. The Detailed Design shall reflect the Contract Specification and Drawings.

7.2.7 The design and visual character of the prototypes is important and shall be maintained. Hence, there shall be no variation in the final surface finish of similar materials, which shall remain visually consistent, including colour and texture, regardless of orientation or natural grain within agreed tolerances and agreed samples by the Project Architect. The choice of colour and texture are left to the Project Architect and this choice can be modified at any moment after signature of the deal, if modified before production.

7.2.8 Provide submittals outlined within each section of this document.

7.2.9 Provide Working Drawings and technical information to demonstrate compliance with the Design Drawings and Specification. The Contractor's final Detailed Design shall be based on the Design Drawings which indicate generic solutions and may not cover all conditions. Associated risk assessment shall be submitted as part of the documentation.

7.2.10 Where proprietary products are to be installed, be responsible for providing any modification, additional bracing, reinforcing, suitable fixings, etc. to ensure that the products meet the requirements of this document for the circumstances and situation in which they shall be expected to perform. Be responsible for conveying any concerns that the manufacturers may have expressed regarding the suitability of products for the purpose intended.

7.2.11 No portion of the Works shall commence without acceptance of the required submittals by the project architect.

7.2.12 Comply with health and safety requirements including the production and submission of system risk assessment analysis reports.

7.2.13 Be responsible for ensuring that items specified are installed correctly such that the performance requirements specified are fully satisfied for the service life required. All fixings and other aspects not fully detailed or specified shall be regarded as the Contractor's responsibility.

7.2.14 Be responsible for the final selection of products and associated components, which shall be used solely for the purpose intended by the manufacturer; which shall satisfy the requirements of this document.

7.2.15 Be responsible for the carrying out of all testing required by this document.

7.2.16 Coordinate with the work of others including all interfacing as required.

7.2.17 Provide warranties as required by this document.

7.2.18 Provide warranties as required by the project.

7.2.19 Submit relevant documents to statutory authorities as required to comply with the requirements of this document.

7.2.20 Provide details, calculations and any other relevant information to the project architect for submission to and approval by the local authorities. Make any adjustments required by the local authorities, following submissions, to the satisfaction of the project architect.

7.2.21 In addition to submissions for the local authority be responsible for submitting structural, deflection and other calculations and technical information, where required (as requested in this document) for review by the Project Architect. Such submissions shall demonstrate compliance with this document.

7.2.22 Set out the prototypes and accurately coordinate all related Works.

7.2.23 The Contractor shall submit to the acceptance of the design team and the Client, the identity of the approved organization that will approve the contractor's documentation for construction which will be carried out by the contractor and validate the tests and the mock-up which will be carried out by the contractor.

STEP 7.3   Contractor's proposal

7.3.1   The Contractor's Proposals for the prototypes will be reviewed during the Evaluation by the Project Architect. Attend evaluation meetings as required and make adjustments and alterations to the Contractor's Proposals to agree the main design principles to the satisfaction of the Project Architect prior to the possible Contract award. The contractor is to provide the Project Architect with access to the design office and personnel during the Design Evaluation.

7.3.2   The Contractor's Proposals as a minimum shall include:

7.3.2.1   Full details of systems, materials and suppliers.

7.3.2.2   Details of any specialist involvement such as provisions for accommodation of the accepted building maintenance system.

7.3.2.3   Details of Working Drawings programme.

7.3.2.4   Mock-ups of systems and samples available in the same way as those indicated in this document materials.

7.3.2.5   Technical statements confirming performance compliance.

7.3.2.6   Independent test certification.

7.3.2.7   Details of guarantees and warranties including details of predicted service lives for primary and secondary components.

7.3.2.8   Summary of deviations from the Design Drawings and Specification.

7.3.2.9   Commissioning information as relevant.

7.3.2.10   Health and Safety design risk assessment.

7.3.3   The Contractor shall establish an ongoing relationship with the Project Architect of the period of production of the Contractor's working drawings.

STEP 7.4   Contractor's working drawings

7.4.1   Although the Design Drawings show considerable detail and dimensions, no warranty or representation is given by the Project Architect as to the accuracy of such dimensions or the adequacy or buildability of such details. Should the Contractor adopt the details or arrangements indicated on the Design Drawings, it shall be deemed that he has checked their buildability and performance in terms of this document, all relevant regulations and codes of practice, and manufacturers' recommendations for any products referred to.

7.4.2   Comply with all relevant codes of practice, standards, fire regulations, local building codes, safety regulations and any other regulations applicable to the installation, together with all relevant statutory rules, regulations applicable to both the design and execution of the prototypes.

7.4.3   Prepare a programme for the Detailed Design showing all tasks and submissions and submit for acceptance by the Project Architect.

7.4.4   Produce Working Drawings, supported by calculations for review by the Project Architect.

7.4.5   Submit to the Project Architect 3 copies of all design/ production information, in accordance with the Contract Conditions,

7.4.6   The Working Drawings shall finalise all manufacturing, interface and installation details.

7.4.7   Ensure that any necessary amendments are made until the Project Architect confirms that resubmission is not required, submit copies of amended drawings and related documents, and ensure incorporation of necessary amendments.

7.4.8   This document shall not be altered without the Project Architect's prior written consent.

7.4.9   Select suitable materials, sizes, thicknesses, types and locations of fixings and sealants, all in accordance with specified standards and ensure that they are used for the purpose intended by the manufacturer.

7.4.10   Any necessary support structure shall incorporate all movements and tolerances to which it is subjected.

7.4.11   Submit descriptions of relevant structural performance principles of the prototypes, including how and where loads are transmitted to the primary structure and the accommodation of tolerances.

7.4.12   Show details of all fixing requirements to interfacing elements of the Works, which shall be agreed with the Project Architect prior to commencement of the installation.

7.4.13   Coordinate all interfaces.

STEP 7.5   Systems and materials

7.5.1   The components of the entire assembly shall be covered by a single source warranty. Therefore, approval shall be obtained from the manufacturer for all materials to be used.

7.5.2 The works shall be designed and installed as complete integrated systems, including all necessary support structure, bracketry, fixing rails and plates, angles, cleats, grouting, fixings and fastenings, rivets, clips, vapour control barriers, insulation, damp-proof membranes, breather and other membranes, intumescent firestops and cavity barriers, acoustic breaks, pressed metal components, closures, seals and sealants, gaskets, fillers, tapes, spacers, packers, shims, isolators and all other accessories and components necessary to complete the installation.

7.5.3 Where this document identifies preferred systems and materials, these shall be confirmed as being suitable for their specified and intended purpose with the Tender return. If no such specific confirmation is received, then the submission of the Tender return itself shall constitute such a confirmation. If the preferred systems and materials are considered unsuitable, advise at the time of Tender.

7.5.4 Acceptance of alternative proposals by the Project Architect shall not relieve the Contractor from responsibility to provide suitable systems, materials, components and assemblies, which shall be used as intended by the manufacturer and in compliance with the Contract Documents.

7.5.5 If, with the Tender return, the Contractor submits no such alternative proposal to any of the preferences indicated in the Tender Documents, then those proposed in this document and on the Design Drawings shall be deemed to be acceptable and be warranted by the Contractor.

7.5.6 The works shall accommodate all architectural and functional features indicated on the Design Drawings, whilst maintaining the specified performance.

7.5.7 Dimensions indicated on the Design Drawings are nominal and indicative of the design intent. The Contractor shall maintain these dimensions and clearly state them on the Working Drawings. Any deviations to the indicated dimensions shall be stated with the Tender return.

7.5.8 Rain-screen systems shall perform through back draining and ventilation with pressure equalisation principles.

7.5.9 An air gap shall be provided to the rear of the cladding panels to form a cavity to suit rain-screen principles.

7.5.10 Finishes:

7.5.10.1 All metal components shall be corrosion protected.

7.5.10.2 Visible aluminium components shall be either powder coated or anodised as indicated on the Design Drawings or as described.

7.5.10.3 Colour(s) shall be to the acceptance of the Project Architect. The choice of colour and texture is left to the Project Architect and this choice can be modified at any time before the beginning of fabrication.

7.5.11 Additional integrated components that may be required, such as lightning protection, shall be concealed.

STEP 7.6	Detailed design, fabrication and installation tolerances

7.6.1 This document together with the corresponding Design Drawings indicate the dimensional tolerances (referred to as tolerances to which the Contractor shall work for the Detailed Design, manufacture, sub-assembly, setting out and installation of the Works.

7.6.2 The Working Drawings shall clearly demonstrate how manufacturing and construction tolerances are to be accommodated.

7.6.3 Take account of various specified tolerances and their effect on the Works. Inform the Project Architect of any apparent tolerance omissions, inconsistencies or incompatibilities.

7.6.4 Maintain the tolerances as defined and demonstrate, upon request by the Project Architect, the means by which specified tolerances shall be assured and, where appropriate, which specialist equipment and/or methods shall be used.

7.6.5 All dimensions shall be checked at the agreed location for installation, confirming all dimensions critical to the prototypes. Measurements shall be taken, agreed location for installation, in sufficient time to enable corrective action to be taken to the prototypes, to ensure an accurate fit within agreed or implied tolerances.

7.6.6 Refer to and take account of the Structural Engineer's Movements and Tolerances information.

7.6.7 Confirm common reference points and agree with the Project Architect. Carry out dimensional checks prior to the commencement of manufacture as necessary.

7.6.8 Ensure that any dimensions are compatible and consistent with other relevant design dimensions and accumulated tolerances and movements. State and/ or show, on the Working Drawings, the provisions made which are intended to accommodate the accumulated tolerances of adjoining or adjacent trades.

7.6.9 Inform the Project Architect of any work that does not meet the specified tolerances.

7.6.10 The Works shall be free from deformation outside of specified tolerances and shall not be subject to warping, twisting and/ or perishing but remain stable, firm, free from vibrations, knocking, rattles and/ or whistles, squeaks or other such noises, taking into account known or specified conditions.

7.6.11 Details shall be provided for acceptance by the Project Architect of the Contractor's proposed methods for achieving and constantly monitoring the fabrication and erection tolerances during all stages of the prototypes. Detailed records of the constant control and tolerance achieved shall be submitted to the Project Architect.

7.6.12 In the event of there being any discrepancy in the values of existing datum reference points, datum levels, buildings, foundations or other features to which the Works are related, determine and report such a discrepancy to the Project Architect and obtain written instructions before proceeding.

7.6.13 The permissible tolerances stated in this document shall be progressively checked up to handover. Where two or more different tolerances can be derived by calculation and/ or from the Design Drawings for the same dimension, the least tolerance shall apply which shall be confirmed by the Contractor to the Project Architect. Tolerances shall not be cumulative.

STEP 7.7 Substitution during tender

7.7.1 Should the Contractor, after consideration of all the criteria which in his specialist knowledge are relevant to the design and construction of the Works, wish to make proposals for changes in any details, dimensions or materials shown in the Design Drawings or referred to in this document, then such proposals shall be provided as separate alternative options and returned with the Tender. In no way shall any proposal fail to meet the minimum performance requirements herein specified.

7.7.2 A request for a substitution shall be deemed to be a warranty by the Contractor to the client that such substitutions meet the requirements of this document and as such must be confirmed in writing as equal by the Contractor and accepted in writing by the Project Architect. Admissibility of any request for substitution after Tender shall be at the sole discretion of the Project Architect and may be rejected without reason given.

7.7.3 In the case that any substitution alters the specified requirements, submit sufficient information on substituted materials to allow evaluation by the Project Architect on any deviations from this document.

STEP 7.8 Interfaces

7.8.1 Complete the Detailed Design of all interfaces with adjoining trades prior to commencement of manufacture.

7.8.2 Ensure that all interfaces are fully co-ordinated prior to commencement.

STEP 8.0 Submittals

STEP 8.1 Submittals generally

8.1.1 No portion of the Works shall commence without acceptance of the required submittals by the Project Architect. All submittal replies at Tender should be verified by the Project Architect.

8.1.2 A schedule of submittals shall be provided for agreement with the Project Architect. Schedule to indicate the dates on which the Project Architect shall receive the required submittals. The schedule shall be correlated with the master programme and allow a reasonable amount of time for the review of each submittal. Critical decision dates shall be indicated for selection of finishes and colours. The schedule of submittals shall be revised and resubmitted as necessary.

8.1.3 Provide submittals in accordance with the following:

8.1.3.1 Addressing of Submittals: Submittals shall be delivered to the premises of the Project Architect.

8.1.3.2 Identification of Submittals: Each submittal shall be individually identified with the project name, respective specification reference, supplier's/ manufacturer's name and product reference as appropriate. Each submittal shall be accompanied by a transmittal form containing similar information; together with the purpose for which the submittal is being made. Space shall be provided on each item submitted for stamping by the Project Architect.

8.1.3.3 Numbering of Submittals: Submittals shall be numbered consecutively and that numbering system shall be retained throughout all revisions and re-submittals.

8.1.3.4 Completeness of Submittals: All relevant information shall be included within each submittal to define completely and explain each separate system of work. Submittals may be combined from various sections as necessary and furnished at one time as a single submission.

8.1.3.5 Variations and Substitutions: Submittals that differ from the requirements of the Design Drawings and this document shall be so identified.

8.1.4 Submission and Return of Working Drawings/ Documents:

8.1.4.1 Allow for a sufficient period (a minimum of 5 working days) between the first submission of a drawing/ document and receipt of comments. Allow for resubmissions for each item to achieve an 'A' or 'B' status.

8.1.4.2 Provide a list of Working Drawings proposed.

8.1.4.3 Information specifically requested for each element of the Works shall be provided. Additional information may be required by the Project Architect on inspection of the Contractor's submittals to allow for accurate comments to be made.

8.1.4.4 Initial reviews of submittals from the Contractor shall made using the following proformas:

8.1.5 The Contractor's submittals shall be reviewed by the Project Architect during the Evaluation, and any alteration and/ or agreements reached shall be incorporated into the Contract documentation.

8.1.6 Provide submittals at the time of Tender as listed in this document.

8.1.7 After Contract award provide Working Drawings, samples, quality benchmarks, calculations and test reports as requested in this document and other relevant data.

8.2.1 Provide Tender submittals in accordance with the requirements of this document.

8.2.2 Submit a design response with the Tender proposal, to include all profiles of typical conditions, with dimensions.

8.2.3 The Tender design response shall include:

8.2.3.1 Samples where specified.

8.2.3.2 QA/ QC programme.

8.2.3.3 List of proposed Working Drawings.

8.2.3.4 Summary of deviations from this document.

8.2.3.5 Outline technical specifications reflecting proposed materials/ systems.

8.2.3.6 A list of proposed suppliers and sub-Contractors intended to be used.

8.3.1 The Project Architect shall review submittals for general and practical conformance with the requirements of the Design. Submittals which meet these requirements shall be stamped or marked in accordance with the procedure described herein. Submittals which are incomplete or erroneous, or which are not required, will be returned and a new submittal made as necessary. The Project Architect's review shall not be exhaustive and shall not relieve the Contractor of the responsibility for any omission or deficiencies or from the responsibility to coordinate the work with that of others (which includes the taking of relevant site dimensions as necessary).

8.3.2 Submittals which provide supplementary information to substantiate the technical performance of building systems, components and materials including, but not necessarily limited to, supplementary product literature, certifications, statements of manufacturer's review and pre-assembled testing and inspection reports, will be stamped 'Record Document' by the Contractor before submission.

8.3.3 Re-submittals shall be made under the procedure for initial submittals; identifying changes made since previous submittals.

8.4.1 Following Contract award, the required number of Working Drawings, and where specifically requested in writing, relevant structural, thermal and acoustic calculations and other data, shall be submitted to the Project Architect for review in accordance with the Conditions of Contract.

8.4.2 The Project Architect will review the Working Drawings for compliance with this document and the Design Drawings in visual and overall functional matters only. The Detailed Design and construction of components shall remain the responsibility of the Contractor.

8.4.3 The Project Architect's review of the Working Drawings shall not relieve the Contractor of his responsibility for errors, or for supplying components and materials to the full satisfaction of the Project Architect.

8.4.4 The Working Drawings shall be fully dimensioned in metric, to an agreed scale appropriate to the detail, and include:

8.4.4.1 Full size details and graphic representation describing materials, components and equipment, construction, finishes, provision for movements, fabrication and installation tolerances.

8.4.4.2 Layouts, locations and assemblies of all types of construction detail and junctions, details of materials, method of jointing, details of all connections and fixing and sealing methods, finishes and all pertinent information related to:
- Method of fabrication and construction.
- Proper relation to adjoining work.
- Finishes.
- Amplification of details.
- Minor changes to the Design to suit actual conditions.

8.4.5 Submit Working Drawings in accordance with the Conditions of Contract and do not commence fabrication of components until formally returned by the Project Architect with either 'A' or 'B' stamped on each of the Working Drawings. Ensure that space is left clear on each of the Working Drawings for stamping by the Project Architect.

8.4.5.1 Drawing stamped 'A': Fabrication, manufacture or construction may proceed in accordance with the drawing submitted.

8.4.5.2 Drawing stamped 'B': Fabrication, manufacture or construction may proceed in accordance with the drawings submitted subject to the Contractor taking necessary action based on the Project Architect's comments and all annotations added to the returned drawings. Unless indicated to the contrary on such drawings, the work shall comply with the Contract Documents. To achieve 'A' status, the required number of copies of amended drawings shall be sent to the Project Architect.

8.4.5.3 Drawings stamped 'C' – No work shall be fabricated, manufactured or installed. Submit new drawings to the project architect for review until re-submission is not required.

8.4.6 The Project Architect's final comment on the Working Drawings ('A') shall be conditional upon receipt of all documentation, certification, acceptances in respect of anchorages, fire stop assemblies, samples and test reports, etc. as defined in this document.

8.4.7 The receipt of Working Drawings by the Contractor from the Project Architect marked A or B shall not constitute agreement of a variation.

8.4.8 When preparing the Working Drawings consult the current Architectural, Structural and Services Design Drawings, adjusting the Working Drawings to allow for any changes to site tolerances and/ or discrepancies where applicable.

8.4.8.1 If, before commencing or during the preparation of the Working Drawings the design intent of the Design Drawings and/ or Specification may be affected, or where other elements of the Works may be affected, notify the Project Architect immediately.

8.4.9 Where applicable, the Working Drawings may utilise the manufacturer's standard details provided that they comply with the design intent.

8.4.10 The Project Architect shall have the right at all reasonable times to visit the Contractor's (or his specialist sub-Contractors) design office to check on progress.

8.4.11 The Working Drawings shall be annotated in English and titled in the manner determined for the Contract, with the title block fully indicating the part of the Works to which they apply.

8.4.12 Information contained in any of the Design Drawings shall be treated as confidential and shall not be utilised for any purpose other than for the Works. Such information shall not be communicated to third parties for other purposes without the specific acceptance of the Project Architect.

8.4.13 Maintain on site a full set of Design Drawings, Working Drawings and technical specifications.

8.4.14 Upon completion of the design, manufacture and installation phases, provide the Project Architect the appropriate number of As-built Drawings, in accordance with the Conditions of Contract.

8.4.15 No Working Drawings shall be accepted if produced to a reduced size.

8.4.16 The Working Drawings shall be fully coordinated with interfacing trades.

STEP 8.5 Other Submittals to be provided by the Contractor after Contract Award

8.5.1 Product Data: All relevant technical data that documents the primary performance of each system, system component and/ or material in the Works. Primarily, product data shall consist of a material schedule, together with manufacturer's literature, which is necessary to identify clearly the primary function, quality and performance of each product. The schedule shall include the specific location(s) of use and any related Working Drawings. Product data shall be custom prepared for the project and made specific for the Works.

8.5.2 Certifications: Provide independently certified reports verifying compliance of each element or component with the requirements of the Design Drawings and Specification. These reports shall include the chemical and physical properties of various building materials.

8.5.3 QA/ QC Programme: Provide a programme to satisfy the requirements of this document, the Contract conditions or any other documents referred to in the Contract Documentation.

8.5.4 Pre-construction Testing Reports:

8.5.4.1 Provide technical reports recording test results systems, components and materials as required by the Design Drawings, this document, the Project Architect or a testing laboratory, prior to commencement of installation.

8.5.4.2 These reports shall state compliance with the technical requirements of this document and include, where appropriate, test certificates.

8.5.5 Maintenance/ Operation Manuals: Manuals prepared by the Contractor for Client / building user's maintenance and operation of the various prototypes and/ or components thereof.

8.5.6 Supplementary Product Literature: Such literature may include manufacturer's catalogue information, product specifications, standard illustrations, diagrams and standard details. The supplementary product literature shall describe physical characteristics such as size, weight, finish, material analysis, electrical requirements and other information such as load tables, test results, assessments and industry quality standards.

8.5.7 Technical Calculations: These shall consist of technical engineering calculations which document technical performance of various systems, system components and/ or materials, as required by the Design Drawings and Specifications.

8.5.8 Guarantees and warranties: Provide copies of all relevant example guarantees and warranties available for installed materials and products.

8.5.8.1 Prepare and submit health and safety design risk assessments for review.

8.5.8.2 All submittals provided shall be written in the English language.

STEP 8.6 As-built Drawings and manuals to be provided by the Contractor at project completion

8.6.1 Upon completion of the Works and when deemed necessary by the Project Architect, provide As-built Drawings in a computer format, agreed with the Project Architect, showing the Works as finally fabricated and erected in accordance with the 'A' status Working Drawings.

8.6.2 The As-built Drawings referred to above shall include any site variances or installation adjustments or variations and any actual site or setting out dimensional modifications as installed.

8.6.3 As-built Drawings shall be produced to a relevant and agreed scale and shall be used to complement the example Maintenance Manual for the specific purpose of locating the elements within the overall structure.

STEP 8.7 Project specific requirements: Information to be provided with tender

Submit the following information:

8.7.1 Typical plan, section and elevation drawings at suitable scales.

8.7.2 Typical detailed drawings at large scales for all elements of the system.

8.7.3 Technical information and example certification demonstrating compliance with specification of proposed incorporated products and finishes.

8.7.4 Example certification, reports and calculations demonstrating compliance with Specification of proposed composite rain-screen.

8.7.5 Proposals for connections to and support from the building structure and building components.

8.7.6 Proposals for amendments to primary supporting structure and for secondary supporting structure additional to that indicated on preliminary Design Drawings.

8.7.7 Schedule of builder's work, special provisions and special attendance by others.

8.7.8 Examples of standard documentation from which a future project quality plan will be prepared.

8.7.9 Preliminary fabrication and installation method statements and programme.

8.7.10 Schedule of products and finishes with a design life expectancy less than that specified, with proposals for frequencies and methods of replacement.

8.7.11 Proposals for replacing damaged or failed products.

8.7.12 Areas of non-compliance with this document.

8.7.13 Reference to work of a similar nature carried out by the tenderer on other contracts, particularly those carried out in the region, with relevant dates, and project addresses sufficient to enable inspections to be made.

8.7.14 The typical detailed drawings at large scales, referred to in sub clause above, shall include, as a minimum, the Contractor's proposals for the junctions indicated on the following drawings:

8.7.14.1 Project Architect's drawings as listed on the drawing register.

8.7.14.2 The technical information and certification, referred to in sub clause c) above, shall include, as a minimum, details of the time/ temperature regime for the heat soaking of toughened glass, with information on the method for the control and monitoring of the regime.

STEP 8.8   Samples, Mock-ups, prototypes and quality benchmarks

8.8.1 Information to be Provided Before Testing or Fabrication

Submit the following information:

8.8.1.1 Detailed drawings to fully describe fabrication and installation.

8.8.1.2 Detailed calculations to prove compliance with design/ performance requirements.

8.8.1.3 Project specific fabrication, handling and installation method statements.

8.8.1.4 Certification for incorporated components manufactured by others confirming their suitability for proposed locations.

8.8.1.5 Recommendations for spare parts for future repairs or replacements.

8.8.1.6 Recommendations for safe dismantling and recycling or disposal of products.

8.8.2 Contractor's Working Drawings

To be submitted, as per Drawing Register provided by Project Architect.

8.8.2.1 Setting-out and control points.

8.8.2.2 Toleranced dimensions indicating both the location of components and the width of all joints.

8.8.2.3 Identification of components.

8.8.2.4 Details of isolation, packing and shimming.

8.8.2.5 The locations of all sealants, with details of position, type, and size of backing rods, bond-release tapes, and the like.

8.8.2.6 Embedment, spacing and edge distances for fixings.

8.8.2.7 The type, size, and spacing of all welds.

8.8.3 Detailed Calculations
To include, as a minimum:

8.8.3.1 Structural Calculations: For all sections, connections, anchorages, support assemblies.

8.8.3.2 Thermal Calculations: To support the claimed insulation values of all vision panels, spandrel panels, frame sections, and other insulated components.

8.8.3.3 Condensation Prediction Calculations: To identify the probability of internal, external, or interstitial condensation forming and, where the calculations indicate that condensation is likely to occur, the quantitative rate of formation together with an explanation as to how the proposed design eliminates any damage or inconvenience caused by the condensation so formed.

8.8.3.4 Acoustic Calculations: To support the claimed acoustic values of vision panels, spandrel panels, frame sections, and other components.

8.8.4 **Project-Specific Method Statements**

8.8.4.1 To include, as a minimum:

8.8.4.2 Manufacturer's recommendations for the use of proprietary fixings.

8.8.4.3 Information on all bolts and fixings requiring specific torques together with details of the required torque levels.

8.8.4.4 Information on the location and use of locking nuts and washers, engagement of serrations.

8.8.4.5 Information for glazing procedures, including the position of setting blocks, orientation of glass, and any specific requirements of the glazing supplier.

8.8.4.6 Information on the cleaning and, if required, priming procedures for all sealants.

8.8.4.7 Details of points which are susceptible to damage, or which should not be loaded during installation.

STEP 8.9 Scope of checking of Contractor's submittals by the Project Architect

This article applies to any submission made by the contractor at any point either during tender or following contract signature.

8.9.1 The scope of contractor's submittals for prototypes that will be checked by the Project Architect (in addition to samples) is as follows:
- Working drawing submittals: General arrangement sections, elevations
- Working drawing submittals: General arrangement plans
- Working drawing submittals: System drawings and calculations
- Drawings of prototypes and typical junction/interface details
- Checking compliance with coordination drawings
- Submittals: Test mock-ups

8.9.2 Upon receipt of the submittals as listed above, the following items will be checked by the Project Architect for compliance with the tender documents as follows:
- Compliance with the scope of the project set out in the tender documents.
- Compliance with the methodology set out in this specification for both design of the components/assemblies and for accompanying structural/environmental calculations that support the design. The calculation methodology adopted for each system would be checked in terms of: standards applied, inputs considered, compliance of design criteria with specification, transparency in the procedure adopted for calculations, compliance of the procedure to standards considered, compliance of results obtained with design criteria assumed.

8.9.3 **Calculations are to be submitted by the Contractor as follows:**
All the calculations submitted by the Contractor for individual systems shall comply with, but are not limited to, the checklists below. All the calculations submitted shall follow the template outlined below and be presented in the same way, using the headings below. If one item is not applicable to a certain calculation, specify that it is not applicable under the heading.

8.9.4 **Checklist for Structural Calculations to be submitted by the Contractor:**

8.9.4.1 **Structural system description:** The Contractor is to provide a brief text description of the system and its structural behaviour explaining clearly the structural concept and the support conditions.

8.9.4.2 **Materials:** The Contractor is to provide list of materials used and mechanical properties.

8.9.4.3 **Summary of results:** The Contractor is to provide the summary of the calculation results in tabulated format, comparing the values found to the design criteria set and establishing whether the system is suitable or not.

8.9.4.4 **Structural system and support conditions:** The Contractor is to provide diagram illustrating the static structural scheme used, only including the necessary information (please omit from the diagram all the details of the system that are not relevant to the specific calculation)

8.9.4.5 **Design criteria:** The Contractor is to provide design criteria used to evaluate the system (e.g. maximum allowed stress and maximum allowed deflection values) and how these have been established, providing references to standards used.

8.9.4.6 **Load cases:** The Contractor is to provide the design values for all the load cases utilised in the calculation and specify how these have been obtained (reference sources, such as standards, wind tunnel test report, etc.).

The Contractor is to show graphically how these have been applied to the system and provide a load path diagram for each load case.

In the load path diagram (to be provided for each load case applied) the Contractor is to show the main forces acting on each component involved in transferring the loads to the supports shall be clearly shown and labelled.

The following load cases are generally expected: dead loads, live loads, wind loads, snow loads, thermal loads, seismic loads. The Contractor is to specify the design value for all these loads for each system analysed, providing appropriate sources.

8.9.4.7 **Load combinations:** The Contractor is to specify all the load combinations used for both Serviceability Limit States and Ultimate Limit States (according to Eurocode 1). The Contractor is to specify the load safety factors and combination factors used for each load case considered.

8.9.4.8 **Analysis:** The Contractor is to provide calculations including all the steps required and writing down the expressions using letters (algebraic formula) before converting those into the corresponding numbers.

8.9.4.9 If a FEA Software package is used for structural calculations, the Contractor is to provide the following in addition to the items above:
*   brief introductory text describing the methodology used
*   name of software utilised and version
*   graphical output from the software showing the how the system has been set up and how the meshing has been defined
*   graphical output from software illustrating clearly how each load case has been applied to the component analysed
*   graphical output from the software showing outputs for deflections and stresses for each load case considered and for all the load combinations. For frames and metal structures, please also provide graphical outputs for bending moment, shear force and axial force diagrams for each load case applied and for all the load combinations. The results shall include clear legends with readable values (High-resolution images).

8.9.5 **Checklist for Environmental Calculations:**

8.9.5.1 **System description:** The Contractor is to provide a brief text description of the system and its environmental / thermodynamic behaviour explaining clearly how the concept proposed meets the performance required.

8.9.5.2 **Materials:** The Contractor is to provide list of materials used and appropriate thermal properties.

8.9.5.3 **Summary of results:** The Contractor is to provide the summary of the calculation results in tabulated format, comparing the values found to the design criteria set and establishing whether the system is suitable or not.

8.9.5.4 **Thermodynamic system and boundary conditions:** The Contractor is to provide diagram illustrating the system analysed and the boundary conditions set for the system, providing appropriate substantiation and only including only the relevant details affecting the thermal performance of the system (please omit from the diagram all the details of the system that are not relevant to the specific calculation).

8.9.5.5 **Design criteria:** The Contractor is to provide design criteria used to evaluate the system and how these have been established, providing references to standards used.

8.9.5.6 **Scenarios analysed:** The Contractor is to provide the design values for all the scenarios analysed in the calculation and specify how these have been obtained (reference sources, such as standards, MEP Engineer report, etc.). Any design scenario must be substantiated, illustrating how this has been obtained.

The Contractor is to provide clear diagrams showing the inputs and boundary conditions considered for each calculation scenario.

8.9.5.7 **Analysis:** The Contractor is to provide calculations including all the steps required and writing down the expressions using letters (algebraic formula) before converting those into the corresponding numbers.

The Contractor is to refer to appropriate chapters in the standards used for the calculation methodologies (Eurocodes or US standards).

8.9.5.8 If a FEA Software package is used for environmental calculations, the Contractor is to provide the following in addition to the items above:
• Brief introductory text describing the methodology used
• name of software utilised and version
• Graphical output from the software showing how the system has been set up and how the meshing has been defined.
• Graphical output from software illustrating clearly how each calculation scenario has been considered
• Graphical output from the software showing outputs for relevant thermodynamic quantities (e.g. temperature distributions, relative humidity values, heat flows, etc.). The results shall include clear legends with readable values (high–resolution images).

8.9.6 The Contractor is to not include results in tabulated form as these are generally not clear, extremely lengthy and awkward to check. All graphical outputs are to be provided to a high level of resolution. Any anomaly or modelling assumptions in the FE model shall be clearly stated in the introduction or annotated on the output diagrams.

8.9.7 The correctness of the numerical results of the calculations for components/assemblies will not be checked by the Project Architect. It is the responsibility of the Contractor to ensure that components and assemblies are sized adequately to meet the performance requirements of this specification.

8.9.8 The Contractor is to ensure that the sizing of all components and assemblies take into account all issues of workmanship associated with the specific techniques and methods used by the Contractor in the fabrication and installation of the prototypes. Appropriate factors of safety should be applied to calculations to ensure that the Contractor's own expectations of methods and techniques, including but not limited to workmanship, fabrication and installation are met in the prototypes.

8.9.9 Should a full set of checks for calculations for the detailed design of the works, as undertaken by the Contractor, be required by the Client, in order to ensure not only general compliance with scope and methodology set in the specification but also the correctness of the results, then a third party checking engineer will be appointed by the Client to undertake this task. The checking task may be undertaken for a single system, or several systems, as required by the Client. Checks for this task would be undertaken on a line by line basis of all calculations required for the structural design of the complete scope of each system.

STEP 8.10 Verification of submittals in relation to tender documentation.

8.10.1 No portion of the prototypes shall commence without verification of the required submittals by the Project Architect

STEP 9.0 **Samples**

In this section two types of samples are required:
• Samples provided during tender.
• Samples provided after award of tender.

STEP 9.1 **Samples generally**

9.1.1 Samples shall include various products, fabricated items, equipment, devices, appliances or components thereof, as may be required to satisfy the visual appearance and technical requirements of the Design.

9.1.2 Samples shall be reviewed for their visual characteristics only and where moving or operating elements are involved, the Project Architect shall be given the opportunity to review working samples.

9.1.3 Ranges of samples shall be provided where a considerable range of colour, graining, texture, smoothness and other characteristics may be anticipated in the Works.

9.1.4 Where custom colours are specified, samples shall be submitted illustrating precise colours, textures, patterns and finishes for review by the Project Architect and the Client. The choice of colour and texture is left to the project architect and the client this choice can be modified at any moment after signature of the deal, if modified before production.

STEP 9.2 **Samples before award to tender**

9.2.1 Samples provided with the Tender or during the Evaluation prior to Contract award.

9.2.2 Samples shall be as described on the Design Drawings and Specification which are required to verify the visual appearance of such items for compliance with the requirements of the Design Drawings and Specification.

9.2.3 Pre-contract samples shall be labelled and kept by the Project Architect as a record of materials agreed for Contract until completion/ handover.

9.2.4 Samples shall include relevant trade literature and technical specifications.

STEP 9.3 **Samples after award to tender**

9.3.1 Samples provided during the Detailed Design shall be checked against the Pre-contract samples, where applicable, and this document to ensure that quality and type have been maintained.

9.3.2 At the appropriate time provide the Project Architect with samples listed in particular Specification sections, which shall be kept as a record of materials to be incorporated in the Works and used as references for controlling consistency throughout the Works.

9.3.3 Post contract samples shall comprise materials in their final form.

STEP 9.4 **Project specific requirements:**

Pre-contract Samples

In accordance with Section 5.2, pre-contract samples of the following samples shall be provided:

Rain-screen samples:

9.4.1 The samples to be of size 300mm x 200mm; the rain-screen panels to have finishes and textures as specified and also at least one visible joint with the adjacent panel.

9.4.2 The samples shall incorporate the support system of the rain-screen.

9.4.3 All visible fixings (fixings are visible when they should be part of the design and be approved by the Project Architect).

9.4.4 Glazing samples:

9.4.4.1 Examples of proposed types of finish and colours.

9.4.4.2 300mm length of each type of proposed framing.

9.4.4.3 Glass samples 300mm x 300mm of all proposed glass types.

9.4.4.4 All fixings.

9.4.4.5 All proposed gasket types, extrusions, caps, trims and flashings.

9.4.4.6 Integrated opening mechanisms, where required.

9.4.4.7 All visible fixings (where visible fixings form part of the design intent).

9.4.4.8 Proposed ironmongery and hardware.

9.4.4.9 Operating mechanisms, switches and controls, including mounting.

9.4.5 Balustrade samples:

9.4.5.1 1000mm length of each type of balustrade and handrail.

9.4.5.2 All visible fixings.

STEP 9.5 **Samples after tender award**

In accordance with Section 5.3, post contract award samples of the following shall be provided:

9.5.1 Rain-screen samples:

9.5.1.1 Samples of size 300mm x 200mm sample(s) of accepted rain-screen tiles/ panels in specified finish and texture, as applicable, and indicated joint relationship with adjacent tiles/ panels.

9.5.1.2 Samples of rain-screen support system.

9.5.1.3 All visible fixings (where visible fixings form part of the design intent).

9.5.2 Glazing samples:

9.5.2.1 300mm length of each type of framing, with accepted finishes and colours, including the interface method of attachment) with the glazing and solid infill panel and joints. The choice of colour and texture is left to the project architect and the client, this choice can be modified at any moment after signature of the deal, if modified before production.

9.5.2.2 All accepted gasket types, extrusions, caps, trims and flashings, including at least one joint and one corner joint and including accepted finishes and colours where applicable.

9.5.2.3 Integrated blinds and mechanisms, where required.

9.5.2.4 Accepted ironmongery and hardware.

9.5.2.5 All visible fixings (where visible fixings form part of the design intent).

9.5.2.6 Samples of fastening devices and anchors.

9.5.2.7 Operating mechanisms, switches and controls, including mounting.

9.5.2.8 Certification for incorporated components manufactured by others confirming their suitability for proposed locations in the facade system.

9.5.3 Balustrade samples:

9.5.3.1 Sample of 1000mm length of each type of balustrade and handrail.

9.5.3.2 All visible fixings.

STEP 10.0 Prototypes

General
In this section there are two types of prototypes required:
Visual mock-ups provided prior to tender award.
Performance prototypes provided after tender award.

STEP 10.1 Visual prototypes

10.1.1 During the phase of submission of tender, as described in this document, the Contractor will provide a 1: 1 samples, for evaluation by the Project Architect. The samples are to be provided to an agreed location. The samples are required to use the materials and fixing system proposed by the contractor. All materials and components must meet the requirements of this document. The prototype must be completed at the agreed location.

10.1.2 After contract award, as described in this document, the Contractor will provide material samples and connection samples for approval / validation by the Project Architect.

10.1.3 Some prototypes will be produced either on-site or off-site, not necessarily using the prescribed material in this document, but representing the design intent.

10.1.4 Other prototypes will be produced to confirm the general visual intent including colour, size and texture. The choice of colour and texture is left to the Project Architect. This choice can be modified at any moment before the start of fabrication.

STEP 10.2 Performance prototypes

10.2.1 Prior to manufacture of elements of the prototypes, construct off site, full scale three-dimensional sections where described in the particular Specification sections and/or indicated on the Design Drawings utilising final specified materials but not necessarily final production techniques. The Contractor will provide 1: 1 scale prototypes, for approval/ validation by the Project Architect.

10.2.2 Where necessary, the prototypes shall be tested fully to ensure that the systems meet the performance requirements of this document by application of the maximum applied loads, climatic conditions and structural movements, and/ or be used as a Quality Assurance/ Quality Control standard. Manufacture of materials/ products for inclusion in the Works shall not commence until the Project Architect's written acceptance of the prototypes has been received.

10.2.3 Working Drawings for the prototypes shall be submitted in accordance with the requirements of this document.

10.2.4 Any modifications required to the prototypes shall be recorded to show their final construction.

10.2.5 Programme tests to enable any necessary adjustments without delay to the Works programme.

STEP 10.3 Project-specific requirements:

Prototype requirements after tender award:

Provide prototypes as follows:

10.3.1 ES.01

10.3.2 ES.02

10.3.3 Etcetera

STEP 10.4 Prototype requirements for testing after tender award

Prototypes shall be provided which combine the following types into a single mock-up where possible:

10.4.1 ES.01

10.4.2 ES.02

10.4.3 Etcetera

STEP 10.5 Quality benchmark requirements

Provide quality benchmark samples, in location(s) to be agreed with the Project Architect, as follows:

10.5.1 First panel installed on the prototypes.

10.5.2 For balustrades, the first panel installed of each prototype.

STEP 11.0 Testing

STEP 11.1 Testing generally

11.1.1 Provide independently certified tests that demonstrate that the proposed systems meet the performance requirements of this document.

11.1.2 Independently certified test data for off-site testing shall include static and dynamic results.

11.1.3 Where data from previous independently certified tests demonstrate that the proposed systems meet the performance requirements of this document, off-site independent testing need not be undertaken.

11.1.4 Include for all on-site testing specified in this document, which shall be carried out by an accredited independent testing body.

11.1.5 The works shall be tested in accordance with the requirements of the CWCT Standard Test Methods for Systemised Building Envelopes.

STEP 11.2	Testing of performance prototypes

11.2.1 The prototypes shall be mounted in test rigs, which have the same conditions of attachment and support as elements of the works, with a supporting structure similar in stiffness to that supporting the works. The prototypes to be tested shall not be influenced by the test chamber.

11.2.2 Provide details of all jointing, sealing and glazing techniques, materials used, type, number and size of drainage/ ventilation apertures and section properties of the framing members.

11.2.3 The Project Architect shall be given at least 7 days notice prior to the erection and dismantling of the prototype construction, as the Project Architect may elect to observe the assembly and dismantling of the test prototypes.

11.2.4 Tests shall not be carried out without prior notice of at least 7 days being given to the Project Architect.

11.2.5 Prior to testing, sufficient time shall be allowed to permit all chemically curing sealants to achieve their proper cure as recommended by the sealant manufacturer.

11.2.6 Before the test is begun, the external face of the specimen shall be thoroughly washed using a mild additive-free detergent and then rinsed.

11.2.7 Testing shall be carried out by an independent laboratory acceptable to the Project Architect.

11.2.8 The prototypes shall be tested for air permeability, water leakage, and wind load resistance, plus additional structural loading tests as necessary to demonstrate through calculations/ drawings that the works are capable of accommodating the building movements without degrading the performance of the works.

11.2.9 Details of the testing procedures shall be provided to the Project Architect for review and comment.

11.2.10 If the testing data submitted is not deemed to be satisfactory by the Project Architect, project specific laboratory tests shall be carried out to satisfy the requirements of this document; to be agreed with the Project Architect.

11.2.11 The exact nature of the prototype shall be agreed with the Project Architect.

11.2.12 Test certificates shall not relieve the Contractor of his responsibilities regarding the performance and service life requirements of the prototypes.

STEP 11.3	Standard test apparatus and calibration

Submit details of the following equipment intended for use in the testing process:

11.3.1 Test chamber.

11.3.2 Air system.

11.3.3 Water sprays system.

11.3.4 Pressure measuring apparatus.

11.3.5 Air flow-metering system.

11.3.6 Water flow-metering system.

11.3.7 Deflection measuring devices.

11.3.8 Calibration.

STEP 11.4	Testing of performance prototypes

11.4.1 **Performance prototypes test sequence**

11.4.1.1 The Testing Authority shall witness the installation and dismantling of the prototypes, record any variations to the agreed details on a set of the prototype assembly drawings prepared by the Contractor and shall also record the extent of water penetration into the system.

11.4.1.2 Test Sequence:

11.4.1.2.1 Preliminary testing: Prior to the full test sequence, the prototypes shall be pre-tested under static pressure at 50% maximum design wind load, followed by water penetration test at 50% of the pressure specified for final tests. Deficiencies observed in the samples during testing shall be recorded, and appropriate corrections made.

11.4.1.2.2 The testing sequence shall be followed in accordance with the CWCT Standard for Systemised Building Envelopes procedures.

11.4.1.2.3 Further tests shall be carried out in accordance with the CWCT Standard for Systemised Building Envelopes Discretionary Test procedures as necessary.

11.4.1.3 No test shall be carried out unless all previous tests in the sequence have been passed to the satisfaction of the Testing Authority.

11.4.1.4 If any modification is made to the prototype, repeat testing shall be undertaken as detailed in the relevant CWCT procedures. However, if any modification is undertaken that, in the opinion of the independent testing authority or witness, invalidates earlier test results, the sequence shall commence again at the first test. This requirement is not applicable to glass breakage during the wind resistance safety test when replacement of a pane of glass may be carried out without re-starting the whole sequence.

11.4.2 **Air permeability tests**

11.4.2.1 The prototypes shall be tested to determine the air infiltration. A check for regions of concentrated air leakage shall be made after the air permeability test has been completed and such areas marked upon the prototype drawings.

11.4.2.2 Testing shall be carried out in accordance with EN 12153 (ASTM E283-04) for cladding to a test pressure of [insert figure] Pa or 0.25 the design winds pressure, whichever is the greater.

11.4.2.3 In addition, an air exfiltration test shall be carried out on the prototype to check the performance in relation to the whole building's air leakage test requirements.

11.4.3 **Weatherproofing and water tightness tests**

11.4.3.1 Tests shall be carried out adopting either the static or the dynamic procedures, as appropriate to the system type and expected conditions, set out below:

11.4.3.1.1 The static test method is to be carried out in accordance with EN 12155 (ASTM E331 - 00) for cladding, EN 1027 (AAMA 501.1 - 05) for windows and doors, and the requirements of the CWCT Standard for Systemised Building Envelopes.

11.4.3.1.2 The dynamic Test Method is to be carried out in accordance with the requirements of the CWCT Standard for Systemised Building Envelopes or acceptable equivalent European Standard EN 13050 (or XP ENV 13050, ASTM E547 - 00), for testing for water penetration.

Resistance to water penetration when tested shall be in the test pressure class 600Pa or 0.25 the design wind pressure, whichever is the greater, in accordance with the requirements of the CWCT Standard for Systemised Building Envelopes for testing for water penetration by the static and dynamic test method.

11.4.3.2 Performance under Testing

11.4.3.2.1 There shall be no leakage into the internal face of the works at any time during the test or within 15 minutes of completion of the test.

11.4.3.2.2 At the completion of the test there shall be no standing water in locations intended to drain.

11.4.4 **Wind resistance tests**

11.4.4.1 A serviceability test shall be carried out in accordance with EN 12179 (ASTM E1233 / E1233M-14) for cladding, and EN 12211 (ASTM E1233 / E1233M-14) for windows and doors, as modified by the CWCT Standard for Systemised Building Envelopes.

11.4.4.2 A safety test shall be carried out in accordance with the CWCT Standard for Systemised Building Envelopes.

11.4.4.3 Test pressure: The peak test pressure shall be 1.5 times the design wind pressure for the Safety test, and 1.0 times the design wind pressure for the Serviceability test.

11.4.4.4 Performance under Testing:

11.4.4.4.1 At both positive and negative applications of the peak test pressure there shall be no permanent damage to the cladding system. Framing members shall not buckle, panels shall remain securely held, glass and glazing shall not be damaged and gaskets shall not be displaced. The glass itself shall not deflect such that edge cover is insufficient to restrain the glass under peak test pressure or such that spacers become visible

11.4.4.4.2 After loading to the positive and negative peak test pressure, permanent deformation to wall framing members shall not exceed 1/500 of the span measured between points of attachment to the building one hour after the loading has been removed.

11.4.4.4.3 The loads created by specified test conditions shall be accommodated safely, without detriment to the overall design, structural integrity and performance of the works.

11.4.4.4.4 The permanent fixings of any component shall be capable of resisting the combined dead load and maximum wind load with a factor of safety of at least 1.5.

11.4.5 Impact testing

11.4.5.1 Protection from manual attack is to be to EN 1627 Level WK2 (ASTM F588).

11.4.5.2 The extent of any damage determined through testing shall be recorded and, where possible, quantified. Samples shall also be submitted to the Project Architect.

12.4.5.3 A soft body impact test to glazed elements shall be carried out in accordance with EN 12600 (ASTM F3007–13), conforming to the category requirements specified.

11.4.5.4 A soft body impact test to non–glazed elements shall be carried out in accordance with EN 13049 (ASTM E1996–14 / 1886–13a), conforming to the category requirements specified.

11.4.5.5 A large body impact test to roof–lights/ overhead/ horizontal/ inclined systems shall be carried out in accordance with EN 1873 (ASTM E2112–07), conforming with the specified requirements.

11.4.6 Thermal cycling

The prototypes shall be tested in order to determine the effects of thermal movements on the performance of the works, in particular the joints.

11.4.7 Acoustic testing

11.4.7.1 Initial Advance Test:

11.4.7.1.1 The glass configurations shall be identified and any acoustically enhanced configurations that may be necessary shall be incorporated to meet this document.

11.4.7.1.2 Immediately following the appointment of the Contractor, laboratory acoustic tests of the proposed glass configurations shall be arranged, using similar framing to that intended with similar dimensions and mass per metre run of framing. These prototypes shall not be used as visual samples and shall not include glass coatings or heat treatments but shall be used to confirm compliance with the specified acoustic data.

11.4.7.1.3 From initial results of acoustic testing, a detailed acoustic assessment shall be provided of each cladding type for review.

11.4.7.2 The works shall achieve the specified requirements when tested in accordance with EN ISO 10140-3 (ASTM A805M-09).

11.4.7.3 Testing for flanking transmission shall be undertaken in accordance with EN ISO 10848-2 (ASTM E336-14). The test method is designed for suspended ceilings but may for this purpose and in the absence of any other International Test Standards, be adapted to establish the flanking performance of a cladding system. The simulated wall and floor constructions shall not influence the results of these junction tests.

11.4.7.4 Any acoustic tests shall commence at a time agreed with the Project Architect, in a recognised independent laboratory, with a comprehensive test report being submitted, in writing, to the Project Architect within three weeks of completion of the tests.

11.4.7.5 Where existing test data is available from a recognised independent laboratory, it shall be considered acceptable providing the tests have been carried out for the exact system being offered. Test data for similar constructions may be accepted if supporting computations are offered to account for any differences between the proposed and tested construction.

11.4.8 Structural silicone testing and maintenance generally:

11.4.8.1 The requirements of this document with respect to the testing of the structural silicone application shall be complied with.

11.4.8.2 The Project Architect shall be provided with documentary evidence that the selection of sealant takes into account any relevant recommendations by the sealant manufacturer as to the use of the sealant.

11.4.8.3 Compatibility: Test certificates shall be submitted to the Project Architect to confirm compatibility of the sealant used with all substrate materials including aluminium, finishes, glass, glass coatings, and gaskets, setting blocks and backing rods. These certificates shall relate to tests carried out by the sealant manufacturer.

11.4.8.4 Adhesion test data of production samples as tested in accordance with ASTM C 794 shall be submitted to the Project Architect. These shall establish adhesion performance over the temperatures specified in this document.

11.4.8.5 Where the structural silicone bonds glass to the cladding framework, the weakest element in the line of stress shall have a minimum strength of 600kPa or 6 times the design strength, whichever is the greater in accordance with ETAG 01/ 015 or ETAG 002 documents which set out the requirements for use of structural silicone. This criterion shall be proven with a statistical confidence of 99%. For each combination of substrate and design conditions, a report from the sealant manufacturer shall be provided for the tests performed in the following manner:

11.4.8.5.1 Assemble and fully cure under production conditions (not laboratory conditions) a minimum of 12 samples. Each sample shall be a minimum of 150mm long. The sample shall be made of actual substrate material, i.e. glass with actual coating (low E and/ or fritting), aluminium sections with finishes. The joint geometry shall be as accepted by the Project Architect

11.4.8.5.2 Double-sided tape or other spacer material shall be installed such that it does not add to the silicone joint strength.

11.4.8.5.3 After full cure the samples shall be totally immersed in tap water at room temperature for 7 days.

11.4.8.5.4 Samples shall be tested in a tensometer 25 hours after removal from the water immersion tank.

11.4.8.5.5 Each sample shall be subjected to a tensile load test. The crosshead speed shall be 50mm per minute. Testing shall continue until failure occurs or until 830kPa or 6 times the design load, whichever is the greater, is applied to the samples. The maximum stress and mode of failure shall be reported, including percentage area of cohesive failure and any area of voids in the sealant for each sample. Adhesive failure area or void cross section area parallel to the substrate face greater than 20% shall be unacceptable.

11.4.8.5.6 A statistical analysis of results shall indicate a design stress of not less than 600kPa or 6 times the design stress of the sealant, whichever is the greater, with a confidence of 99% over the temperature range as described in this document.

11.4.8.5.7 If the sample set does not meet the requirements of the above criteria, the design of the failed element shall be revised and subjected to a re-test. This procedure shall continue until the above requirements have been met.

11.4.8.5.8 A report of the above testing shall be prepared. No fabrication shall commence until the results have been accepted by the Project Architect

11.4.8.5.9 All test results shall be retained with regard to the structural silicone glazing for a minimum period of 15 years from project completion. These shall be made available to the Project Architect on request.

11.4.8.6 **Maintenance**

An on-going inspection/ maintenance programme for the structural silicone shall be documented and accepted Testing Authorities shall be employed to carry out these inspections which shall include the following:

11.4.8.6.1 Cleaning: Specify acceptable detergents and methods to be used.

11.4.8.6.2 Inspection: Provide forms to be filled out periodically, each pre-dated with the inspection date and an adequate quantity for the design life of the building. The form shall state the full procedure for the inspection.

11.4.8.6.3 Sample Cut-out: Provide forms for periodic cut-out of structural seals and weather seals to check shore hardness and tensile properties of the seal.

11.4.8.6.4 Each of the procedures shall clearly state pass/ fail criteria and indicate action required when a failure is obtained as a result. The Testing Authority shall be required to produce a report based on its findings and recommendations for any remedial works to the Project Architect.

11.4.9 **Seismic building movement test**

11.4.9.1 A mid-height support beam is displaced horizontally and then back to its original position. At each stage, visual observations are made, with the test being conducted three times. Displacements, in terms of mm, are determined as 'probable' or 'credible' displacements. In the 'credible' test, there must be no permanent damage to the framing members, panels or fixings. Glazing beads and cappings must be held securely and gaskets not be displaced. In the probable test, no racking or distortion of members occurs. The panel must then pass the subsequent air and water penetration tests.

11.4.10   Inter-storey movement test

11.4.10.1   The mid-span point of the mid-height support beam is displaced by a fixed distance vertically downwards then back to the centre, tested three times, during which no racking or distortion of the members is allowed to occur. The panel must pass the subsequent air and water penetration tests.

STEP 11.5   Testing of installed works

11.5.1   Air permeability (exfiltration)

11.5.1.1   Provide actual air exfiltration results from tests undertaken that comply with the 'Air-tightness Fan Test' of the building envelope.

11.5.1.2   Air exfiltration rates shall be within the limits specified. Any areas of excessive air leakage identified shall be rectified at the Contractor's expense.

11.5.2   Waterproofing and water-tightness testing

11.5.2.1   Test the weather-tightness of the works using the Site hose test carried out in accordance with the recommendations of the CWCT Standard for Systemised Building Envelopes.

11.5.2.2   If a different method is proposed details of the testing system and a proposed method statement shall be submitted to the Project Architect for acceptance at least one month prior to the proposed testing on Site.

11.5.2.3   Prior to testing ensure that the works have been completed to a stage where the integrity of the system can be tested, that obvious defects have been made good and that the works have been cleared of all materials, debris and dust.

11.5.2.4   Testing shall be carried out when all works are complete including that of all associated trades and interfacing trades.

11.5.2.5   Performance under testing:

11.5.2.5.1   There shall be no leakage through the works at any time during the test.

11.5.2.5.2   If any leaks/ defects occur, mark the location on the works, water shall be drained completely. Prepare a report to be submitted to the Project Architect together with proposals for remedial measures. Any part of the works that is adversely affected shall be replaced or repaired; the design intent shall be maintained.

11.5.2.5.3   After making good any defects, retest locally to verify integrity of repair.

11.5.2.5.4   At completion of the test there shall be no standing water in locations intended to remain dry. Certify the waterproof integrity of the works.

11.5.2.5.5   Invite the Project Architect to witness the tests.

11.5.3   Testing of fixings

11.5.3.1   As the work proceeds, allow for the bolts to be proof load tested as required and witnessed by the Structural Engineer.

11.5.3.2   Tests for composite samples: Provide test results for flexural strength of composite to be used in facade panels in accordance with EN 1570-5 (no ASTM equivalent).

11.5.3.3   Tests for shear resistance and tensile resistance of fixings in composite panel: Provide test results for tests for shear resistance and tensile resistance of fixings.

11.5.3.4   During the execution of the prototypes, make a torsion test on the bolts according to the requirements of the standards and in the presence of structural engineers involved in the project.

11.5.4   Thermal performance testing

11.5.4.1   Thermography testing shall be carried out to ensure that insulation is continuous using a suitable thermal imaging method to be proposed by the Contractor. The testing method shall be subject to acceptance by the Project Architect.

11.5.4.2   Insulation shall be proven to be continuous. Any areas of excessive cooling energy loss identified shall be rectified at the Contractor's expense.

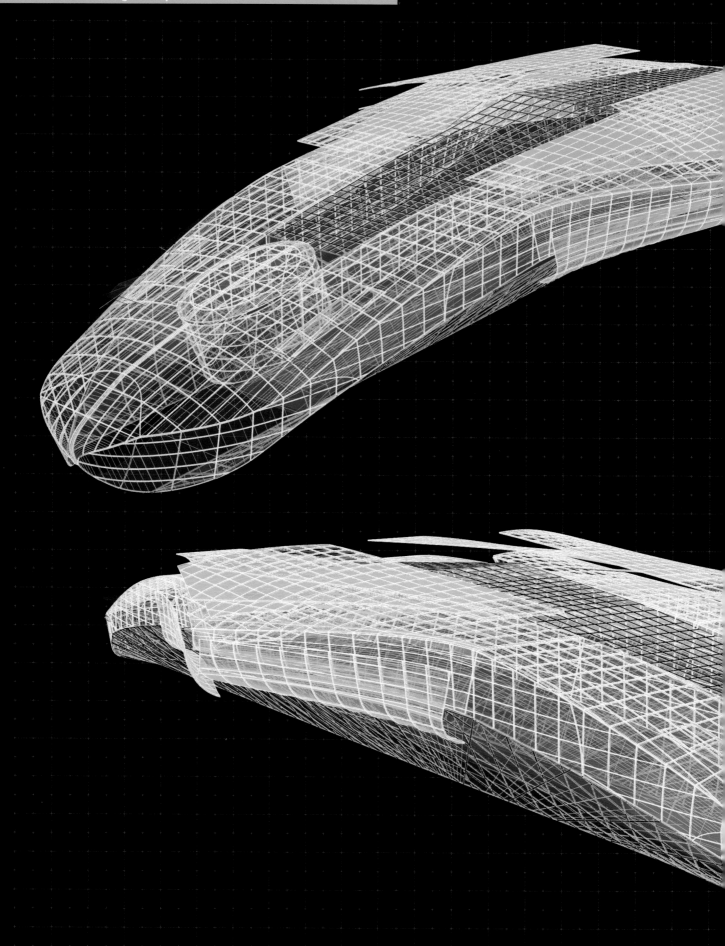

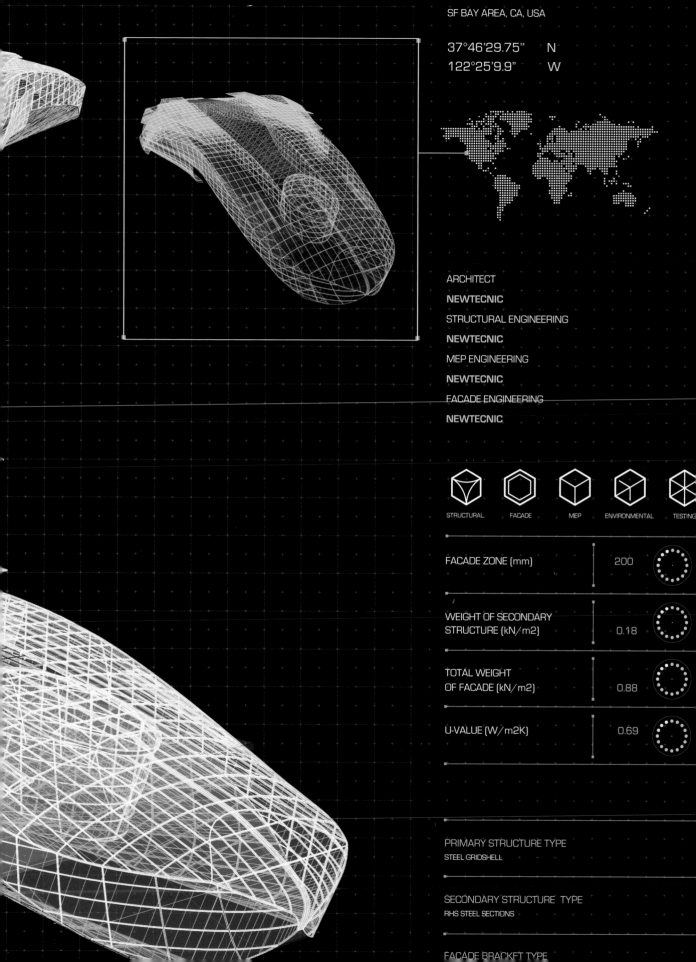

SF BAY AREA, CA, USA

37°46'29.75"   N
122°25'9.9"   W

ARCHITECT
NEWTECNIC

STRUCTURAL ENGINEERING
NEWTECNIC

MEP ENGINEERING
NEWTECNIC

FACADE ENGINEERING
NEWTECNIC

| STRUCTURAL | FACADE | MEP | ENVIRONMENTAL | TESTING |

FACADE ZONE [mm]	200	
WEIGHT OF SECONDARY STRUCTURE [kN/m2]	0.18	
TOTAL WEIGHT OF FACADE [kN/m2]	0.88	
U-VALUE [W/m2K]	0.69	

PRIMARY STRUCTURE TYPE
STEEL GRIDSHELL

SECONDARY STRUCTURE TYPE
RHS STEEL SECTIONS

FACADE BRACKET TYPE

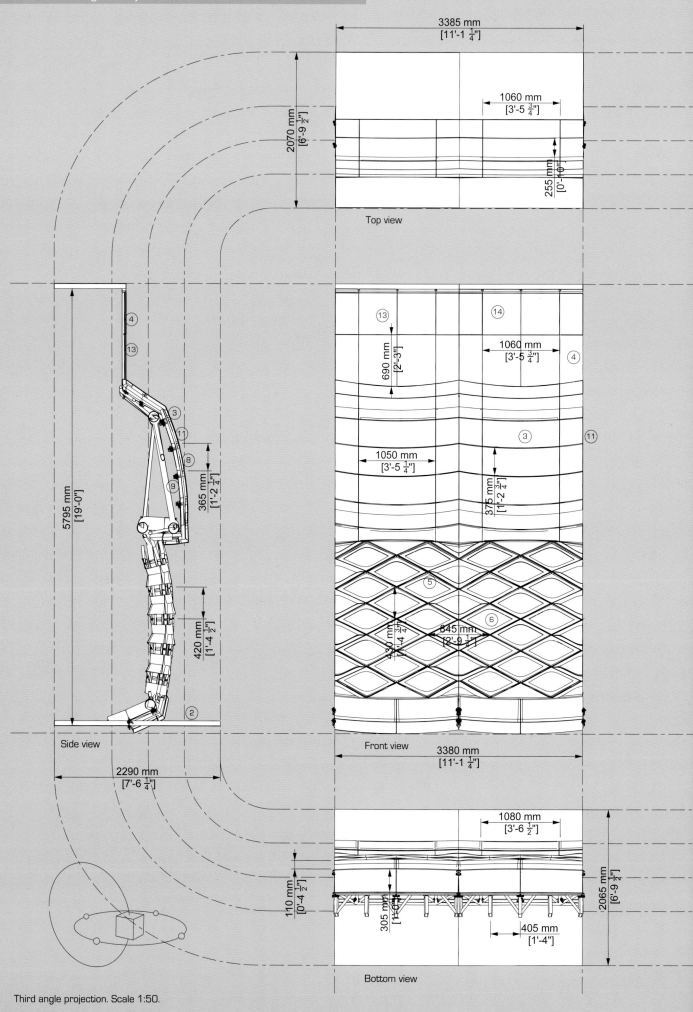

3385 mm
[11'-1 $\frac{1}{4}$"]

1060 mm
[3'-5 $\frac{3}{4}$"]

2070 mm
[6'-9 $\frac{1}{2}$"]

255 mm
[0'-0"]

Top view

① 4

① 13

5795 mm
[19'-0"]

① 3

① 11

① 8

① 9

365 mm
[1'-2 $\frac{1}{4}$"]

420 mm
[1'-4 $\frac{1}{2}$"]

② 2

Side view

2290 mm
[7'-6 $\frac{1}{4}$"]

① 13   ① 14

690 mm
[2'-3"]

1060 mm
[3'-5 $\frac{3}{4}$"]

① 4

① 3   ① 11

1050 mm
[3'-5 $\frac{1}{4}$"]

375 mm
[1'-2 $\frac{3}{4}$"]

① 5

① 6

430 mm
[1'-4 $\frac{3}{4}$"]

845 mm
[2'-9 $\frac{1}{4}$"]

Front view

3380 mm
[11'-1 $\frac{1}{4}$"]

1080 mm
[3'-6 $\frac{1}{2}$"]

110 mm
[0'-4 $\frac{1}{2}$"]

305 mm
[1'-0"]

405 mm
[1'-4"]

2065 mm
[6'-9 $\frac{1}{2}$"]

Bottom view

Third angle projection. Scale 1:50.

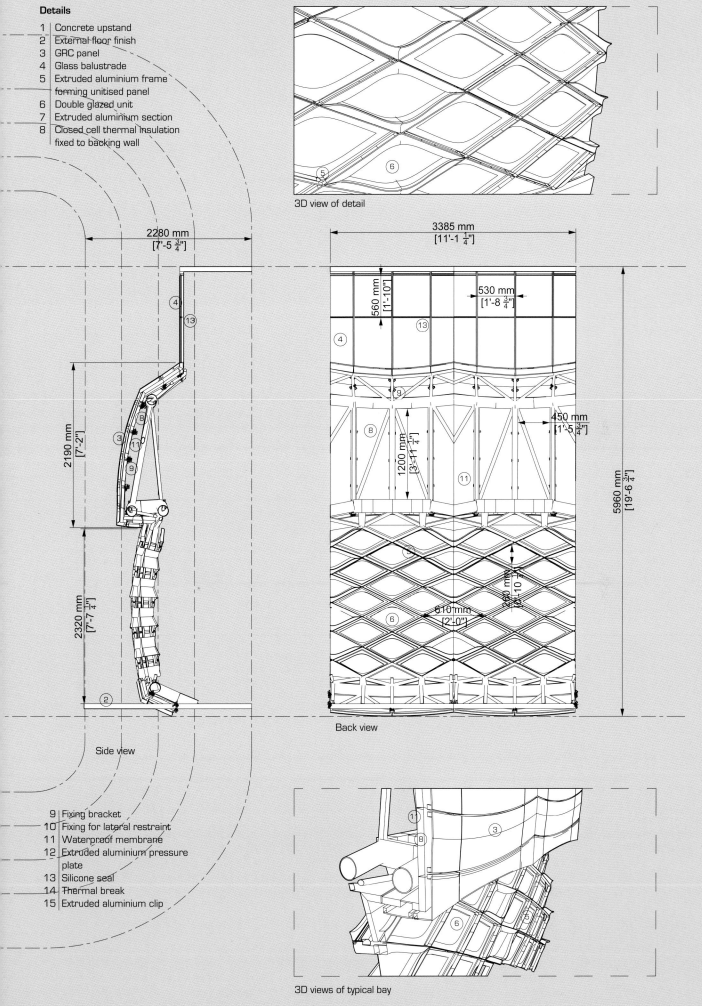

Details

1	Concrete upstand
2	External floor finish
3	GRC panel
4	Glass balustrade
5	Extruded aluminium frame forming unitised panel
6	Double glazed unit
7	Extruded aluminium section
8	Closed cell thermal insulation fixed to backing wall

3D view of detail

2280 mm
[7'-5 3/4"]

2190 mm
[7'-2"]

2320 mm
[7'-7 1/4"]

Side view

3385 mm
[11'-1 1/4"]

560 mm
[1'-10"]

530 mm
[1'-8 3/4"]

450 mm
[1'-5 3/4"]

1200 mm
[3'-11 1/4"]

5960 mm
[19'-6 3/4"]

610 mm
[2'-0"]

Back view

9	Fixing bracket
10	Fixing for lateral restraint
11	Waterproof membrane
12	Extruded aluminium pressure plate
13	Silicone seal
14	Thermal break
15	Extruded aluminium clip

3D views of typical bay

MCCS_57

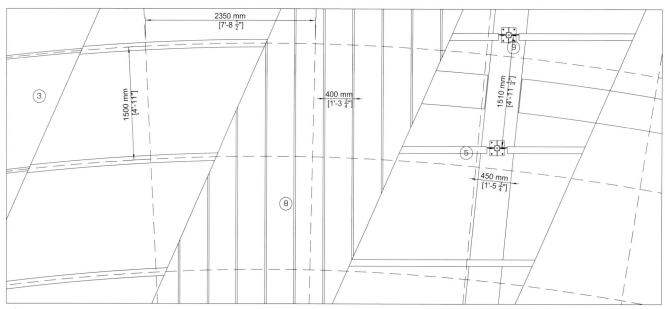

a | Elevation. Facade build-up

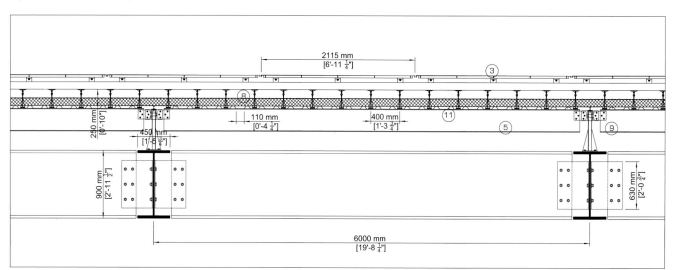

b | Horizontal section. Panel connection with primary structure

Details

1	Concrete upstand	9	Fixing bracket
2	External floor finish	10	Fixing for lateral restraint
3	GRC panel	11	Waterproof membrane
4	Glass balustrade	12	Extruded aluminium pressure
5	Extruded aluminium frame		plate
	forming unitised panel	13	Silicone seal
6	Double glazed unit	14	Thermal break
7	Extruded aluminium section	15	Extruded aluminium clip
8	Closed cell thermal insulation		
	fixed to backing wall		

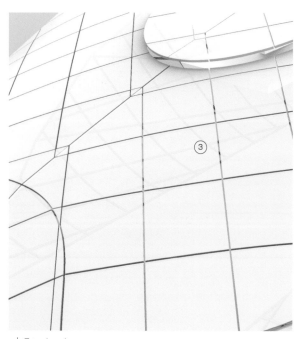

c | Exterior view

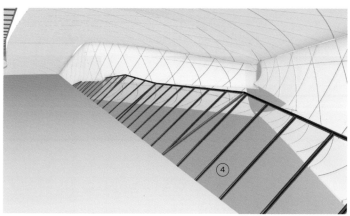

d | Interior view

1:50 scale

1:10 scale

2'-1" 4'-2" 6'-3" 8'-4"

5" 10" 1'-3" 1'-8"

500 1000 1500 2000 2500 mm

1:50 scale

1:10 scale

100 200 300 400 500 mm

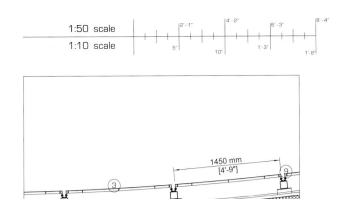

1450 mm
[4'-9"]

100 mm
[0'-3 3/4"]

200 mm
[0'-7 3/4"]

900 mm
[2'-11 1/2"]

1535 mm
[5'-0 1/2"]

450 mm
[1'-5 3/4"]

e | Horizontal section. Rainscreen assembly at curvature

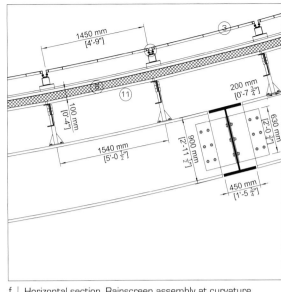

1450 mm
[4'-9"]

100 mm
[0'-4"]

200 mm
[0'-7 3/4"]

630 mm
[2'-0 3/4"]

1540 mm
[5'-0 1/2"]

900 mm
[2'-11 1/2"]

450 mm
[1'-5 3/4"]

f | Horizontal section. Rainscreen assembly at curvature

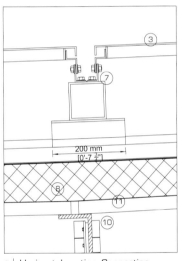

200 mm
[0'-7 3/4"]

g | Horizontal section. Connection

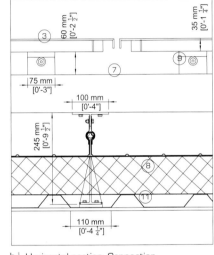

60 mm
[0'-2 1/2"]

35 mm
[0'-1 1/4"]

75 mm
[0'-3"]

100 mm
[0'-4"]

245 mm
[0'-9 1/2"]

110 mm
[0'-4 1/4"]

h | Horizontal section. Connection

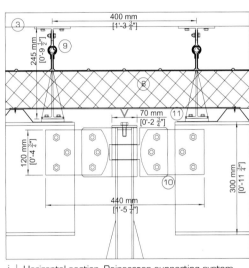

400 mm
[1'-3 3/4"]

245 mm
[0'-9 1/2"]

70 mm
[0'-2 3/4"]

120 mm
[0'-4 3/4"]

300 mm
[0'-11 3/4"]

440 mm
[1'-5 1/2"]

j | Horizontal section. Rainscreen supporting system

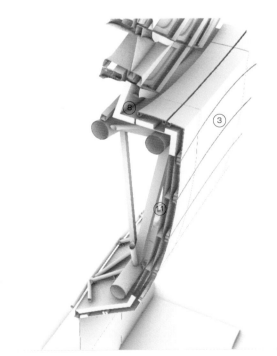

k | Typical bay. 3D view

m | Vertical section. Typical bay

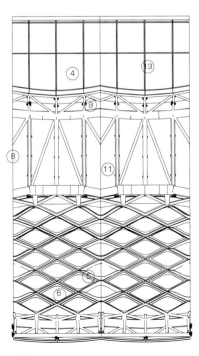

n | Typical bay. Back view

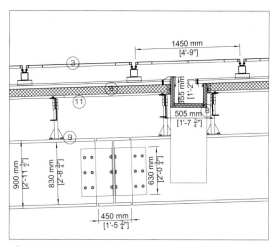

a | Vertical section. Rainscreen with drainage system

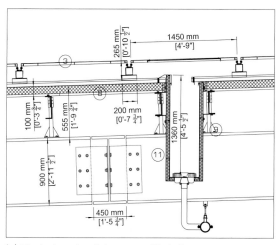

b | Vertical section. Rainscreen with drainage system

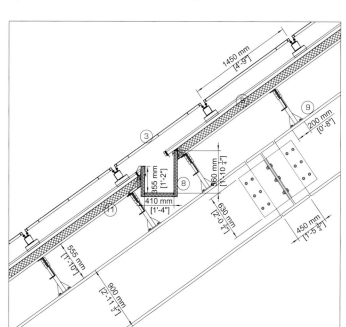

c | Vertical section. Rainscreen with drainage system

Details

1 | Concrete upstand
2 | External floor finish
3 | GRC panel
4 | Glass balustrade
5 | Extruded aluminium frame forming unitised panel
6 | Double glazed unit
7 | Extruded aluminium section
8 | Closed cell thermal insulation fixed to backing wall

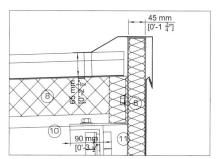

d | Vertical section. Parapet

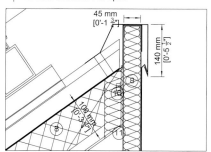

e | Vertical section. Parapet

Compression
-0.35

Tension
0.35

f | Finite element model of a typical bay

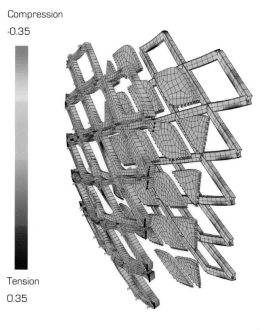

g | Utilization distribution within quadrilateral elements

Facade system	Opaque composite rainscreen with glazing insets
Facade zone	200mm
Primary structure type	Steel gridshell
Secondary structure type	RHS steel sections
Weight of secondary structure (kN/m²)	0.18
Facade bracket type	Spider bracket with four adjustable arms
Number of components in fixing system	14
Weight of facade, including secondary structure (kN/m²)	0.88

1:50 scale

1:10 scale

2'-1"   4'-2"   6'-3"   8'-4"

5"   10"   1'-3"   1'-8"

500   1000   1500   2000   2500   mm

100   200   300   400   500 mm

1:50 scale

1:10 scale

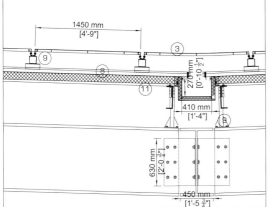

1450 mm
[4'-9"]

270 mm [0'-10½"]

410 mm [1'-4"]

630 mm [2'-0¾"]

450 mm [1'-5¾"]

h | Vertical section. Gutter detail

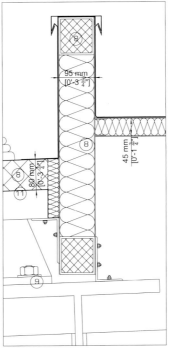

175 mm [0'-7"]

65 mm [0'-2½"]

100 mm [0'-3¾"]

270 mm [0'-10½"]

410 mm [1'-4"]

j | Vertical section. Gutter detail

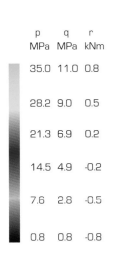

2450 mm [8'-0½"]

410 mm [1'-4"]

100 mm [0'-3¾"]

900 mm [2'-11½"]

450 mm [1'-5¾"]

k | Horizontal section. Connection with frame

9 | Fixing bracket
10 | Fixing for lateral restraint
11 | Waterproof membrane
12 | Extruded aluminium pressure
plate
13 | Silicone seal
14 | Thermal break
15 | Extruded aluminium clip

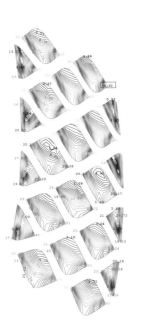

95 mm [0'-3¾"]

45 mm [0'-1¾"]

80 mm [0'-3¾"]

m | Vertical section. Parapet

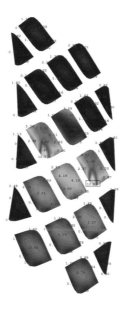

270 mm [0'-10½"]

300 mm [0'-11¾"]

45 mm [0'-1¾"]

n | Vertical section. Parapet

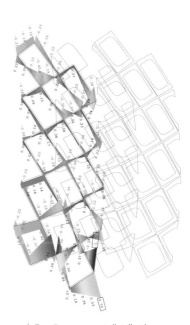

p MPa	q MPa	r kNm
35.0	11.0	0.8
28.2	9.0	0.5
21.3	6.9	0.2
14.5	4.9	-0.2
7.6	2.8	-0.5
0.8	0.8	-0.8

p | Principal shear stress distribution
in glazing panels (MPa)

q | Principal tension stress distribution
in glazing panels (MPa)

r | Bending moment distribution
in steel frame (kNm)

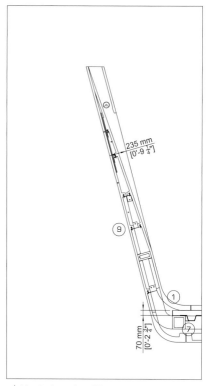

a | Vertical section. Glass balustrade

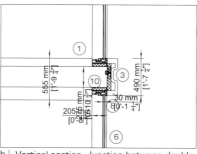

b | Vertical section. Junction between double glazed units at slab edge

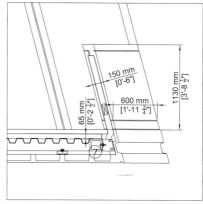

c | Vertical section. Balustrade connection detail

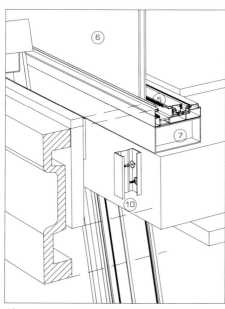

d | 3D view. Connection of opaque glass spandrel connecting to slab edge

Details

1 | Concrete upstand
2 | External floor finish
3 | GRC panel
4 | Glass balustrade
5 | Extruded aluminium frame forming unitised panel
6 | Double glazed unit
7 | Extruded aluminium section
8 | Closed cell thermal insulation fixed to backing wall
9 | Fixing bracket
10 | Fixing for lateral restraint
11 | Waterproof membrane
12 | Extruded aluminium pressure plate
13 | Silicone seal
14 | Thermal break
15 | Extruded aluminium clip

e | Vertical section. Curtain wall glazing connecting to concrete slab

f | Vertical section. Curtain wall glazing connecting to concrete slab

Period	With shading	Without shading	Solar reduction
1 year	8.3 MWh	19.6 MWh	58%

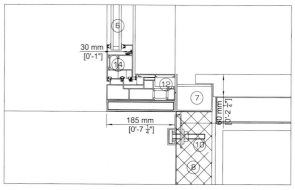

kWh/m²

700
583
467
350
233
117

g | Annual cumulative solar radiation analysis on glazed facade with shading system

h | Annual cumulative solar radiation analysis on glazed facade without shading system

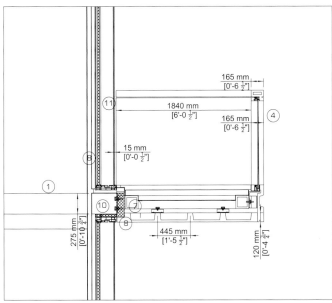

j | Vertical section. Balustrade connection to insulated metal panel

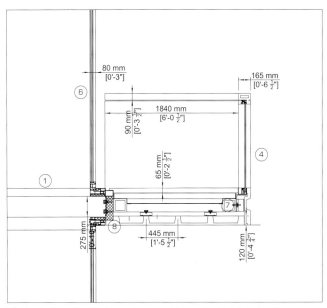

k | Vertical section. Balustrade connection to double glazed units

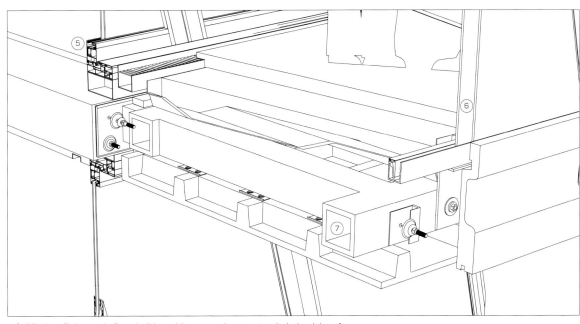

m | 3D view. Balustrade floor buildup with connection to extruded aluminium frame

EXT: 40°C

INT: 22°C

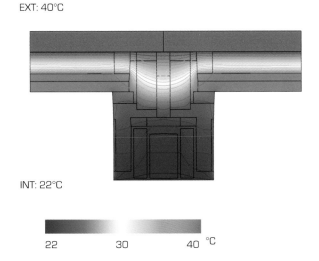

22   30   40 °C

n | Thermal performance analysis of a unitised curtain wall mullion
  | Isotherms showing temperature distribution across assembly

EXT: 0°C

INT: 22°C

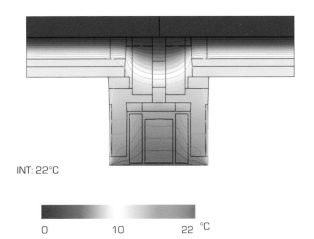

0   10   22 °C

p | Thermal performance analysis of a unitised curtain wall mullion
  | Isotherms showing temperature distribution across assembly

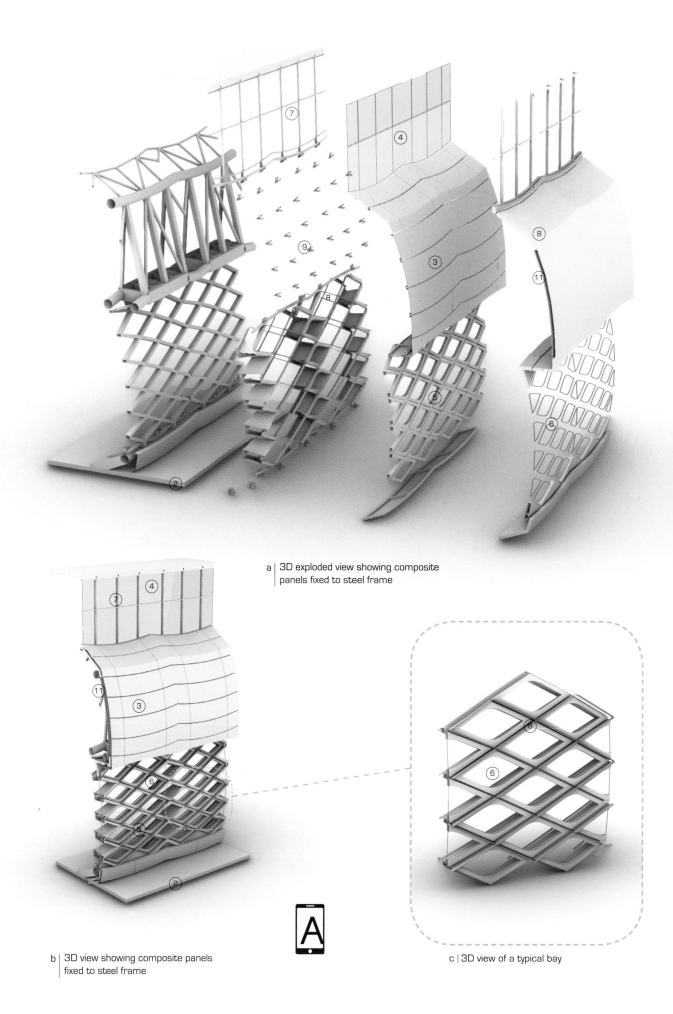

a | 3D exploded view showing composite panels fixed to steel frame

b | 3D view showing composite panels fixed to steel frame

c | 3D view of a typical bay

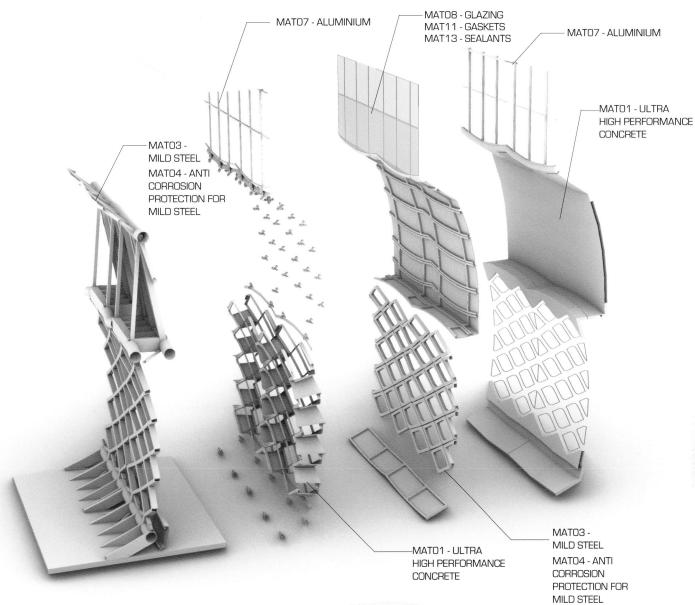

MAT07 - ALUMINIUM

MAT08 - GLAZING
MAT11 - GASKETS
MAT13 - SEALANTS

MAT07 - ALUMINIUM

MAT03 -
MILD STEEL

MAT04 - ANTI
CORROSION
PROTECTION FOR
MILD STEEL

MAT01 - ULTRA
HIGH PERFORMANCE
CONCRETE

MAT01 - ULTRA
HIGH PERFORMANCE
CONCRETE

MAT03 -
MILD STEEL

MAT04 - ANTI
CORROSION
PROTECTION FOR
MILD STEEL

d | 3D exploded view showing facade components with
material specification references

Details

1 | Concrete upstand
2 | External floor finish
3 | GRC panel
4 | Glass balustrade
5 | Extruded aluminium frame
forming unitised panel
6 | Double glazed unit
7 | Extruded aluminium section
8 | Closed cell thermal insulation
fixed to backing wall
9 | Fixing bracket
10 | Fixing for lateral restraint
11 | Waterproof membrane by
others
12 | Extruded aluminium
pressure plate
13 | Silicone seal
14 | Thermal break
15 | Extruded aluminium clip

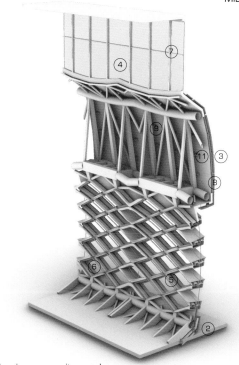

e | 3D view showing composite panels
fixed to steel frame

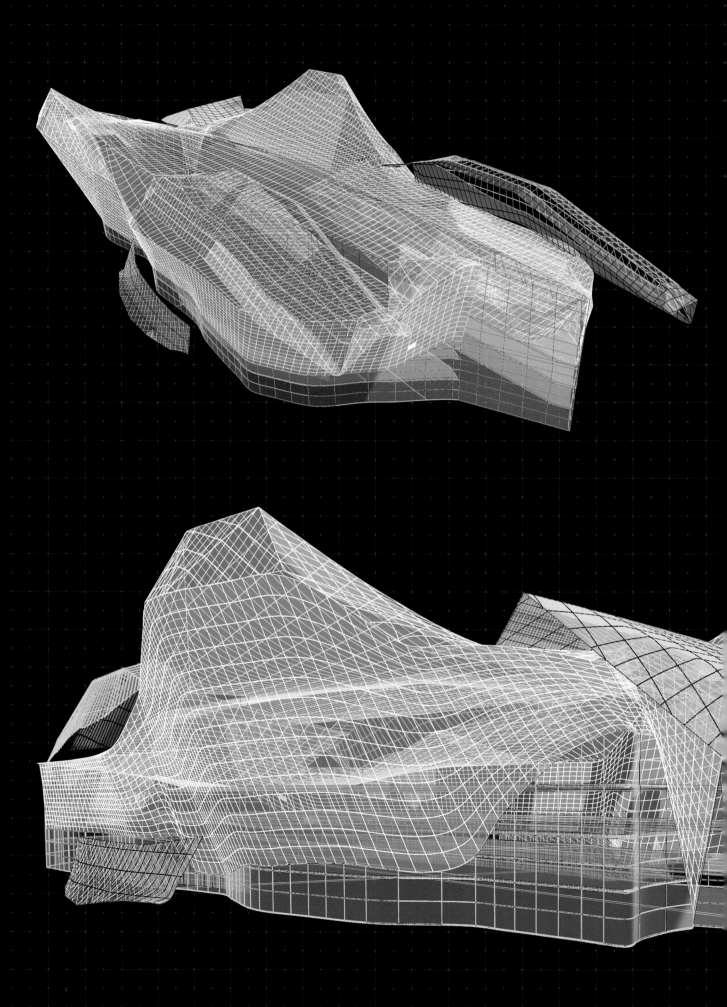

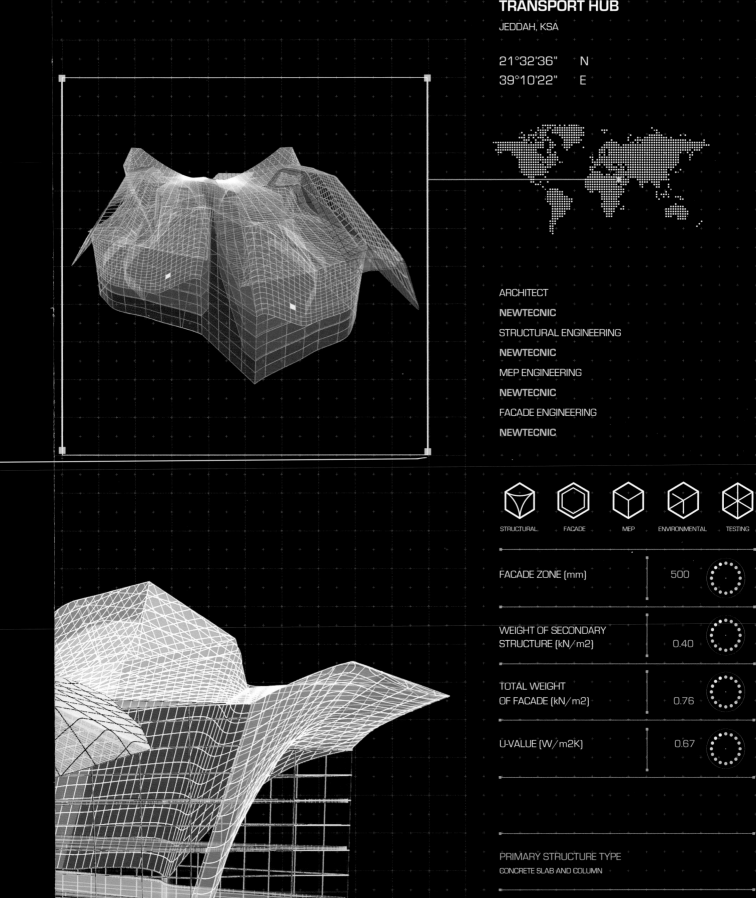

TRANSPORT HUB

JEDDAH, KSA

21°32'36"   N
39°10'22"   E

ARCHITECT
NEWTECNIC
STRUCTURAL ENGINEERING
NEWTECNIC
MEP ENGINEERING
NEWTECNIC
FACADE ENGINEERING
NEWTECNIC

STRUCTURAL   FACADE   MEP   ENVIRONMENTAL   TESTING

FACADE ZONE (mm)	500	
WEIGHT OF SECONDARY STRUCTURE (kN/m2)	0.40	
TOTAL WEIGHT OF FACADE (kN/m2)	0.76	
U-VALUE (W/m2K)	0.67	

PRIMARY STRUCTURE TYPE
CONCRETE SLAB AND COLUMN

SECONDARY STRUCTURE TYPE
CHS STEEL SECTIONS

FACADE BRACKET TYPE
SPIDER BRACKET WITH TWO ADJUSTABLE ARMS

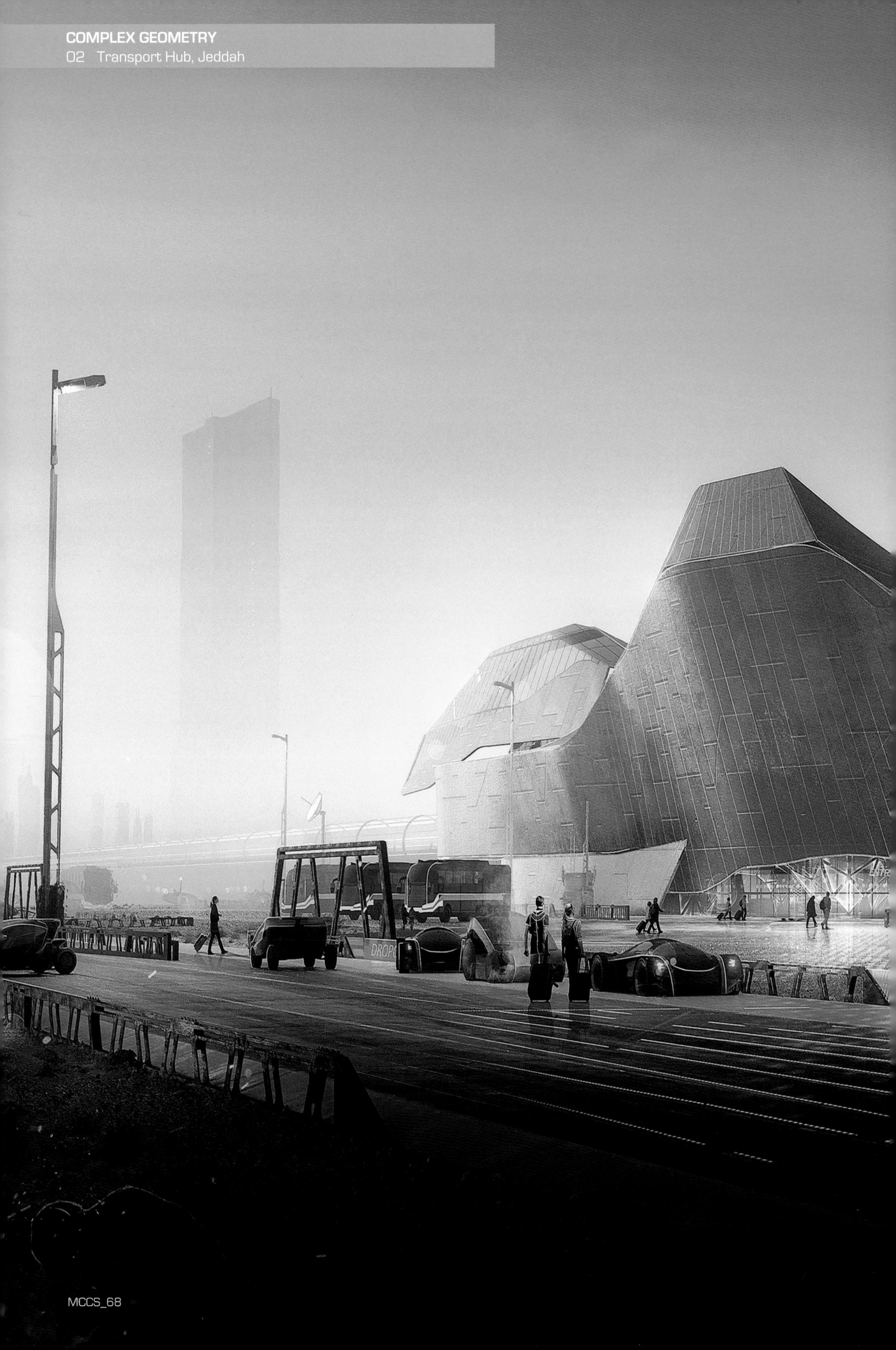

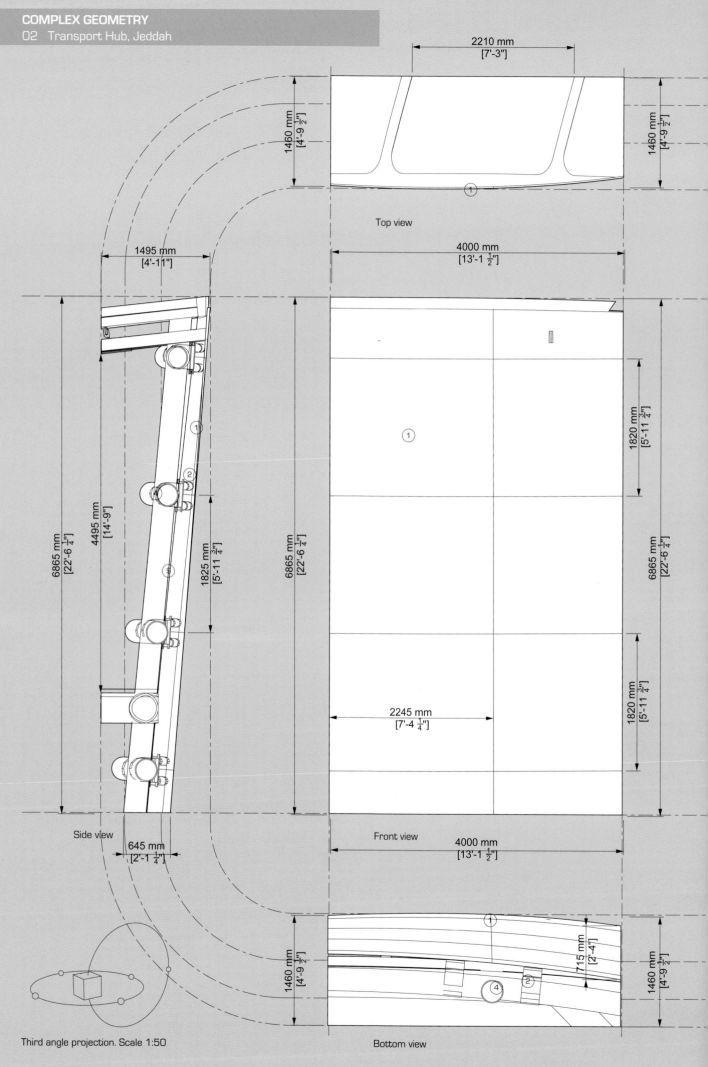

2210 mm
[7'-3"]

1460 mm
[4'-9 $\frac{1}{2}$"]

1460 mm
[4'-9 $\frac{1}{2}$"]

Top view

4000 mm
[13'-1 $\frac{1}{2}$"]

1495 mm
[4'-11"]

1820 mm
[5'-11 $\frac{3}{4}$"]

6865 mm
[22'-6 $\frac{1}{4}$"]

4495 mm
[14'-9"]

6865 mm
[22'-6 $\frac{1}{4}$"]

6865 mm
[22'-6 $\frac{1}{4}$"]

1825 mm
[5'-11 $\frac{3}{4}$"]

1820 mm
[5'-11 $\frac{3}{4}$"]

2245 mm
[7'-4 $\frac{1}{4}$"]

Side view

Front view

4000 mm
[13'-1 $\frac{1}{2}$"]

645 mm
[2'-1 $\frac{1}{4}$"]

1460 mm
[4'-9 $\frac{1}{2}$"]

715 mm
[2'-4"]

1460 mm
[4'-9 $\frac{1}{2}$"]

Third angle projection. Scale 1:50

Bottom view

Details

1. GRC rainscreen cladding panel
2. Adjustable fixing bracket
3. Steel frame
4. Steel support structure
5. Rubber based sheet
6. Metal strap
7. Aluminium support structure
8. Waterproof membrane with 1mm protective aluminium sheet above
9. Thermal insulation

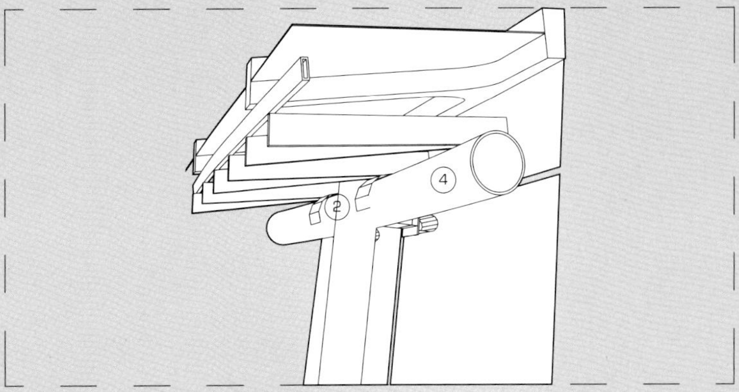

10. Vapour barrier
11. Waterproof membrane
12. Profiled metal deck
13. Steel purlin
14. Steel channel
15. Steel structure

3D view of detail

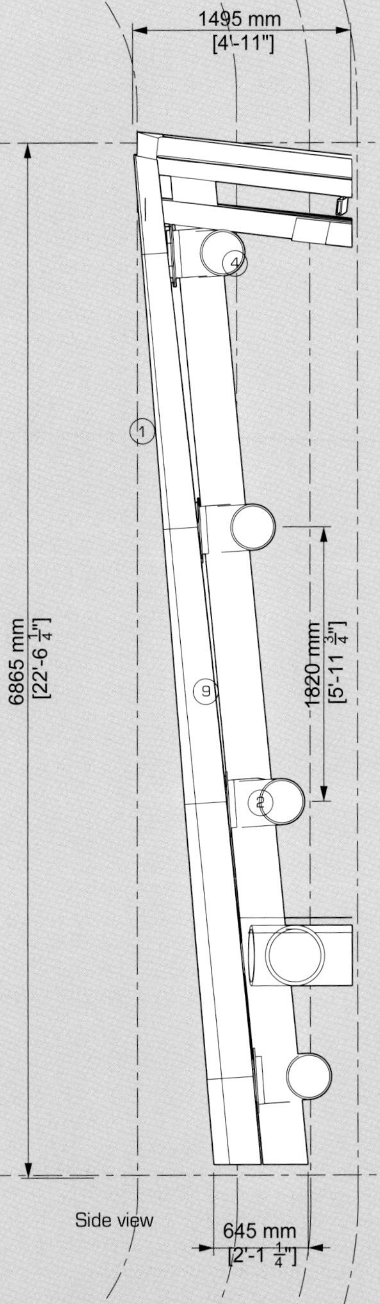

1495 mm [4'-11"]

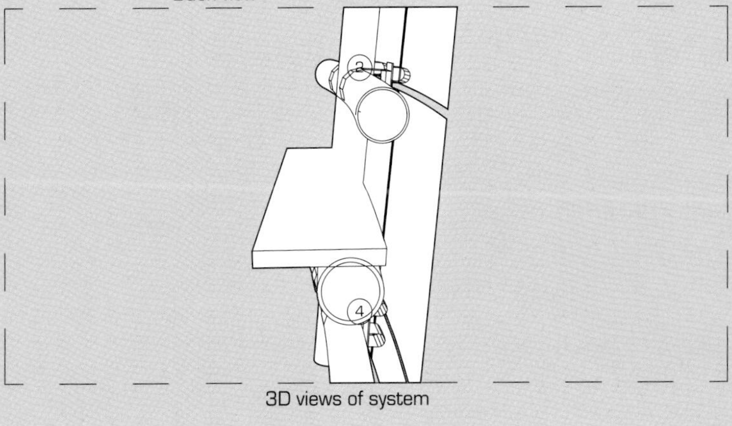

6865 mm [22'-6 1/4"]

1820 mm [5'-11 3/4"]

Side view

645 mm [2'-1 1/4"]

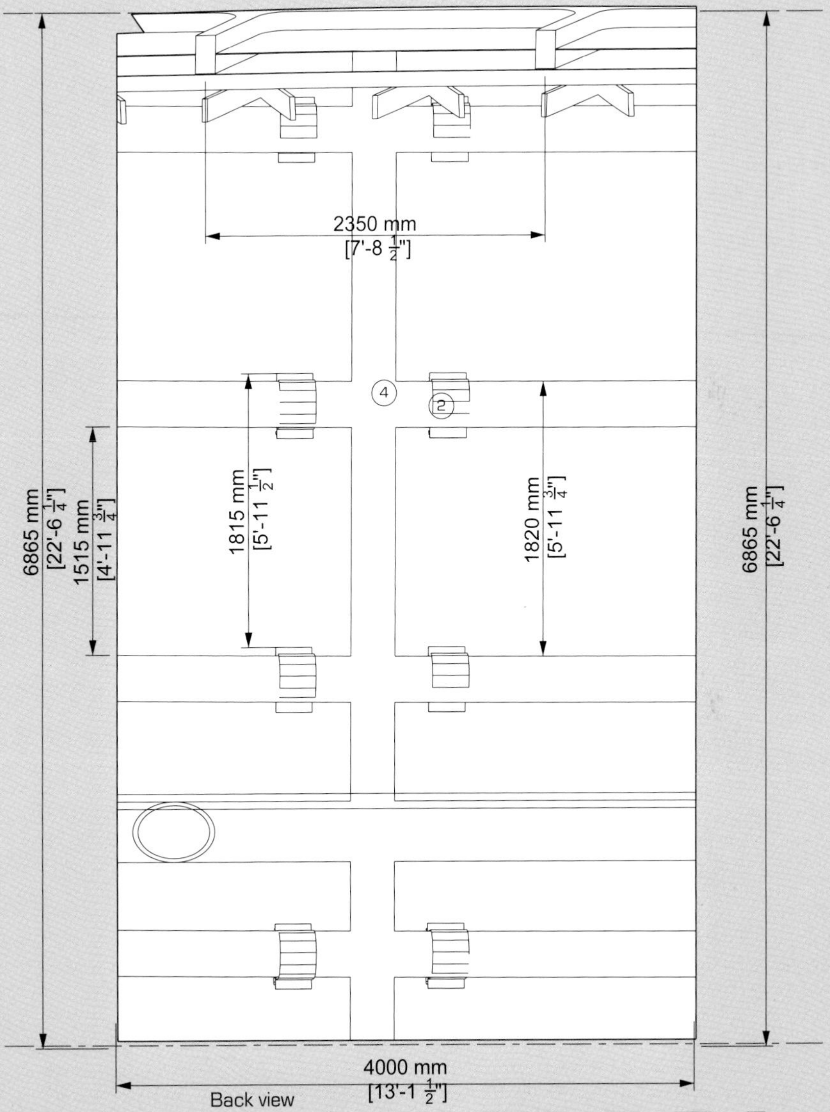

2350 mm [7'-8 1/2"]

6865 mm [22'-6 1/4"]

1515 mm [4'-11 3/4"]

1815 mm [5'-11 1/2"]

1820 mm [5'-11 3/4"]

6865 mm [22'-6 1/4"]

Back view

4000 mm [13'-1 1/2"]

3D views of system

MCCS_71

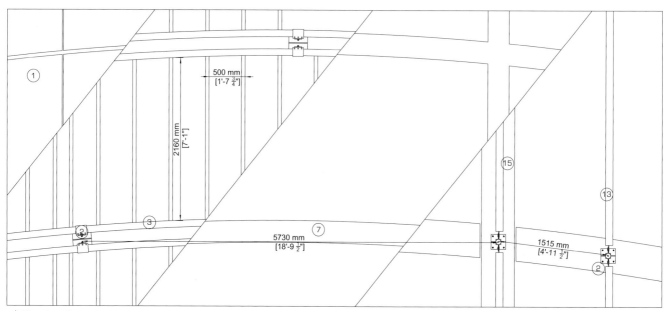

a | Elevation. Facade buildup

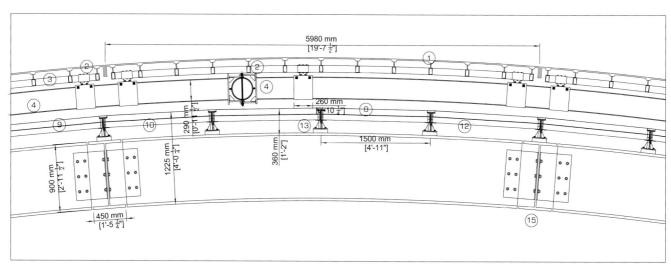

b | Horizontal section. Panel connection with primary structure

c | Exterior view

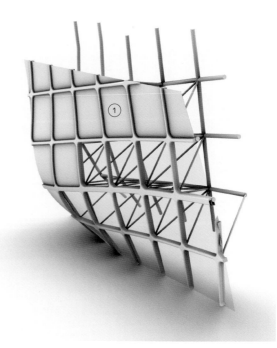

d | Typical bay. 3D view

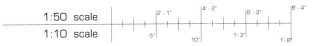

1:50 scale
1:10 scale

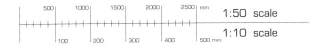

1:50 scale
1:10 scale

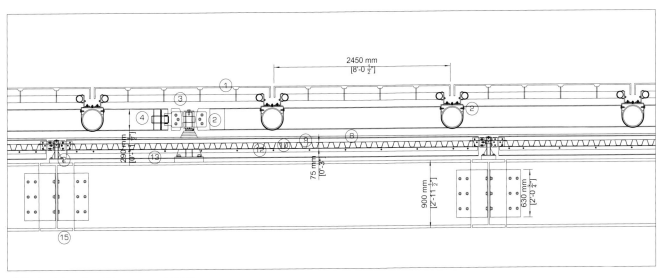

e | Horizontal section. Rainscreen assembly

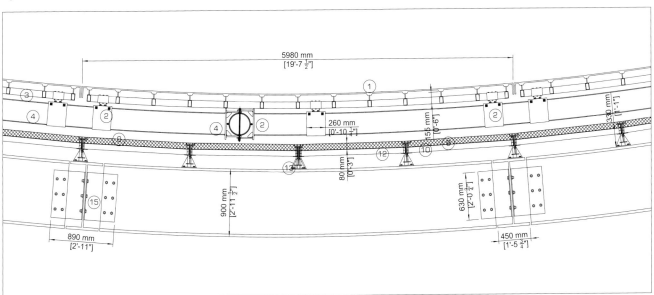

f | Horizontal section. Rainscreen assembly at curvature

Details

1 GRC rainscreen cladding panel
2 Adjustable fixing bracket
3 Steel frame
4 Steel support structure
5 Rubber based sheet
6 Metal strap
7 Aluminium support structure
8 Waterproof membrane with 1mm protective aluminium sheet above
9 Thermal insulation
10 Vapour barrier
11 Waterproof membrane
12 Profiled metal deck
13 Steel purlin
14 Steel channel
15 Steel structure

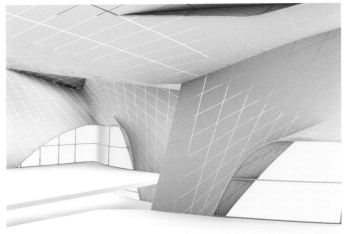

g | Interior view

h | Typical bay: 3D view

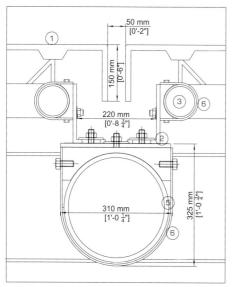

a | Horizontal section. Structure at panel joints

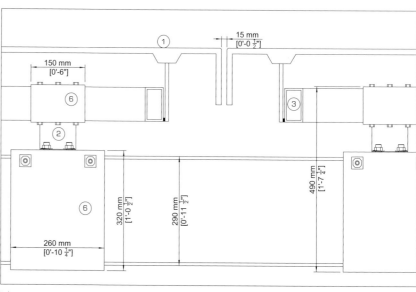

b | Horizontal section. Detail of panel fixing system

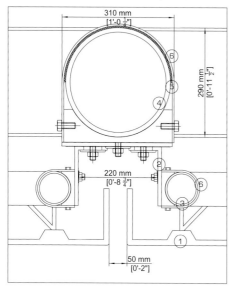

c | Horizontal section. Detail of secondary structure

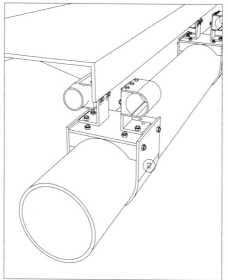

d | 3D view. Connection of opaque panel to secondary structure

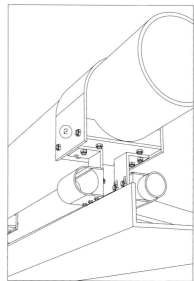

e | Vertical section. Connection of opaque panel to secondary structure

Facade system	Metal rainscreen with full height stick glazing
Facade zone	500mm
Primary structure type	Concrete slab and column
Secondary structure type	CHS steel sections
Weight of secondary structure (kN/m²)	0.4
Facade bracket type	Spider bracket with two adjustable arms
Number of components in fixing system	5
Weight of facade, including secondary structure (kN/m²)	0.76

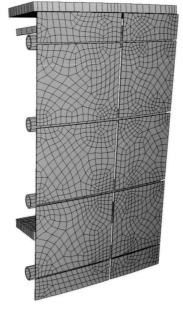

f | Finite element model of a typical bay

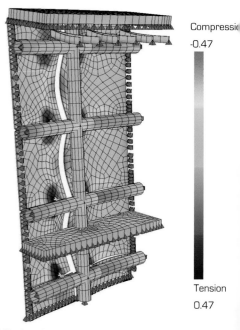

g | Utilization distribution within quadrilateral elements

Compressi
-0.47

Tension
0.47

1:50 scale

1:10 scale

2'-1"   4'-2"   6'-3"   8'-4"

5"   10"   1'-3"   1'-8"

500   1000   1500   2000   2500 mm

100   200   300   400   500 mm

1:50 scale

1:10 scale

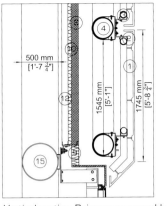

h | Vertical section. Rainscreen assembly

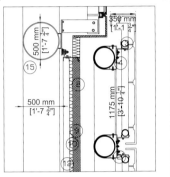

j | Vertical section. Rainscreen assembly

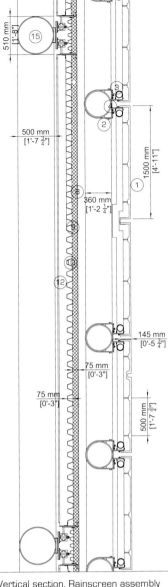

k | Vertical section. Rainscreen assembly

Details

1 | GRC rainscreen cladding panel
2 | Adjustable fixing bracket
3 | Steel frame
4 | Steel support structure
5 | Rubber based sheet
6 | Metal strap
7 | Aluminium support structure
8 | Waterproof membrane with 1mm protective aluminium sheet above

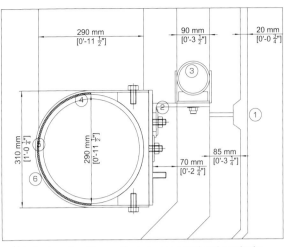

m | Vertical section. Connection between panel and steel tube

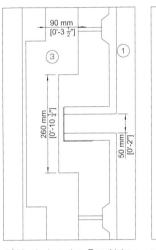

n | Vertical section. Panel joints

p | Vertical section. GRC shadow gap panel

9 | Thermal insulation
10 | Vapour barrier
11 | Waterproof membrane
12 | Profiled metal deck
13 | Steel purlin
14 | Steel channel
15 | Steel structure

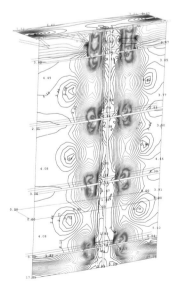

q | Principal shear stress distribution in glazing panels (MPa)

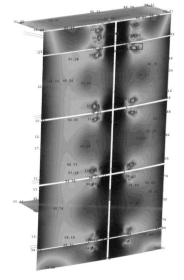

r | Principal tension stress distribution in glazing panels (MPa)

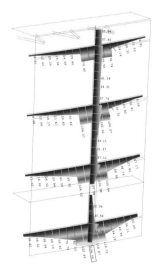

s | Von Mises stress distribution in steel frame (MPa)

q MPa	r MPa	s MPa
27.7	58.2	131.2
22.2	46.8	105.0
16.6	35.4	78.8
11.1	23.9	52.5
5.5	12.5	26.2
0.0	1.1	0.0

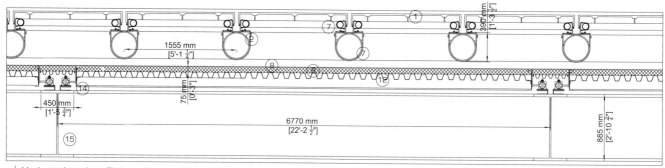

a | Horizontal section. Flat panel connection with secondary structure

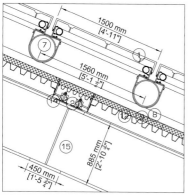

b | Horizontal section. Facade secondary structure

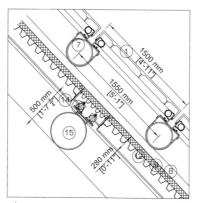

c | Horizontal section. Facade secondary structure

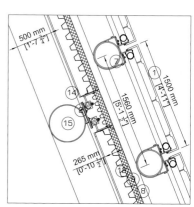

d | Horizontal section. Facade secondary structur

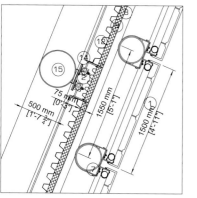

e | Horizontal section. Facade secondary structure

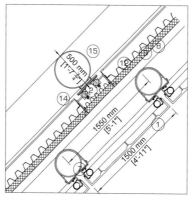

f | Horizontal section. Facade secondary structure

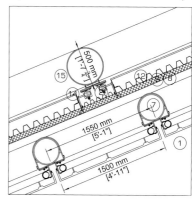

g | Horizontal section. Facade secondary structur

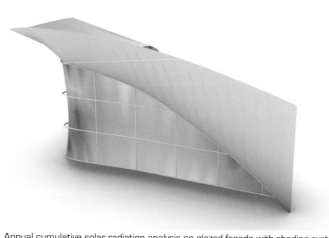

h | Annual cumulative solar radiation analysis on glazed facade with shading system

kWh/m²

1100

917

733

550

367

183

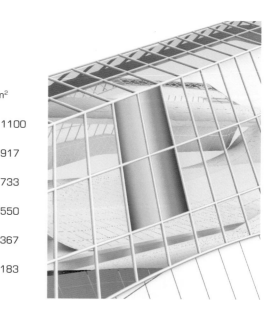

j | Annual cumulative solar radiation analysis on glazed facade without shading system

Period	With shading	Without shading	Solar reduction
1 year	26.7 MWh	30.8 MWh	13%

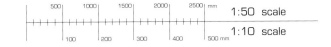

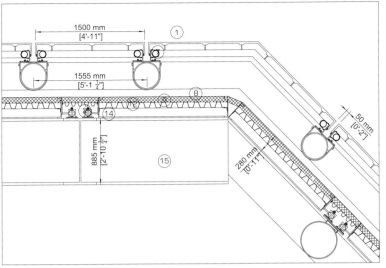

k | Horizontal section. External corner

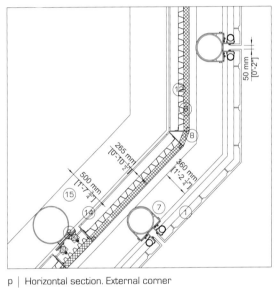

m | Horizontal section. External corner

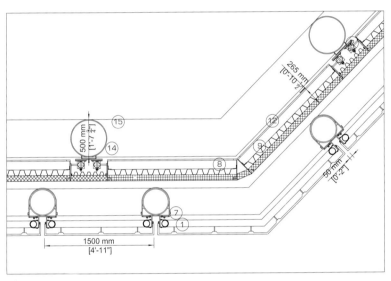

n | Horizontal section. External corner

p | Horizontal section. External corner

Details

1 | GRC rainscreen cladding panel
2 | Adjustable fixing bracket
3 | Steel frame
4 | Steel support structure
5 | Rubber based sheet
6 | Metal strap
7 | Aluminium support structure
8 | Waterproof membrane with 1mm protective aluminium sheet above
9 | Thermal insulation
10 | Vapour barrier
11 | Waterproof membrane
12 | Profiled metal deck
13 | Steel purlin
14 | Steel channel
15 | Steel structure

EXT: 40°C

EXT: 0°C

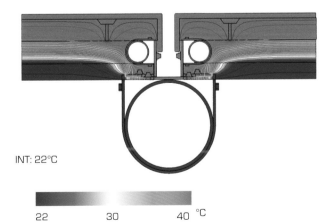

INT: 22°C

q | Thermal performance analysis of rainscreen cladding on steel frame
| Isotherms showing temperature distribution across assembly

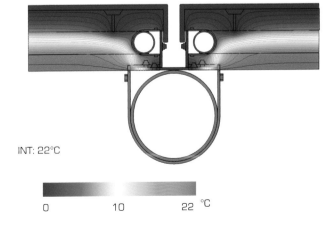

INT: 22°C

r | Thermal performance analysis of rainscreen cladding on steel frame
| Isotherms showing temperature distribution across assembly

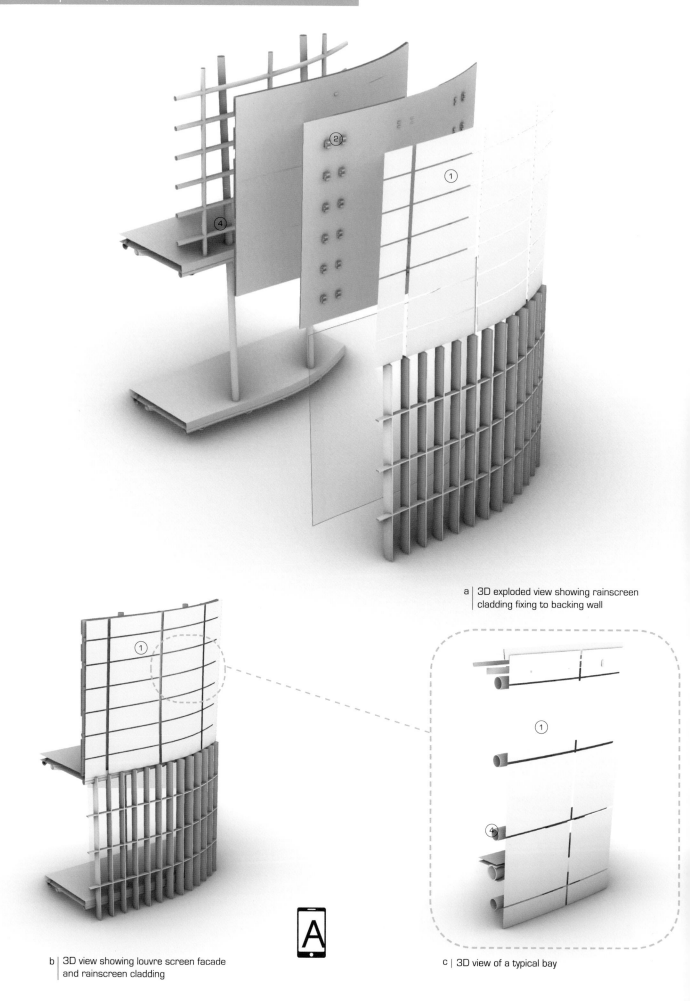

a | 3D exploded view showing rainscreen
cladding fixing to backing wall

b | 3D view showing louvre screen facade
and rainscreen cladding

c | 3D view of a typical bay

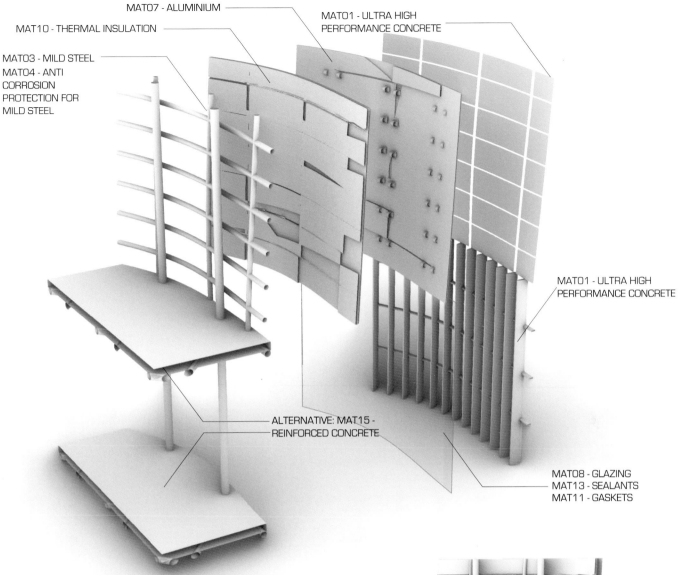

MAT07 - ALUMINIUM

MAT10 - THERMAL INSULATION

MAT01 - ULTRA HIGH
PERFORMANCE CONCRETE

MAT03 - MILD STEEL
MAT04 - ANTI
CORROSION
PROTECTION FOR
MILD STEEL

MAT01 - ULTRA HIGH
PERFORMANCE CONCRETE

ALTERNATIVE: MAT15 -
REINFORCED CONCRETE

MAT08 - GLAZING
MAT13 - SEALANTS
MAT11 - GASKETS

d | 3D exploded view showing facade components with
material specification references

Details

1	GRC rainscreen cladding panel
2	Adjustable fixing bracket
3	Steel frame
4	Steel support structure
5	Rubber based sheet
6	Metal strap
7	Aluminium support structure
8	Waterproof membrane with 1mm protective aluminium sheet above
9	Thermal insulation
10	Vapour barrier
11	Waterproof membrane
12	Profiled metal deck
13	Steel purlin
14	Steel channel
15	Steel structure

e | 3D view showing louvre screen facade
and rainscreen cladding

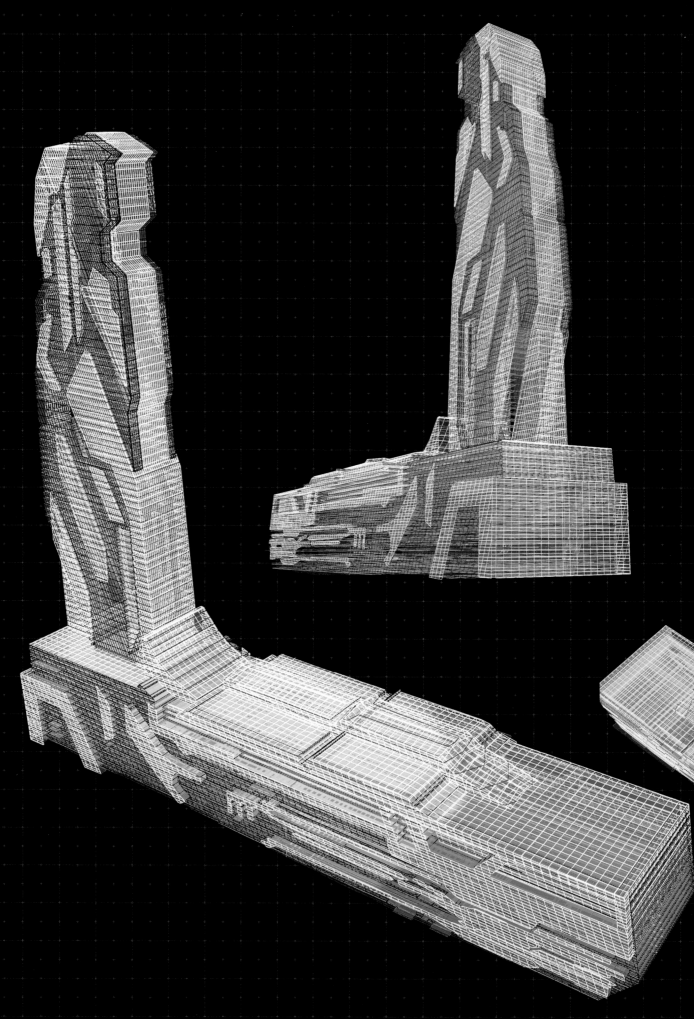

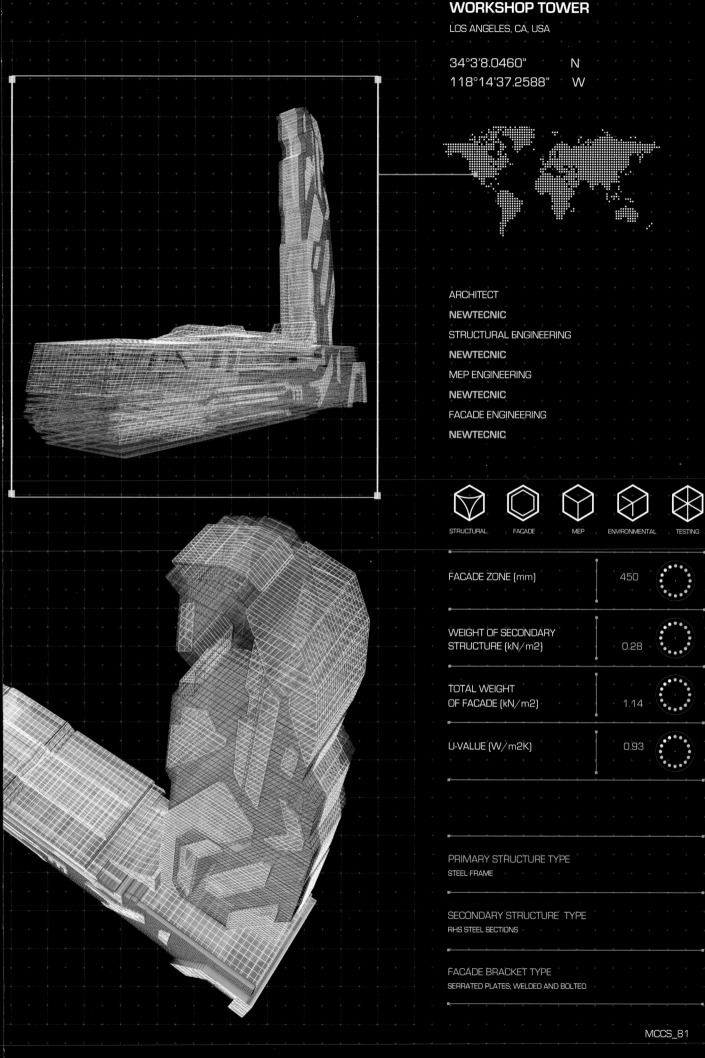

WORKSHOP TOWER

LOS ANGELES, CA, USA

34°3'8.0460"   N
118°14'37.2588"   W

ARCHITECT
NEWTECNIC
STRUCTURAL ENGINEERING
NEWTECNIC
MEP ENGINEERING
NEWTECNIC
FACADE ENGINEERING
NEWTECNIC

STRUCTURAL   FACADE   MEP   ENVIRONMENTAL   TESTING

FACADE ZONE (mm)	450	
WEIGHT OF SECONDARY STRUCTURE (kN/m2)	0.28	
TOTAL WEIGHT OF FACADE (kN/m2)	1.14	
U-VALUE (W/m2K)	0.93	

PRIMARY STRUCTURE TYPE
STEEL FRAME

SECONDARY STRUCTURE TYPE
RHS STEEL SECTIONS

FACADE BRACKET TYPE
SERRATED PLATES; WELDED AND BOLTED

MCCS_83

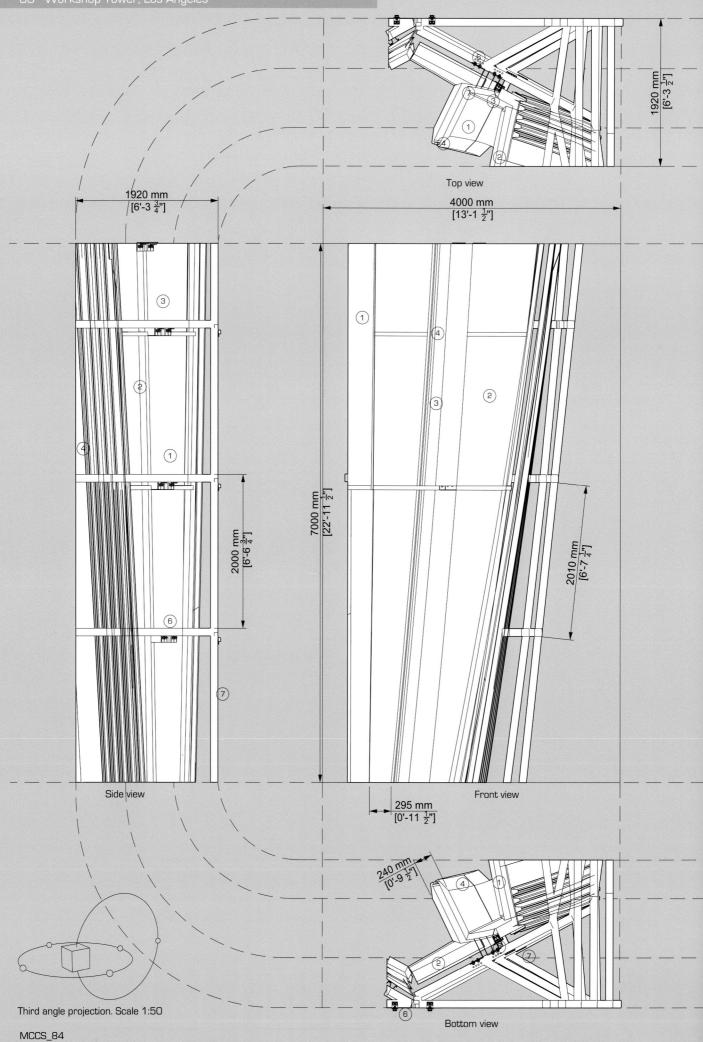

Top view

1920 mm
[6'-3 ¾"]

4000 mm
[13'-1 ½"]

1920 mm
[6'-3 ½"]

7000 mm
[22'-11 ½"]

2000 mm
[6'-6 ¾"]

2010 mm
[6'-7 ¼"]

Side view

Front view

295 mm
[0'-11 ½"]

240 mm
[0'-9 ½"]

Third angle projection. Scale 1:50

Bottom view

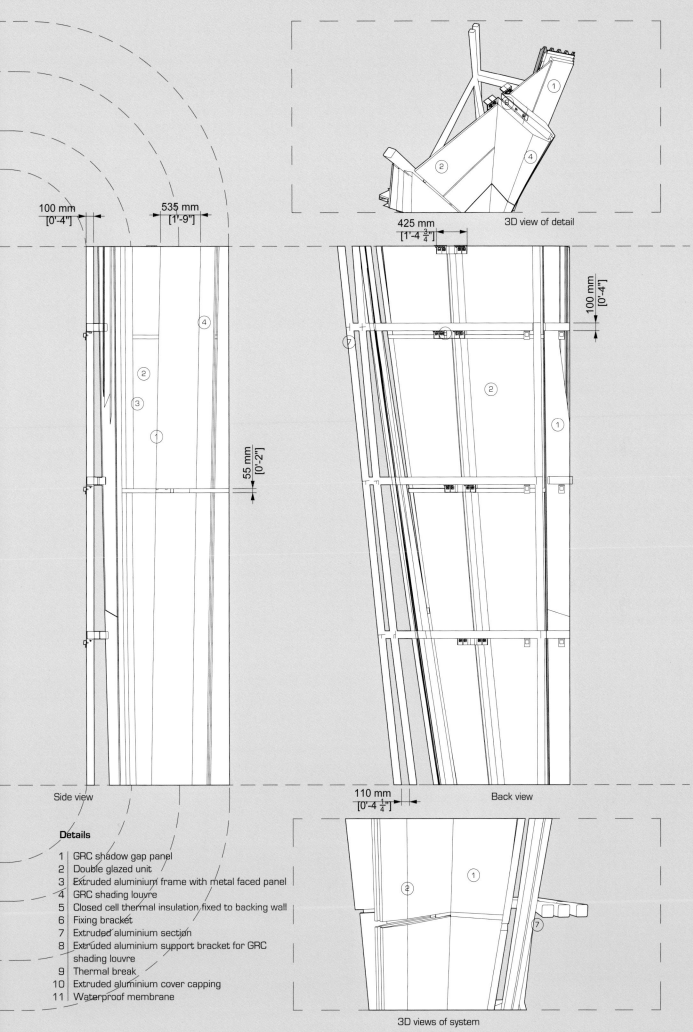

100 mm
[0'-4"]

535 mm
[1'-9"]

425 mm
[1'-4 3/4"]

100 mm
[0'-4"]

55 mm
[0'-2"]

3D view of detail

Side view

110 mm
[0'-4 1/4"]

Back view

Details

1 | GRC shadow gap panel
2 | Double glazed unit
3 | Extruded aluminium frame with metal faced panel
4 | GRC shading louvre
5 | Closed cell thermal insulation fixed to backing wall
6 | Fixing bracket
7 | Extruded aluminium section
8 | Extruded aluminium support bracket for GRC
   shading louvre
9 | Thermal break
10 | Extruded aluminium cover capping
11 | Waterproof membrane

3D views of system

MCCS_85

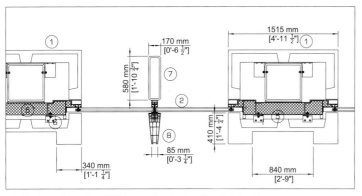

a | Horizontal section. GRC louvre fixed to inside of glazing frame

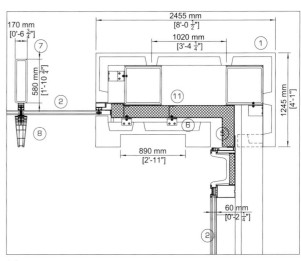

b | Horizontal section. External corner

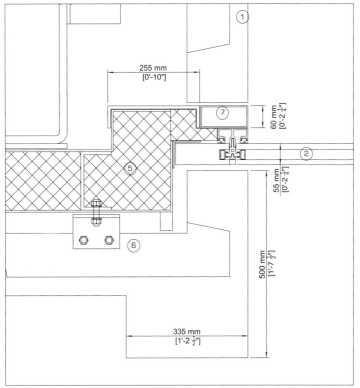

c | Horizontal section. Junction between double glazed unit and opaque panel

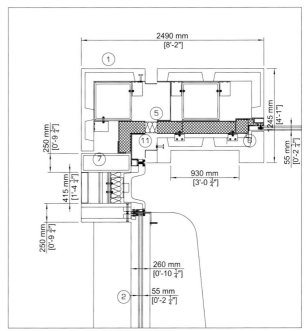

d | Horizontal section. External corner

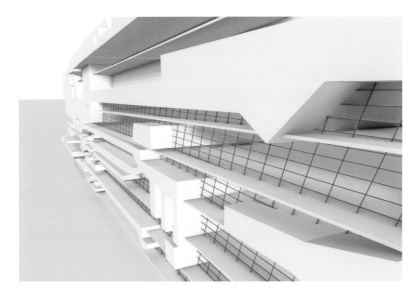

e | Exterior view

f | Typical bay. 3D view

1:50 scale

2'- 1"   4'- 2"   6'- 3"   8'- 4"

5"   10"   1'-3"   1'-8"

1:10 scale

500   1000   1500   2000   2500   mm   1:50 scale

100   200   300   400   500 mm   1:10 scale

Details

1 | GRC shadow gap panel
2 | Double glazed unit
3 | Extruded aluminium frame with metal faced panel
4 | GRC shading louvre
5 | Closed cell thermal insulation fixed to backing wall
6 | Fixing bracket
7 | Extruded aluminium section
8 | Extruded aluminium support bracket for GRC shading louvre
9 | Thermal break
10 | Extruded aluminium cover capping
11 | Waterproof membrane

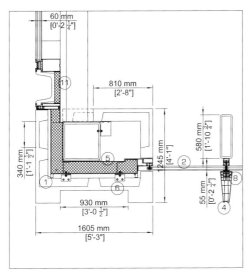

g | Horizontal section. External corner

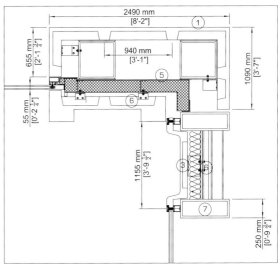

h | Horizontal section. External corner

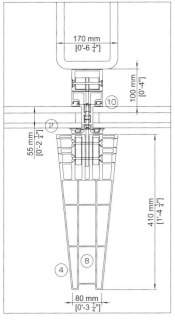

j | Horizontal section. GRC louvre fixed to inside of glazing frame

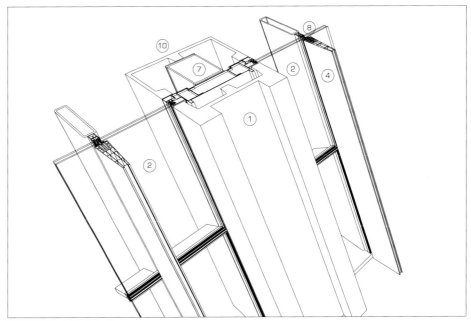

k | 3D view. External louvre

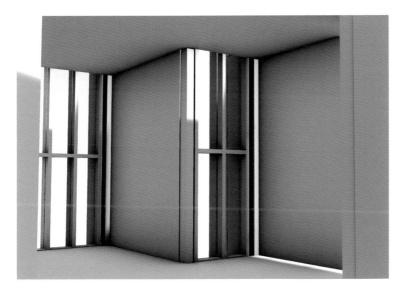

m | Interior view

n | Typical bay. 3D view

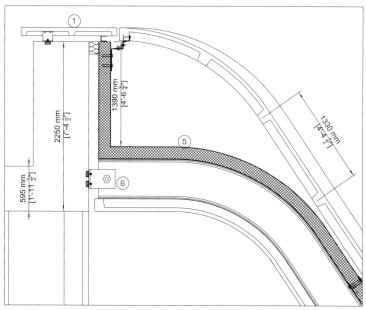

a | Vertical section. Curved external corner panel

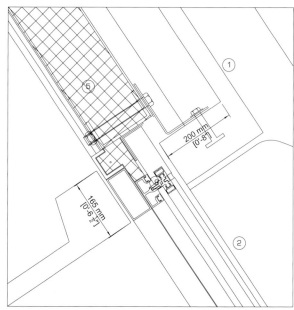

b | Vertical section. Connection of unitised panel and structure

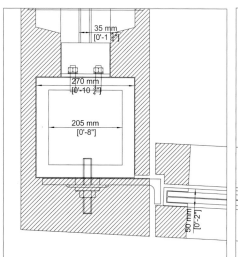

c | Horizontal section. Connection of unitised panel and structure

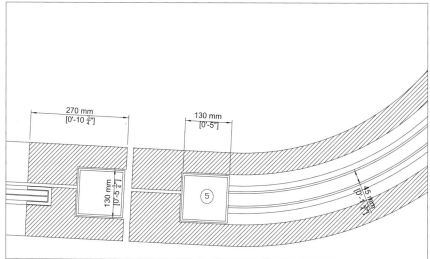

d | Horizontal section. Curved double glazed unit at corner

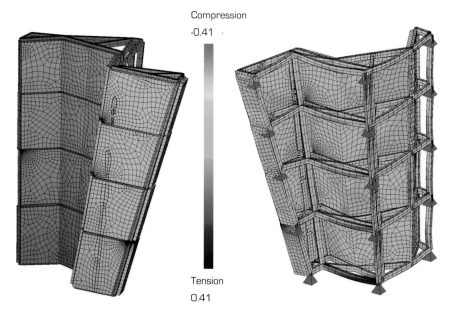

e | Finite element model of a typical bay

f | Utilization distribution within quadrilateral elements

Facade system	Opaque and glazing unitized panels
Facade zone	450mm
Primary structure type	Steel frame
Secondary structure type	RHS steel sections
Weight of secondary structure (kN/m²)	0.28
Facade bracket type	Serrated plates; welded and bolted
Number of components in fixing system	12
Weight of facade, including secondary structure (kN/m²)	1.14

1:50 scale

2'-1" 4'-2" 6'-3" 8'-4"

5" 10" 1'-3" 1'-8"

1:10 scale

500 1000 1500 2000 2500 mm

100 200 300 400 500 mm

1:50 scale

1:10 scale

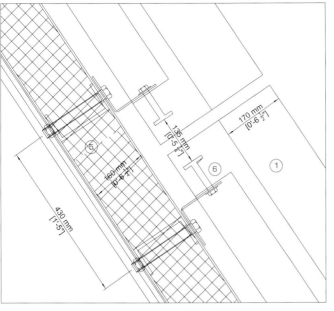

g | Vertical section. Connection of unitised panel and structure

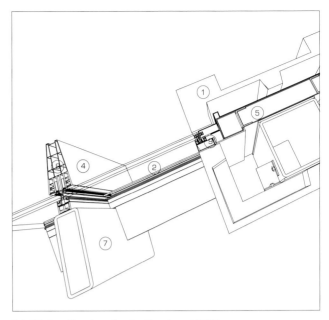

h | 3D view. Curtain wall unit with external GRC louvre

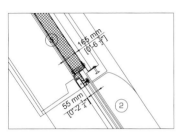

j | Vertical section. Junction between dou-
ble glazed unit and spandrel panel

k | Vertical section. Double glazed unit
connecting to thin frame

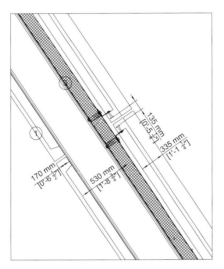

m | Vertical section. Panel to panel connection

Details

1 | GRC shadow gap panel
2 | Double glazed unit
3 | Extruded aluminium frame with metal faced panel
4 | GRC shading louvre
5 | Closed cell thermal insulation fixed to backing wall
6 | Fixing bracket
7 | Extruded aluminium section
8 | Extruded aluminium support bracket for GRC shading louvre
9 | Thermal break
10 | Extruded aluminium cover capping
11 | Waterproof membrane

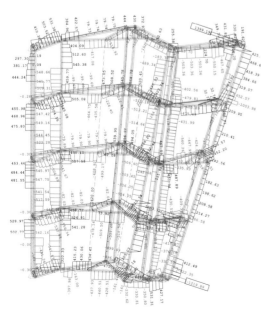

n | Axial force distribution in steel frame (kN)

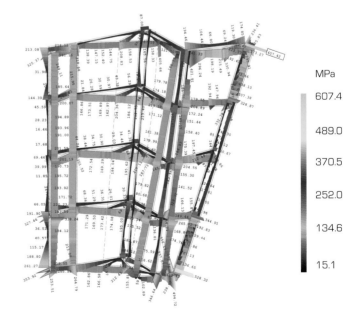

p | Von Mises stress distribution in steel frame (MPa)

MPa

607.4

489.0

370.5

252.0

134.6

15.1

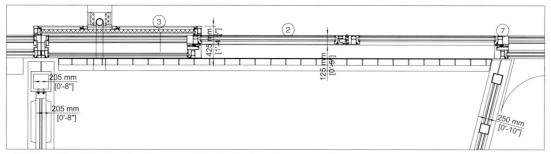

a | Horizontal section. Junction between double glazed unit and opaque panel

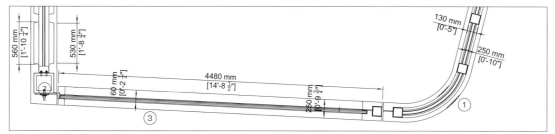

b | Horizontal section. Junction between double glazed unit and opaque panel at external corner

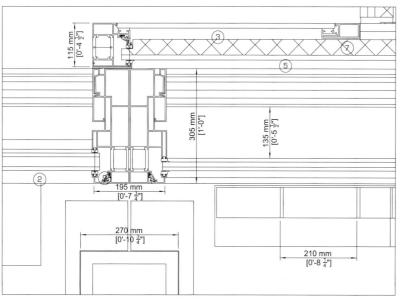

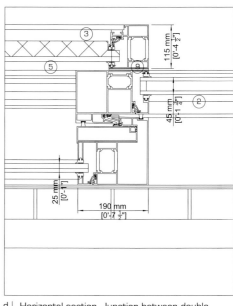

c | Horizontal section. Junction between double glazed unit and opaque panel

d | Horizontal section. Junction between double glazed unit and opaque panel

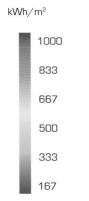

kWh/m²

Period	1 year
With shading	22.4 MWh
Without shading	28 MWh
Solar reduction	20%

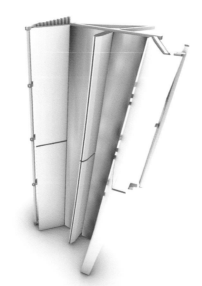

e | Annual cumulative solar radiation analysis on glazed facade with shading system

f | Annual cumulative solar radiation analysis on glazed facade without shading system

1:50 scale

1:10 scale

5"   10"   1'-3"   1'-8"

2'-1"   4'-2"   6'-3"   8'-4"

500   1000   1500   2000   2500 mm

100   200   300   400   500 mm

1:50 scale

1:10 scale

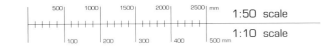

Details

1 | GRC shadow gap panel
2 | Double glazed unit
3 | Extruded aluminium frame with metal faced panel
4 | GRC shading louvre
5 | Closed cell thermal insulation fixed to backing wall
6 | Fixing bracket
7 | Extruded aluminium section
8 | Extruded aluminium support bracket for GRC shading louvre
9 | Thermal break
10 | Extruded aluminium cover capping
11 | Waterproof membrane

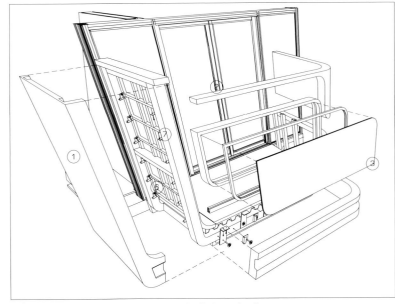

g | 3D view. Exploded components showing balcony detail

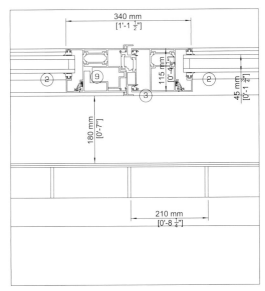

h | Horizontal section. Junction between fully interlocked double glazed units

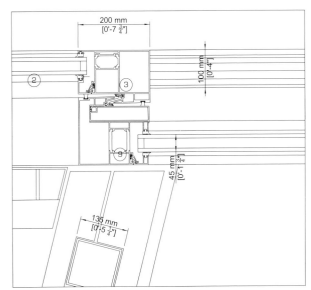

j | Horizontal section. Junction between double glazed units and inward opening window

EXT: 40°C

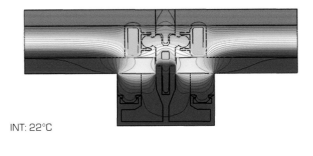

INT: 22°C

22   30   40 °C

k | Thermal performance analysis of a unitised curtain wall mullion
Isotherms showing temperature distribution across assembly

EXT: 0°C

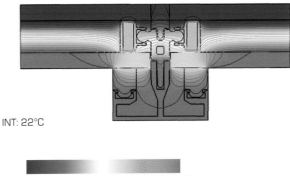

INT: 22°C

0   10   22 °C

m | Thermal performance analysis of a unitised curtain wall mullion
Isotherms showing temperature distribution across assembly

MCCS_91

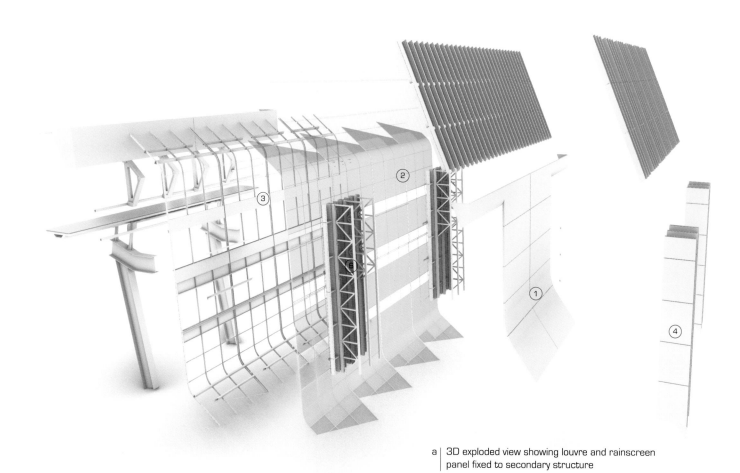

a | 3D exploded view showing louvre and rainscreen
panel fixed to secondary structure

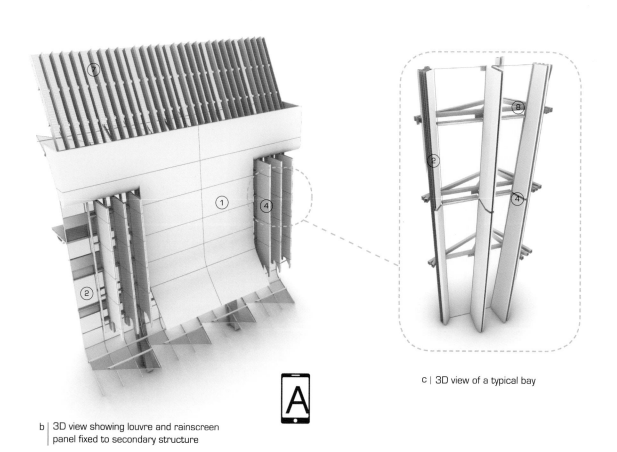

b | 3D view showing louvre and rainscreen
panel fixed to secondary structure

c | 3D view of a typical bay

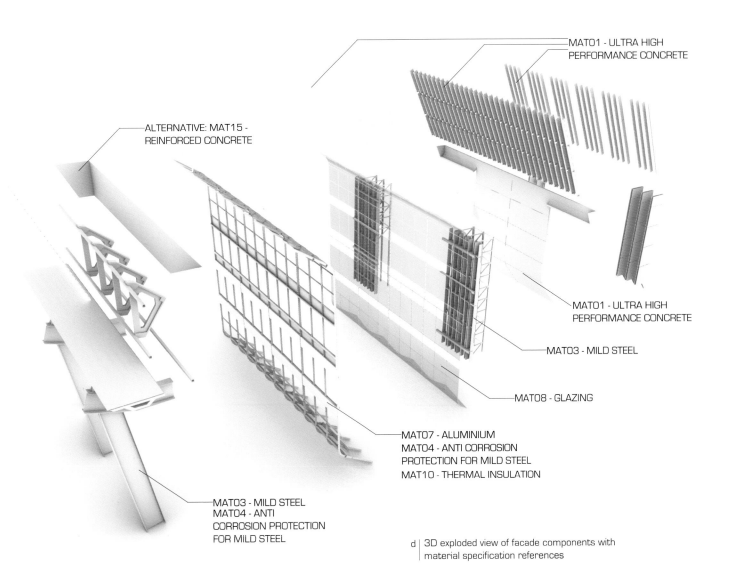

ALTERNATIVE: MAT15 - REINFORCED CONCRETE

MAT01 - ULTRA HIGH PERFORMANCE CONCRETE

MAT01 - ULTRA HIGH PERFORMANCE CONCRETE

MAT03 - MILD STEEL

MAT08 - GLAZING

MAT07 - ALUMINIUM
MAT04 - ANTI CORROSION PROTECTION FOR MILD STEEL
MAT10 - THERMAL INSULATION

MAT03 - MILD STEEL
MAT04 - ANTI CORROSION PROTECTION FOR MILD STEEL

d | 3D exploded view of facade components with material specification references

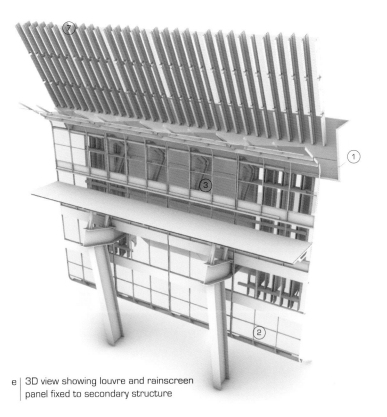

Details

1 | GRC shadow gap panel
2 | Double glazed unit
3 | Extruded aluminium frame with metal faced panel
4 | GRC shading louvre
5 | Closed cell thermal insulation fixed to backing wall
6 | Fixing bracket
7 | Extruded aluminium section
8 | Extruded aluminium support bracket for GRC shading louvre
9 | Thermal break
10 | Extruded aluminium cover capping
11 | Waterproof membrane

e | 3D view showing louvre and rainscreen panel fixed to secondary structure

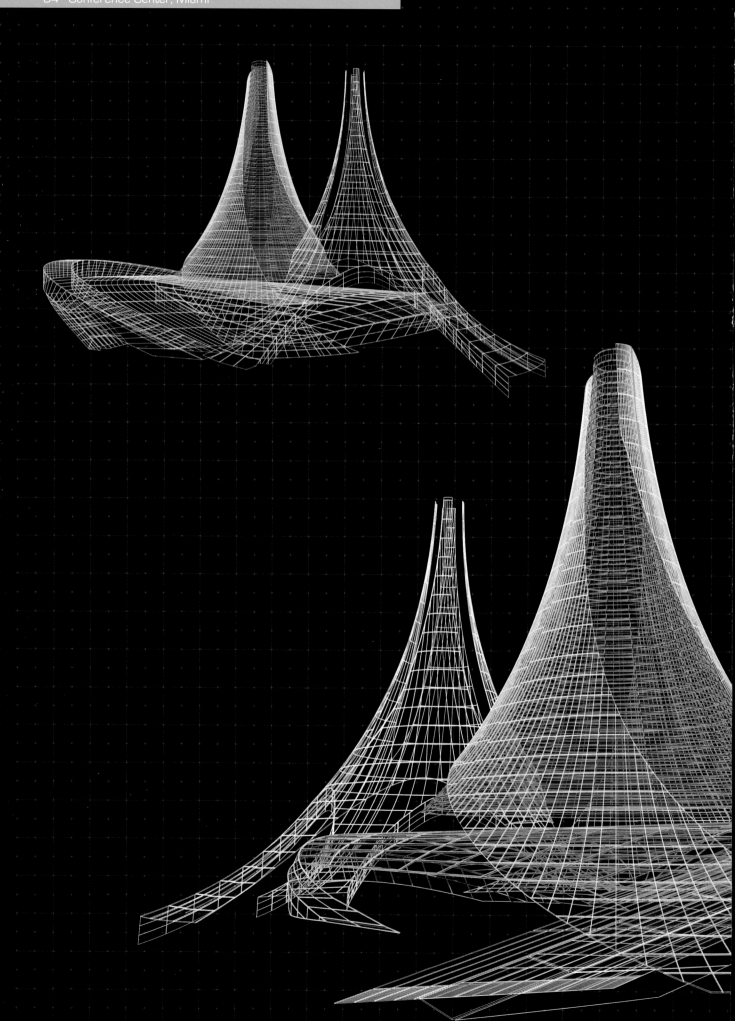

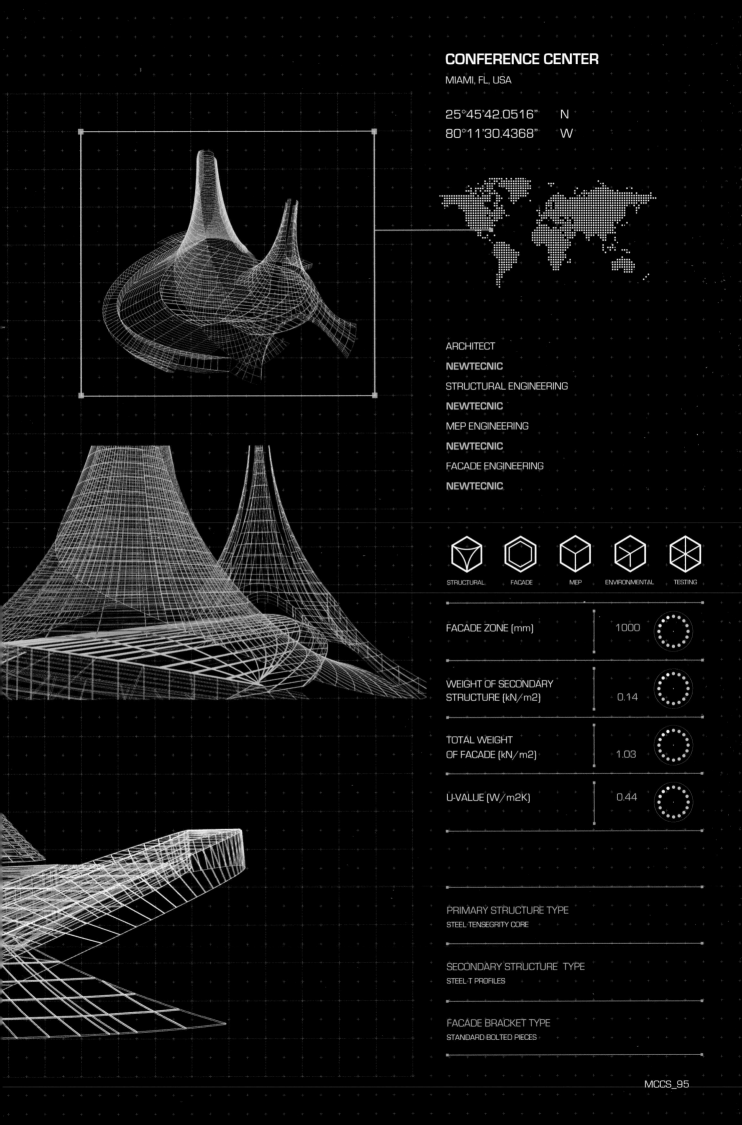

CONFERENCE CENTER

MIAMI, FL, USA

25°45'42.0516"   N
80°11'30.4368"   W

ARCHITECT
NEWTECNIC
STRUCTURAL ENGINEERING
NEWTECNIC
MEP ENGINEERING
NEWTECNIC
FACADE ENGINEERING
NEWTECNIC

STRUCTURAL   FACADE   MEP   ENVIRONMENTAL   TESTING

FACADE ZONE (mm)   1000

WEIGHT OF SECONDARY
STRUCTURE (kN/m2)   0.14

TOTAL WEIGHT
OF FACADE (kN/m2)   1.03

U-VALUE (W/m2K)   0.44

PRIMARY STRUCTURE TYPE
STEEL TENSEGRITY CORE

SECONDARY STRUCTURE TYPE
STEEL T PROFILES

FACADE BRACKET TYPE
STANDARD BOLTED PIECES

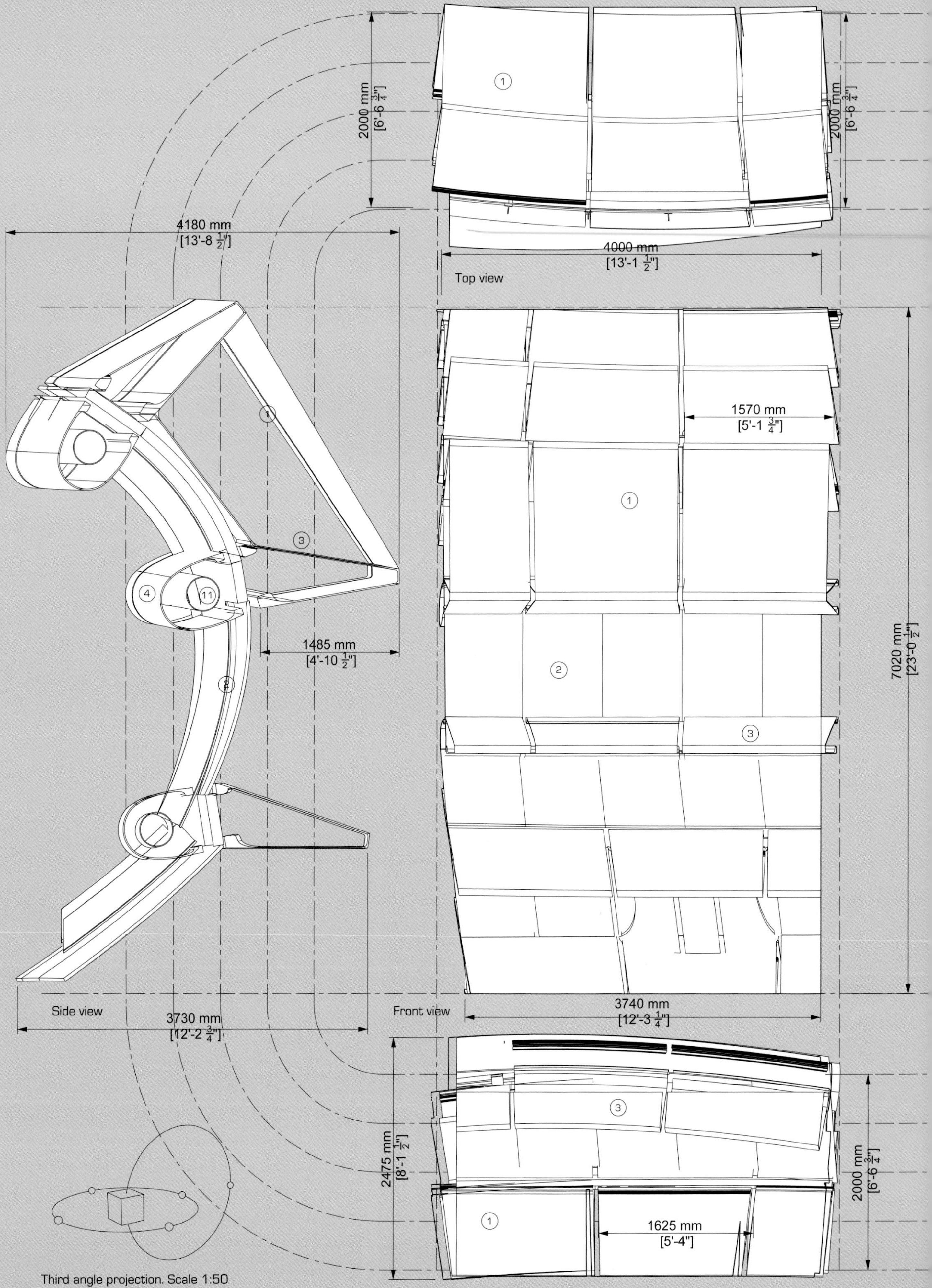

2000 mm
[6'-6 ¾"]

4180 mm
[13'-8 ½"]

2000 mm
[6'-6 ¾"]

①

4000 mm
[13'-1 ½"]

Top view

1570 mm
[5'-1 ¾"]

①

①

③

1485 mm
[4'-10 ½"]

④ ⑪

②

②

③

7020 mm
[23'-0 ½"]

Side view

3730 mm
[12'-2 ¾"]

Front view

3740 mm
[12'-3 ¼"]

③

2475 mm
[8'-1 ½"]

2000 mm
[6'-6 ¾"]

①

1625 mm
[5'-4"]

Third angle projection. Scale 1:50

Bottom view

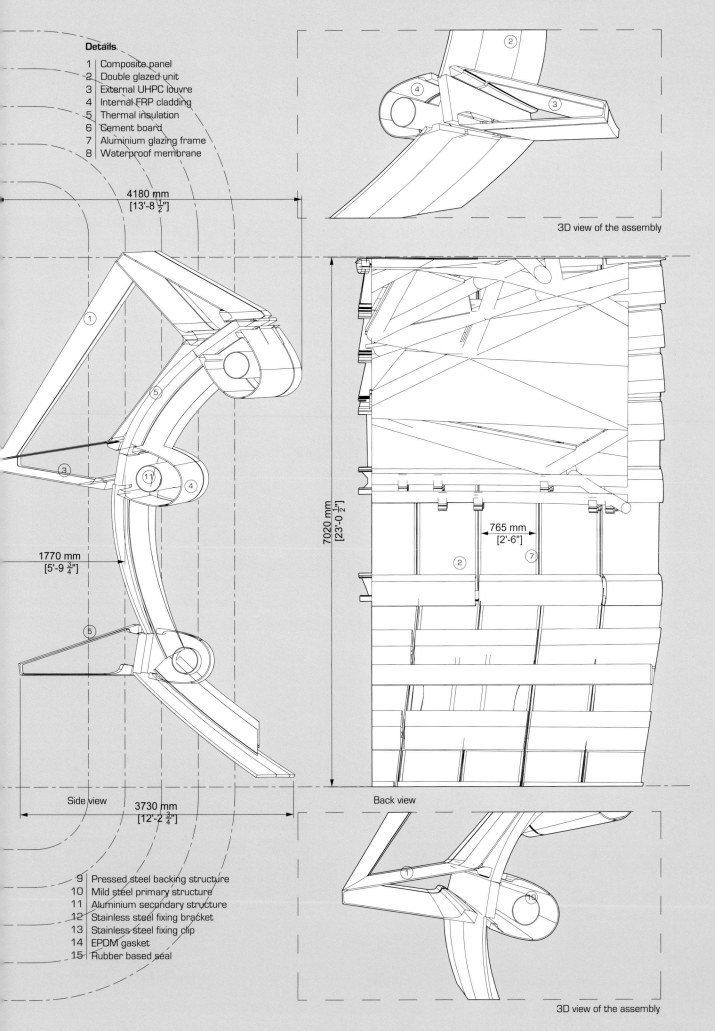

Details

1	Composite panel
2	Double glazed unit
3	External UHPC louvre
4	Internal FRP cladding
5	Thermal insulation
6	Cement board
7	Aluminium glazing frame
8	Waterproof membrane

9	Pressed steel backing structure
10	Mild steel primary structure
11	Aluminium secondary structure
12	Stainless steel fixing bracket
13	Stainless steel fixing clip
14	EPDM gasket
15	Rubber based seal

4180 mm
[13'-8 $\frac{1}{2}$"]

7020 mm
[23'-0 $\frac{1}{2}$"]

1770 mm
[5'-9 $\frac{3}{4}$"]

765 mm
[2'-6"]

3730 mm
[12'-2 $\frac{3}{4}$"]

3D view of the assembly

Side view

Back view

3D view of the assembly

MCCS_99

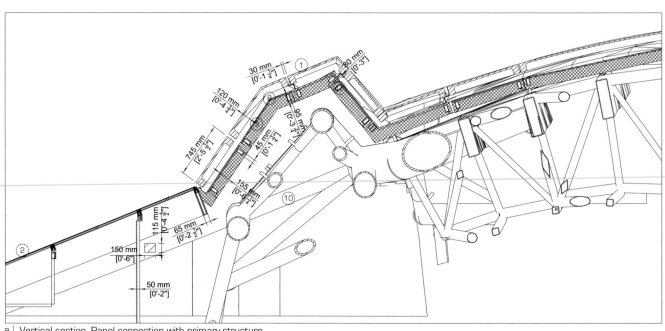

30 mm [0'-1 ¼"]
80 mm [0'-3"]
120 mm [0'-4 ¾"]
95 mm [0'-3 ¾"]
745 mm [2'-5 ½"]
45 mm [0'-1 ¾"]
155 mm [0'-6 ¼"]
115 mm [0'-4 ½"]
65 mm [0'-2 ½"]
150 mm [0'-6"]
50 mm [0'-2"]

a | Vertical section. Panel connection with primary structure

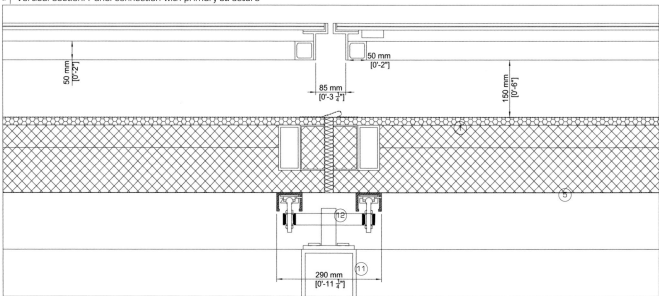

50 mm [0'-2"]
50 mm [0'-2"]
85 mm [0'-3 ¼"]
150 mm [0'-6"]
290 mm [0'-11 ¼"]

b | Horizontal section. Panel connection with primary structure

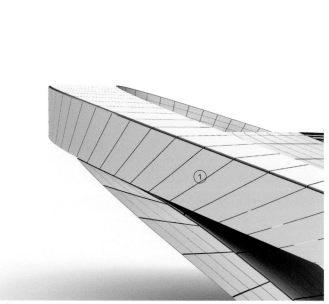

c | Exterior view

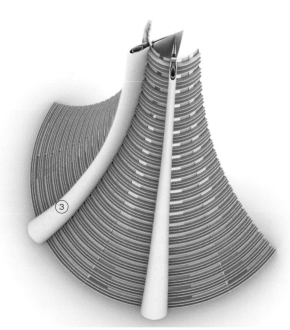

d | Typical Bay. 3D view

1:50 scale
1:10 scale

2'-1" 4'-2" 6'-3" 8'-4"
5" 10" 1'-3" 1'-8"

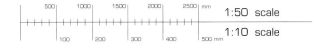

500 1000 1500 2000 2500 mm   1:50 scale
100 200 300 400 500 mm   1:10 scale

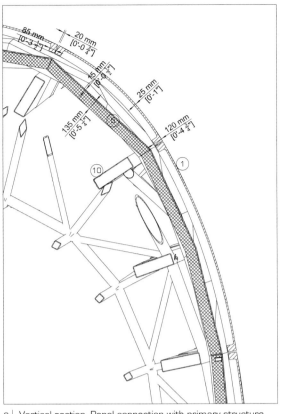

85 mm [0'-3¼"]
20 mm [0'-0¾"]
45 mm [0'-0?"]
25 mm [0'-1"]
135 mm [0'-5¼"]
120 mm [0'-4¾"]

10
1

e | Vertical section. Panel connection with primary structure

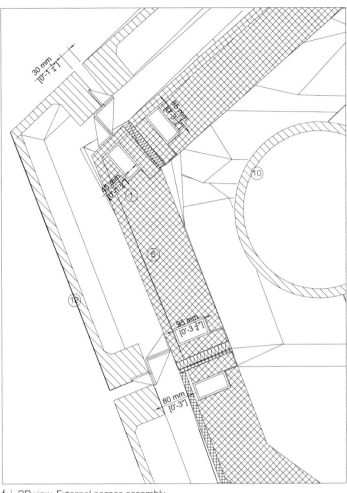

30 mm [0'-1¼"]
85 mm [0'-3?"]
45 mm [0'-1?"]
95 mm [0'-3¾"]
80 mm [0'-3"]

10
1
5
13

f | 3D view. External corner assembly

Details

1 | Composite panel
2 | Double glazed unit
3 | External UHPC louvre
4 | Internal FRP cladding
5 | Thermal insulation
6 | Cement board
7 | Aluminium glazing frame
8 | Waterproof membrane
9 | Pressed steel backing structure
10 | Mild steel primary structure
11 | Aluminium secondary structure
12 | Stainless steel fixing bracket
13 | Stainless steel fixing clip
14 | EPDM gasket
15 | Rubber based seal

3
4
11

g | Typical bay. 3D view

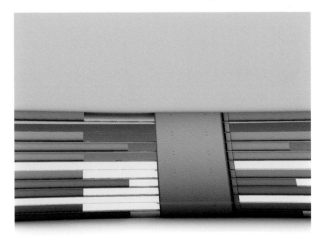

h | Interior view

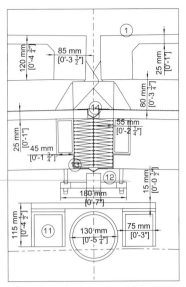

a | Horizontal section. Panel fixing system assembly

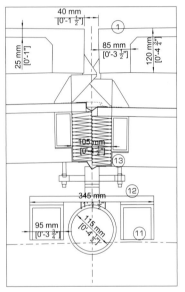

d | Horizontal section. Panel fixing system assembly

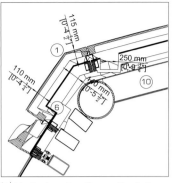

b | Vertical section. Connection between panel and secondary steel tube

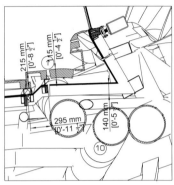

e | Vertical section. Connection between panel and secondary steel tube

Details

1 | Composite panel
2 | Double glazed unit
3 | External UHPC louvre
4 | Internal FRP cladding
5 | Thermal insulation
6 | Cement board
7 | Aluminium glazing frame
8 | Waterproof membrane

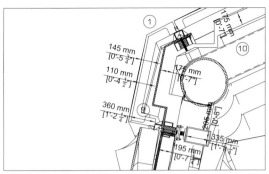

c | Vertical section. Connection between panel and secondary steel tube

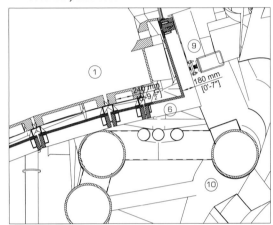

f | Vertical section. Connection between panel and secondary steel tube

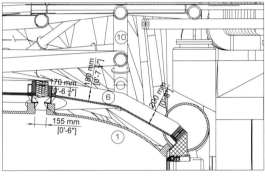

g | Vertical section. Connection between panel and secondary steel tube

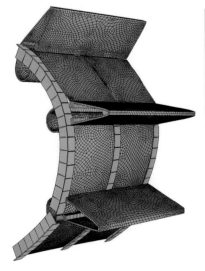

h | Finite element model of a typical bay

Facade system	Unitized glazing with FRP cladding
Facade zone	1000mm
Primary structure type	Steel tensegrity core
Secondary structure type	Steel T profiles
Weight of secondary structure (kN/m²)	0.14
Facade bracket type	Standard bolted pieces
Number of components in fixing system	9
Weight of facade, including secondary structure (kN/m²)	1.03

j | Axial force distribution in steel frame [kN]

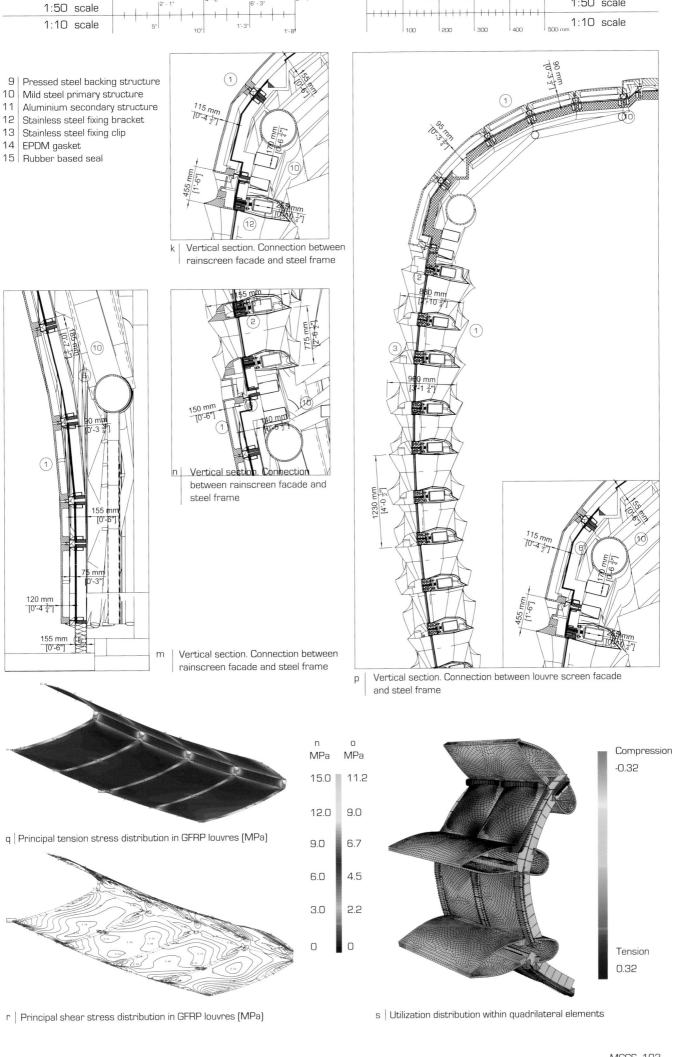

1:50 scale

1:10 scale

2'-1"   4'-2"   6'-3"   8'-4"

5"   10"   1'-3"   1'-8"

500 1000 1500 2000 2500 mm   1:50 scale

100 200 300 400 500 mm   1:10 scale

9 | Pressed steel backing structure
10 | Mild steel primary structure
11 | Aluminium secondary structure
12 | Stainless steel fixing bracket
13 | Stainless steel fixing clip
14 | EPDM gasket
15 | Rubber based seal

k | Vertical section. Connection between rainscreen facade and steel frame

n | Vertical section. Connection between rainscreen facade and steel frame

m | Vertical section. Connection between rainscreen facade and steel frame

p | Vertical section. Connection between louvre screen facade and steel frame

q | Principal tension stress distribution in GFRP louvres (MPa)

r | Principal shear stress distribution in GFRP louvres (MPa)

s | Utilization distribution within quadrilateral elements

n   o
MPa   MPa

15.0   11.2

12.0   9.0

9.0   6.7

6.0   4.5

3.0   2.2

0   0

Compression
-0.32

Tension
0.32

MCCS_103

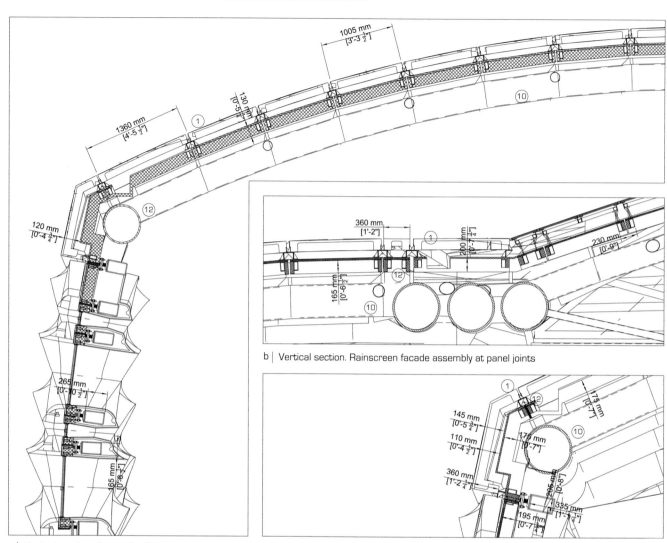

a | Vertical section. Connection between louvre screen
facade and steel frame

b | Vertical section. Rainscreen facade assembly at panel joints

c | Vertical section. Rainscreen facade assembly at external corner

d | Annual cumulative solar radiation analysis
on glazed facade with shading system

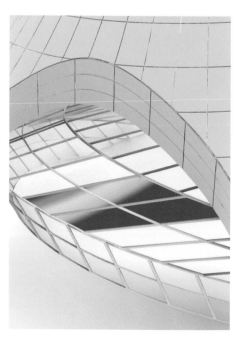

e | Annual cumulative solar radiation analysis
on glazed facade without shading system

kWh/m²

| 900 |
| 750 |
| 600 |
| 450 |
| 300 |
| 150 |

Period	1 year
With shading	15.3 MWh
Without shading	25.2 MWh
Solar reduction	39%

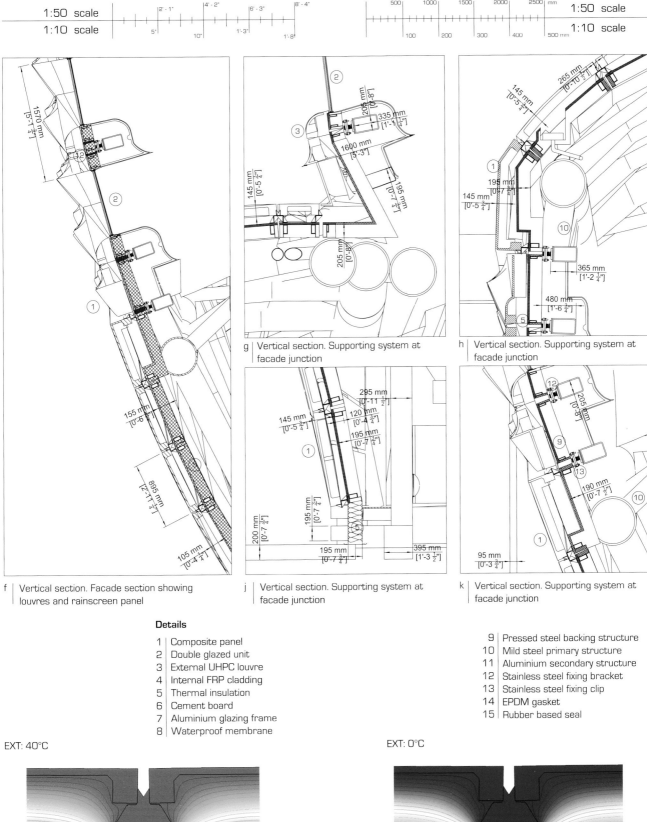

1:50 scale
1:10 scale

2'-1" 4'-2" 6'-3" 8'-4"
5" 10" 1'-3" 1'-8"

500 1000 1500 2000 2500 mm
100 200 300 400 500 mm

1:50 scale
1:10 scale

1570 mm [5'-1 ¾"]

155 mm [0'-6"]

895 mm [2'-11 ¼"]

105 mm [0'-4 ¼"]

f | Vertical section. Facade section showing louvres and rainscreen panel

335 mm [1'-1 ¼"]
205 mm [0'-8"]
1600 mm [5'-3"]
145 mm [0'-5 ¼"]
195 mm [0'-7 ¾"]
205 mm [0'-8"]

g | Vertical section. Supporting system at facade junction

295 mm [0'-11 ½"]
120 mm [0'-4 ¾"]
145 mm [0'-5 ¾"]
195 mm [0'-7 ¾"]
195 mm [0'-7 ¾"]
200 mm [0'-7 ¾"]
195 mm [0'-7 ¾"]
395 mm [1'-3 ½"]

j | Vertical section. Supporting system at facade junction

265 mm [0'-10 ½"]
145 mm [0'-5 ¾"]
195 mm [0'-7 ¾"]
145 mm [0'-5 ¾"]
365 mm [1'-2 ¼"]
480 mm [1'-6 ¾"]

h | Vertical section. Supporting system at facade junction

205 mm [0'-8"]
190 mm [0'-7 ½"]
95 mm [0'-3 ¾"]

k | Vertical section. Supporting system at facade junction

Details

1	Composite panel
2	Double glazed unit
3	External UHPC louvre
4	Internal FRP cladding
5	Thermal insulation
6	Cement board
7	Aluminium glazing frame
8	Waterproof membrane

9	Pressed steel backing structure
10	Mild steel primary structure
11	Aluminium secondary structure
12	Stainless steel fixing bracket
13	Stainless steel fixing clip
14	EPDM gasket
15	Rubber based seal

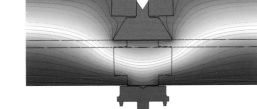

EXT: 40°C
INT: 22°C

22   30   40 °C

m | Thermal performance analysis of panels supported by secondary steel Isotherms showing temperature distribution across assembly

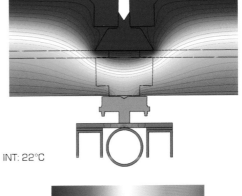

EXT: 0°C
INT: 22°C

0   11   22 °C

n | Thermal performance analysis of panels supported by secondary steel Isotherms showing temperature distribution across assembly

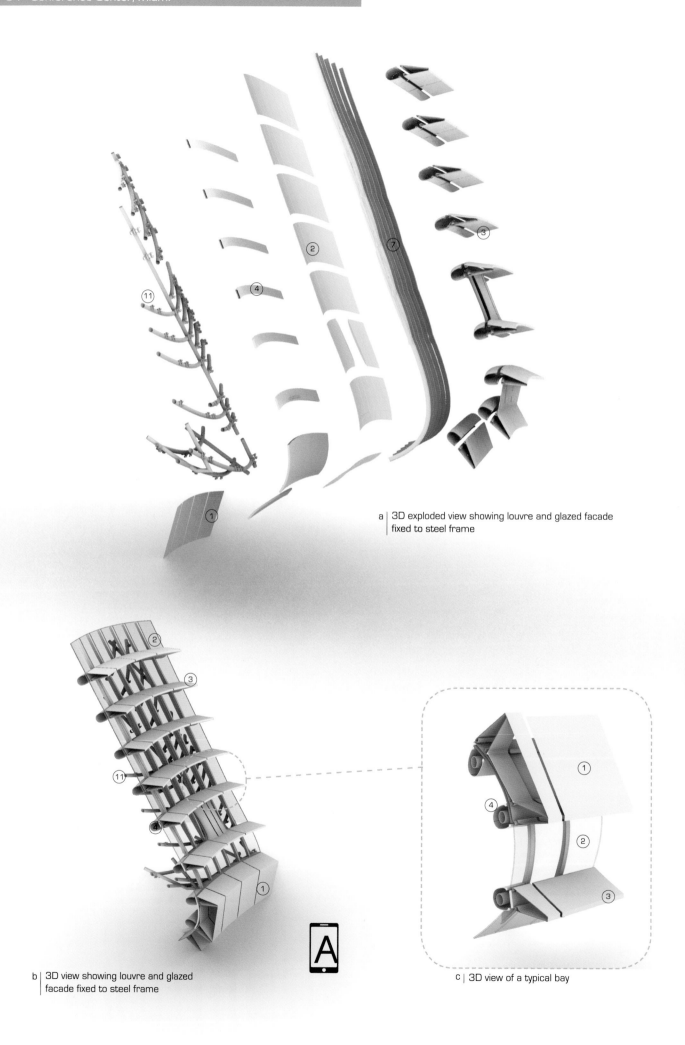

a | 3D exploded view showing louvre and glazed facade
fixed to steel frame

b | 3D view showing louvre and glazed
facade fixed to steel frame

c | 3D view of a typical bay

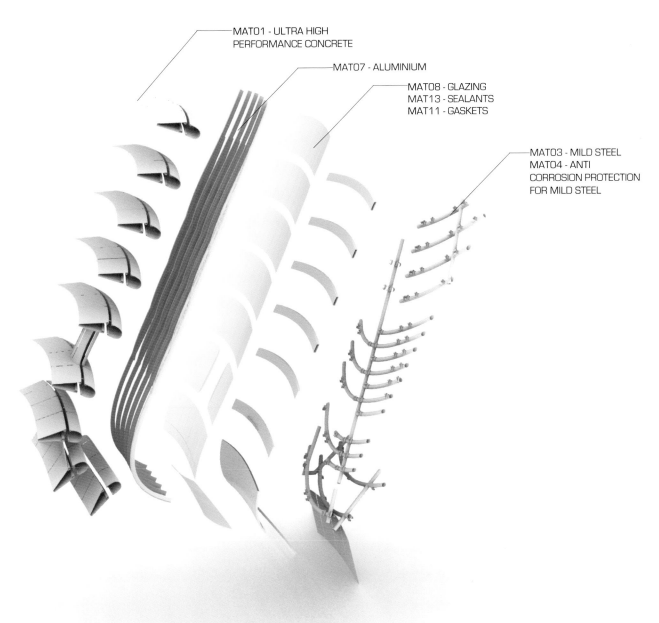

MAT01 - ULTRA HIGH
PERFORMANCE CONCRETE

MAT07 - ALUMINIUM

MAT08 - GLAZING
MAT13 - SEALANTS
MAT11 - GASKETS

MAT03 - MILD STEEL
MAT04 - ANTI
CORROSION PROTECTION
FOR MILD STEEL

d | 3D exploded view of facade components with material
specification references

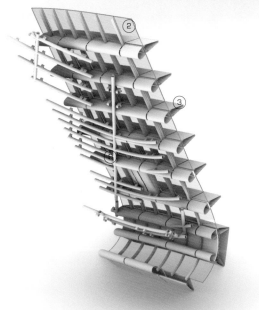

Details

1 | Composite panel
2 | Double glazed unit
3 | External UHPC louvre
4 | Internal FRP cladding
5 | Thermal insulation
6 | Cement board
7 | Aluminium glazing frame
8 | Waterproof membrane
9 | Pressed steel backing structure
10 | Mild steel primary structure
11 | Aluminium secondary structure
12 | Stainless steel fixing bracket
13 | Stainless steel fixing clip
14 | EPDM gasket
15 | Rubber based seal

e | 3D view showing louvre and glazed
facade fixed to steel frame

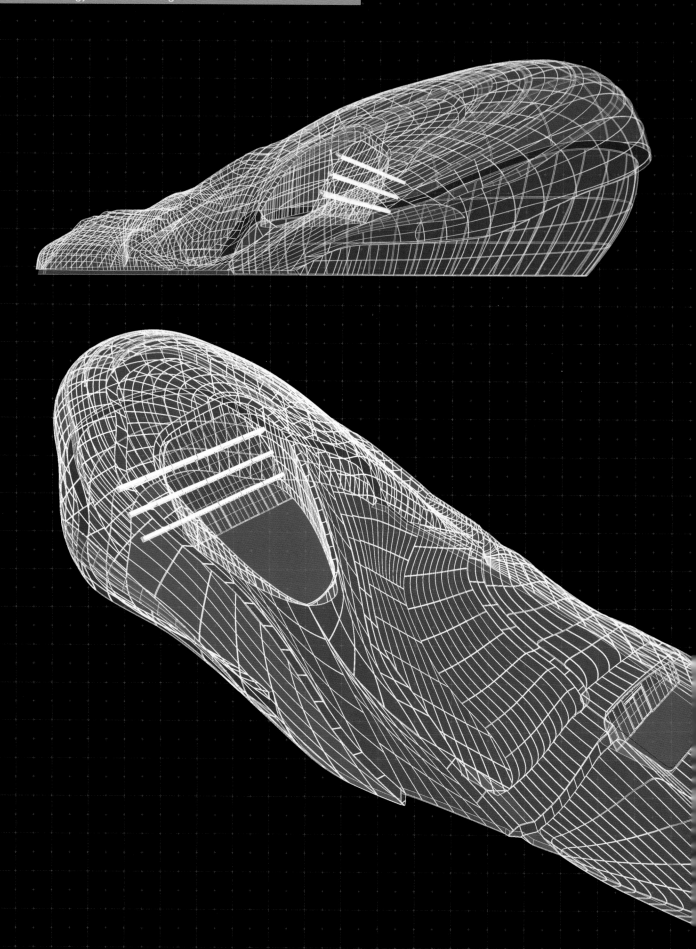

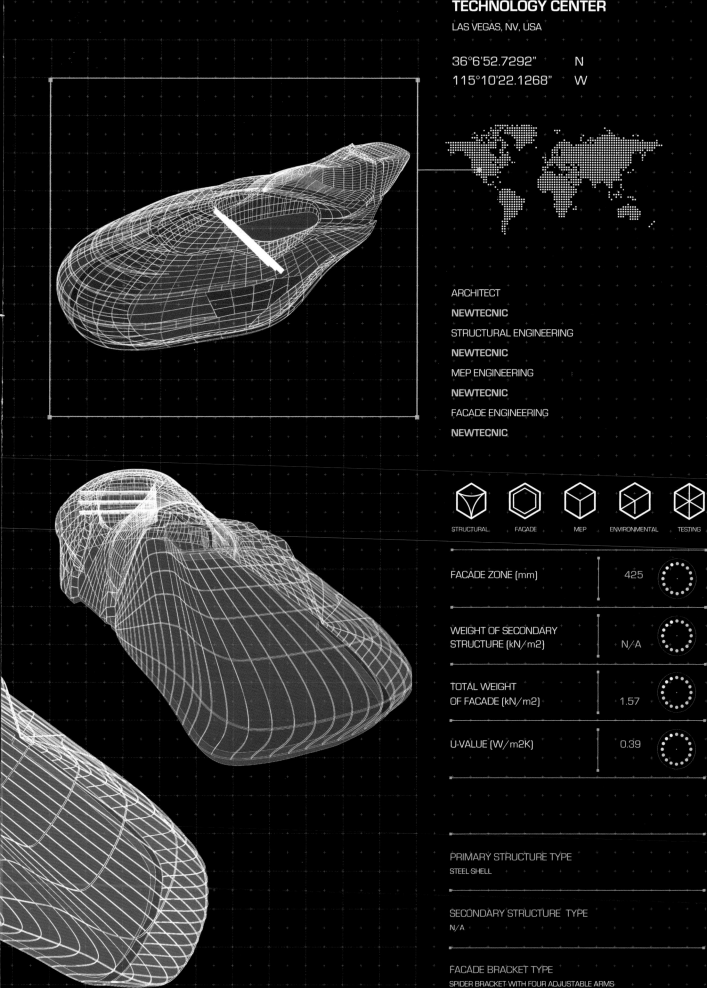

TECHNOLOGY CENTER

LAS VEGAS, NV, USA

36°6'52.7292"   N
115°10'22.1268"   W

ARCHITECT
NEWTECNIC
STRUCTURAL ENGINEERING
NEWTECNIC
MEP ENGINEERING
NEWTECNIC
FACADE ENGINEERING
NEWTECNIC

STRUCTURAL   FACADE   MEP   ENVIRONMENTAL   TESTING

FACADE ZONE (mm)	425	
WEIGHT OF SECONDARY STRUCTURE (kN/m2)	N/A	
TOTAL WEIGHT OF FACADE (kN/m2)	1.57	
U-VALUE (W/m2K)	0.39	

PRIMARY STRUCTURE TYPE
STEEL SHELL

SECONDARY STRUCTURE TYPE
N/A

FACADE BRACKET TYPE
SPIDER BRACKET WITH FOUR ADJUSTABLE ARMS

MCCS_111

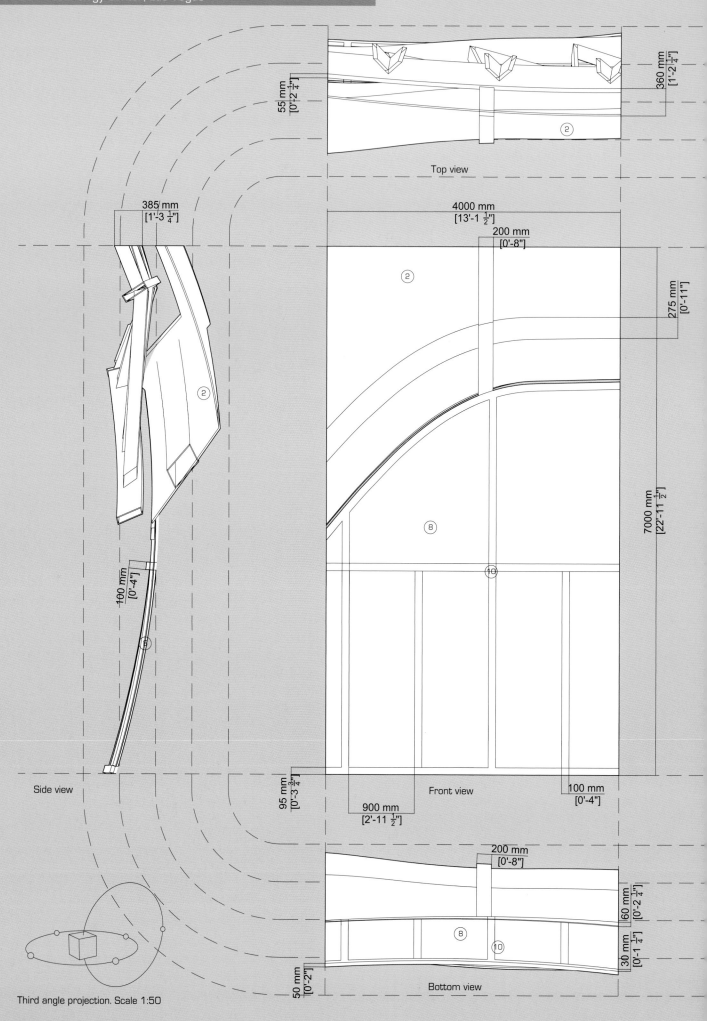

Top view

385 mm
[1'-3 ¼"]

4000 mm
[13'-1 ½"]

200 mm
[0'-8"]

55 mm
[0'-2 ¼"]

360 mm
[1'-2 ¼"]

275 mm
[0'-11"]

7000 mm
[22'-11 ½"]

100 mm
[0'-4"]

95 mm
[0'-3 ¾"]

900 mm
[2'-11 ½"]

100 mm
[0'-4"]

Side view

Front view

200 mm
[0'-8"]

60 mm
[0'-2 ¼"]

30 mm
[0'-1 ¼"]

50 mm
[0'-2"]

Bottom view

Third angle projection. Scale 1:50

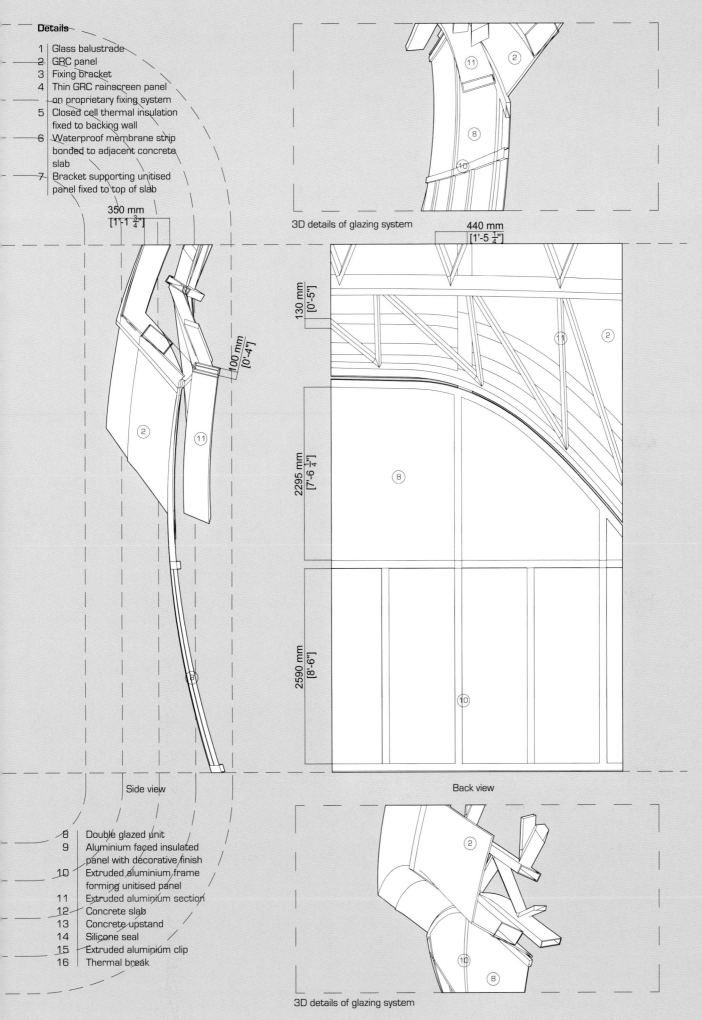

Details

1	Glass balustrade
2	GRC panel
3	Fixing bracket
4	Thin GRC rainscreen panel on proprietary fixing system
5	Closed cell thermal insulation fixed to backing wall
6	Waterproof membrane strip bonded to adjacent concrete slab
7	Bracket supporting unitised panel fixed to top of slab

350 mm
[1'-1 $\frac{3}{4}$"]

100 mm
[0'-4"]

Side view

8	Double glazed unit
9	Aluminium faced insulated panel with decorative finish
10	Extruded aluminium frame forming unitised panel
11	Extruded aluminium section
12	Concrete slab
13	Concrete upstand
14	Silicone seal
15	Extruded aluminium clip
16	Thermal break

3D details of glazing system

440 mm
[1'-5 $\frac{1}{4}$"]

130 mm
[0'-5"]

2295 mm
[7'-6 $\frac{1}{4}$"]

2590 mm
[8'-6"]

Back view

3D details of glazing system

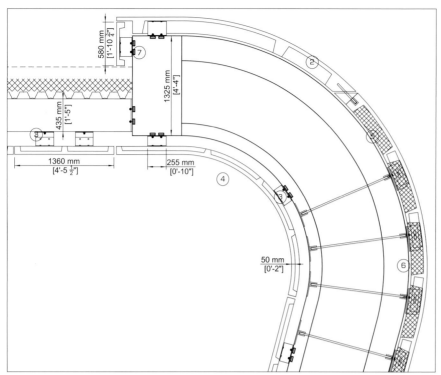

a | Horizontal section. Rainscreen cladding at external corner

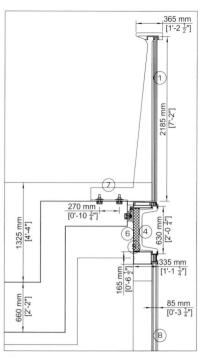

b | Vertical section. Glass balustrade

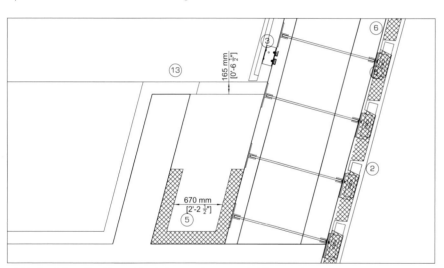

c | Horizontal section. Connection between rainscreen cladding to primary structure

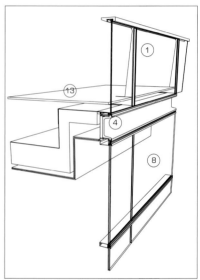

d | 3D view. Glass balustrade

e | Exterior view

f | Interior view

1:50 scale

2'-1" 4'-2" 6'-3" 8'-4"

500 1000 1500 2000 2500 | mm

1:50 scale

1:10 scale

5" 10" 1'-3" 1'-8"

100 200 300 400 500 mm

1:10 scale

Details

1 | Glass balustrade
2 | GRC panel
3 | Fixing bracket
4 | Thin GRC rainscreen panel on proprietary fixing system
5 | Closed cell thermal insulation fixed to backing wall
6 | Waterproof membrane strip bonded to adjacent concrete slab
7 | Bracket supporting unitised panel fixed to top of slab
8 | Double glazed unit
9 | Aluminium faced insulated panel with decorative finish
10 | Extruded aluminium frame forming unitised panel
11 | Extruded aluminium section
12 | Concrete slab
13 | Concrete upstand
14 | Silicone seal
15 | Extruded aluminium clip
16 | Thermal break

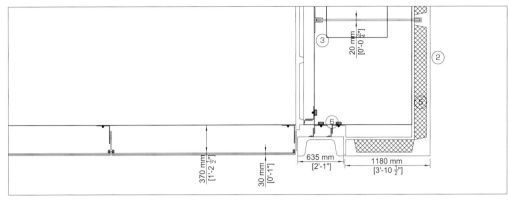

g | Horizontal section. External corner showing insulated panels and unitised double glazed panels

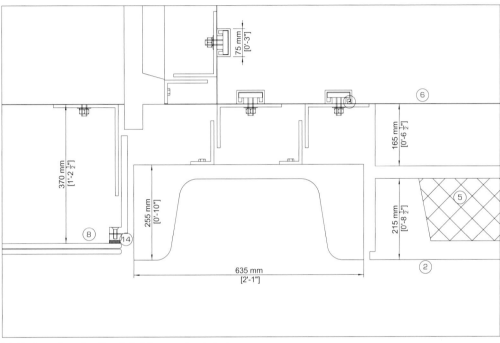

h | Horizontal section. Small cladding panel and shadow gap

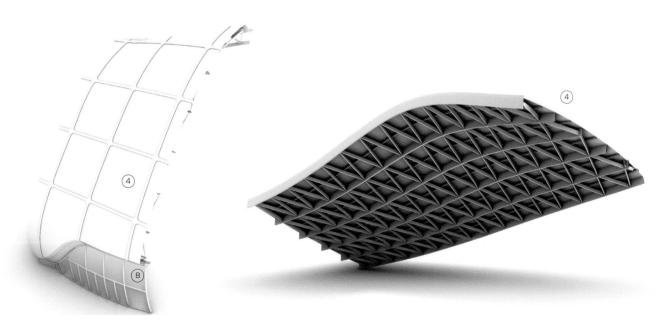

j | Typical bay. 3D view

k | Typical bay. 3D view

MCCS_115

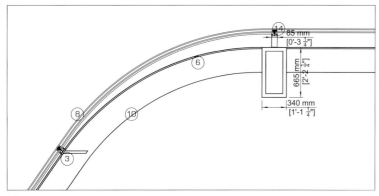

a | Vertical section. Unitised double glazed panels at external corner

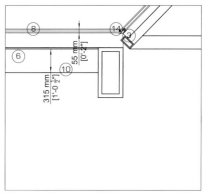

b | Vertical section. Connection of unitised double glazed panels to structure

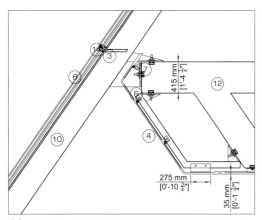

c | Vertical section. Inclined unitised double glazed unit

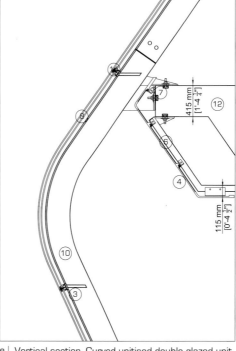

d | Vertical section. Inclined unitised double glazed unit

e | Vertical section. Curved unitised double glazed unit

Details

1 | Glass balustrade
2 | GRC panel
3 | Fixing bracket
4 | Thin GRC rainscreen panel on proprietary fixing system
5 | Closed cell thermal insulation fixed to backing wall
6 | Waterproof membrane strip bonded to adjacent concrete slab
7 | Bracket supporting unitised panel fixed to top of slab
8 | Double glazed unit
9 | Aluminium faced insulated panel with decorative finish
10 | Extruded aluminium frame forming unitised panel
11 | Extruded aluminium section
12 | Concrete slab
13 | Concrete upstand
14 | Silicone seal
15 | Extruded aluminium clip
16 | Thermal break

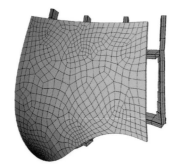

f | Finite element model of a typical bay

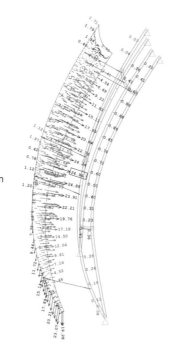

g | Utilization distribution within quadrilateral elements

Compression
-0.68

Tension
0.68

h | Nodal displacements distribution in GRC panels (mm)

Facade system	Monolithic open-joined GRC rain-screen
Facade zone	425mm
Primary structure type	Steel shell
Secondary structure type	-
Weight of secondary structure (kN/m²)	-
Facade bracket type	Spider bracket with four adjusta-ble arms
Number of compo-nents in fixing system	8
Weight of facade, including secondary structure (kN/m²)	1.57

1:50 scale
1:10 scale

2'-1" 4'-2" 6'-3" 8'-4"
5" 10" 1'-3" 1'-8"

500 1000 1500 2000 2500 mm
100 200 300 400 500 mm

1:50 scale
1:10 scale

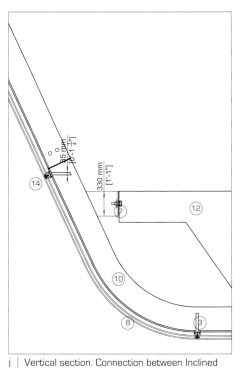

j | Vertical section. Connection between Inclined unitised double glazed panels to slab

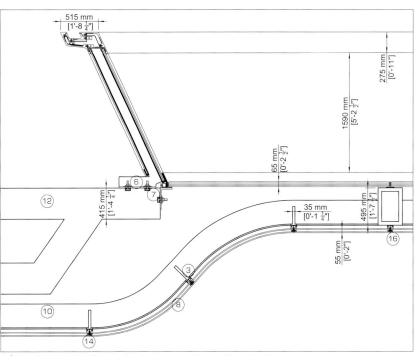

k | Vertical section. Connection between Inclined unitised double glazed panels to slab

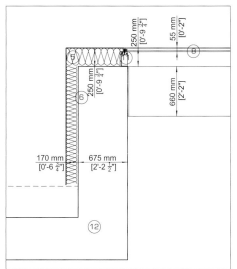

m | Horizontal section. Unitised double glazed unit assembly at parapet level with insulated cladding

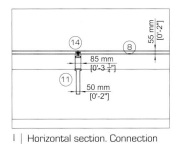

l | Horizontal section. Connection between unitised double glazed unit

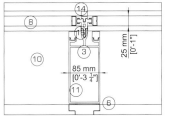

n | Horizontal section. Connection between unitised double glazed unit

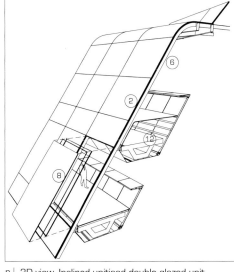

p | 3D view. Inclined unitised double glazed unit

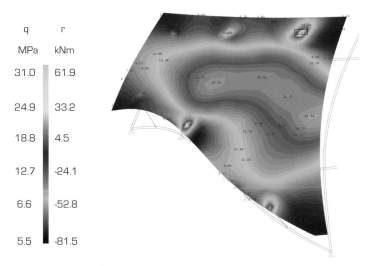

q	r
MPa	kNm
31.0	61.9
24.9	33.2
18.8	4.5
12.7	-24.1
6.6	-52.8
5.5	-81.5

q | Principal tension stress distribution in GRC panels (MPa)

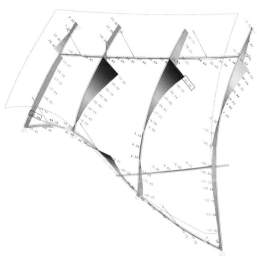

r | Bending moment distribution in steel frame (kNm)

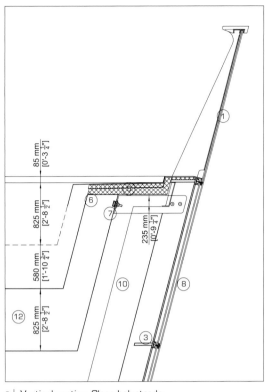

a | Vertical section. Glass balustrade

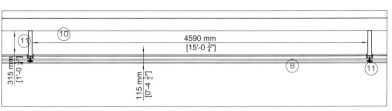

b | Horizontal section. Double glazed unit

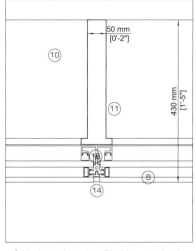

c | Horizontal section. Double glazed unit

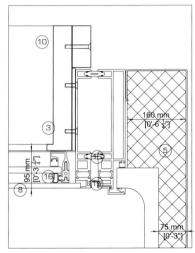

d | Horizontal section. Double glazed unit

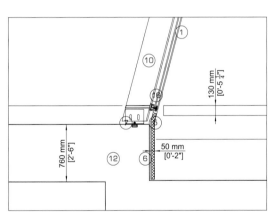

e | Vertical section. Bottom detail of double glazed unit

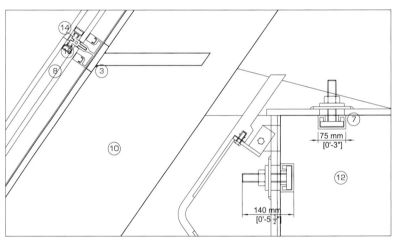

f | Vertical section. Connection of unitised double glazed unit to slab edge

kWh/m²

1300

1083

867

650

433

217

Period	With shading	Without shading	Solar reduction
1 year	25.2 MWh	36.4 MWh	31%

g | Annual cumulative solar radiation analysis on glazed facade with shading system

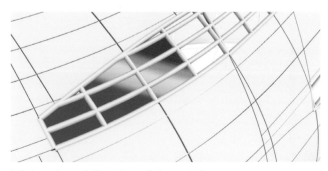

h | Annual cumulative solar radiation analysis on glazed facade without shading system

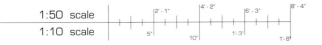

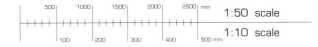

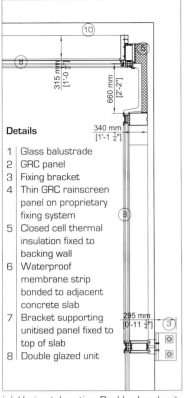

Details

1 Glass balustrade
2 GRC panel
3 Fixing bracket
4 Thin GRC rainscreen panel on proprietary fixing system
5 Closed cell thermal insulation fixed to backing wall
6 Waterproof membrane strip bonded to adjacent concrete slab
7 Bracket supporting unitised panel fixed to top of slab
8 Double glazed unit

j | Horizontal section. Double glazed unit

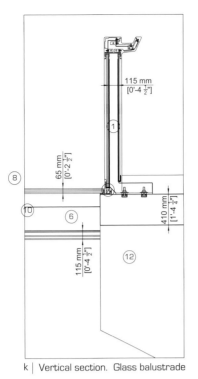

k | Vertical section. Glass balustrade

m | Vertical section. Junction of double glazed unit to slab edge

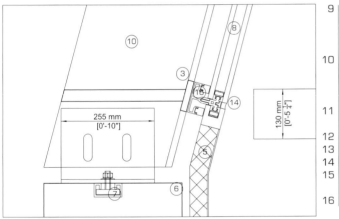

n | Vertical section. Double glazed unit

9 Aluminium faced insulated panel with decorative finish
10 Extruded aluminium frame forming unitised panel
11 Extruded aluminium section
12 Concrete slab
13 Concrete upstand
14 Silicone seal
15 Extruded aluminium clip
16 Thermal break

p | 3D view. Parapet level

EXT: 40°C

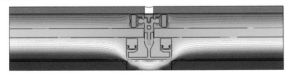

INT: 22°C

22   30   40 °C

EXT: 0°C

INT: 22°C

0   10   22 °C

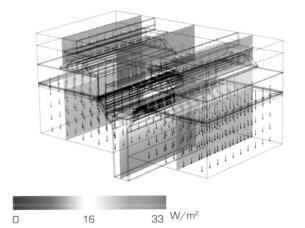

0   16   33 W/m²

q | Left: Thermal performance analysis of a unitised curtain wall mullion
Isotherms showing temperature distribution across assembly

r | Top: Thermal performance analysis of a bracket connection
Total energy flux across assembly varies at different build-ups

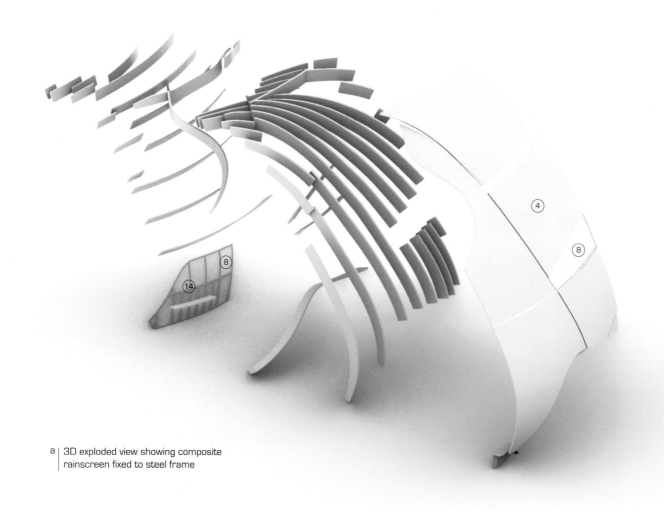

a | 3D exploded view showing composite
rainscreen fixed to steel frame

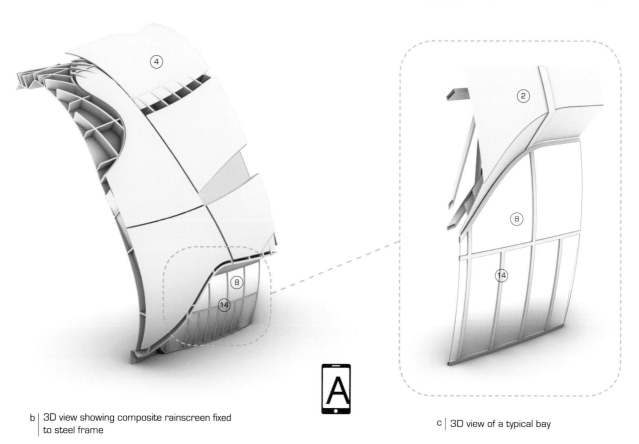

b | 3D view showing composite rainscreen fixed
to steel frame

c | 3D view of a typical bay

MAT03 - MILD STEEL
MAT04 - ANTI CORROSION
PROTECTION FOR MILD STEEL

MAT01 - ULTRA HIGH
PERFORMANCE CONCRETE

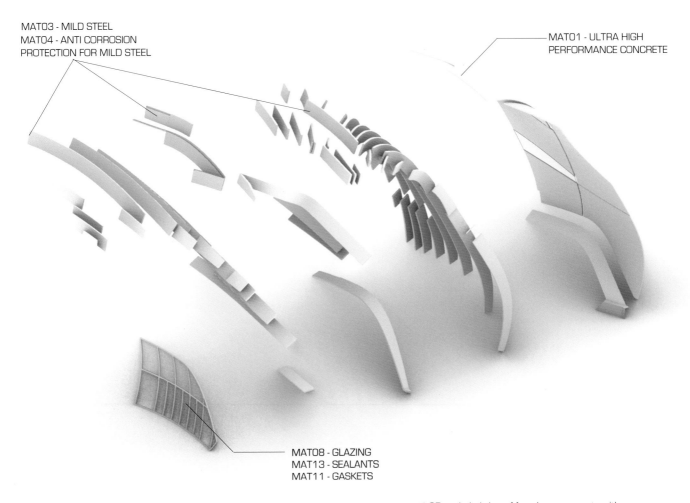

MAT08 - GLAZING
MAT13 - SEALANTS
MAT11 - GASKETS

d | 3D exploded view of facade components with
material specification references

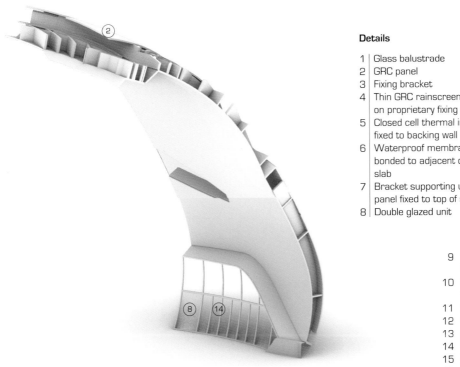

Details

1 | Glass balustrade
2 | GRC panel
3 | Fixing bracket
4 | Thin GRC rainscreen panel
on proprietary fixing system
5 | Closed cell thermal insulation
fixed to backing wall
6 | Waterproof membrane strip
bonded to adjacent concrete
slab
7 | Bracket supporting unitised
panel fixed to top of slab
8 | Double glazed unit

9 | Aluminium faced insulated
panel with decorative finish
10 | Extruded aluminium frame
forming unitised panel
11 | Extruded aluminium section
12 | Concrete slab
13 | Concrete upstand
14 | Silicone seal
15 | Extruded aluminium clip
16 | Thermal break

e | 3D view showing composite rainscreen
fixed to steel frame

ON

uston

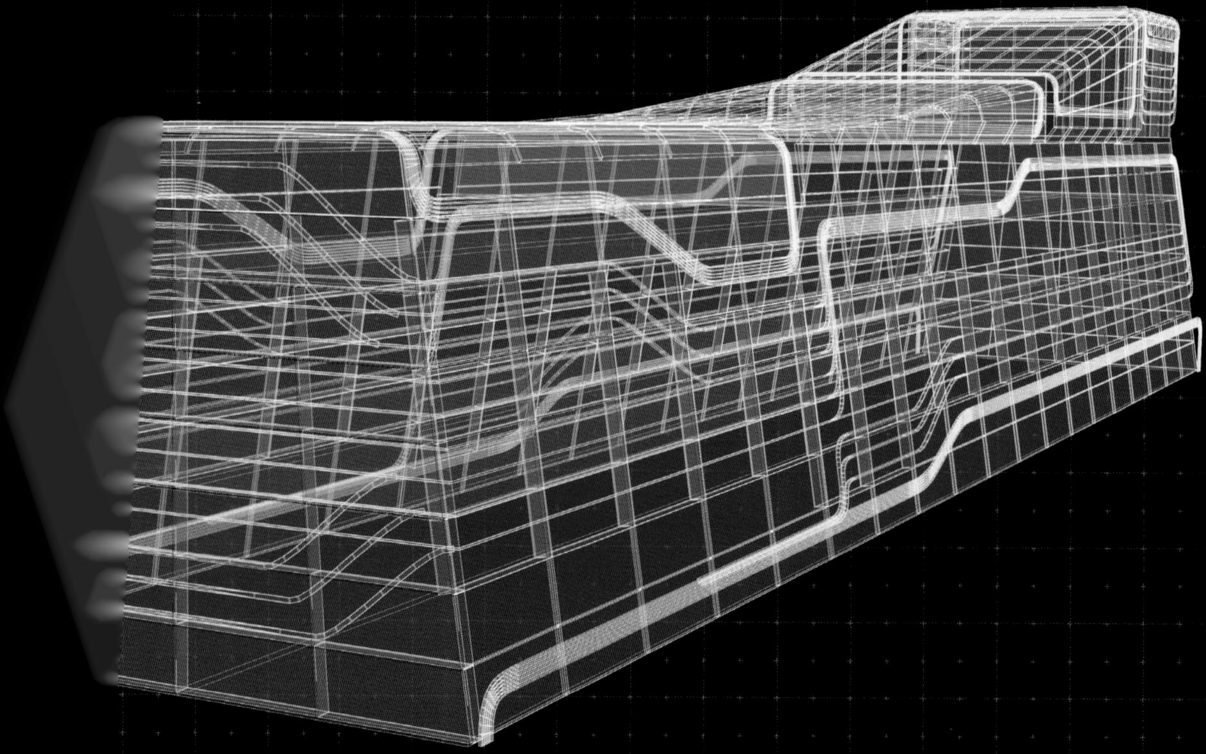

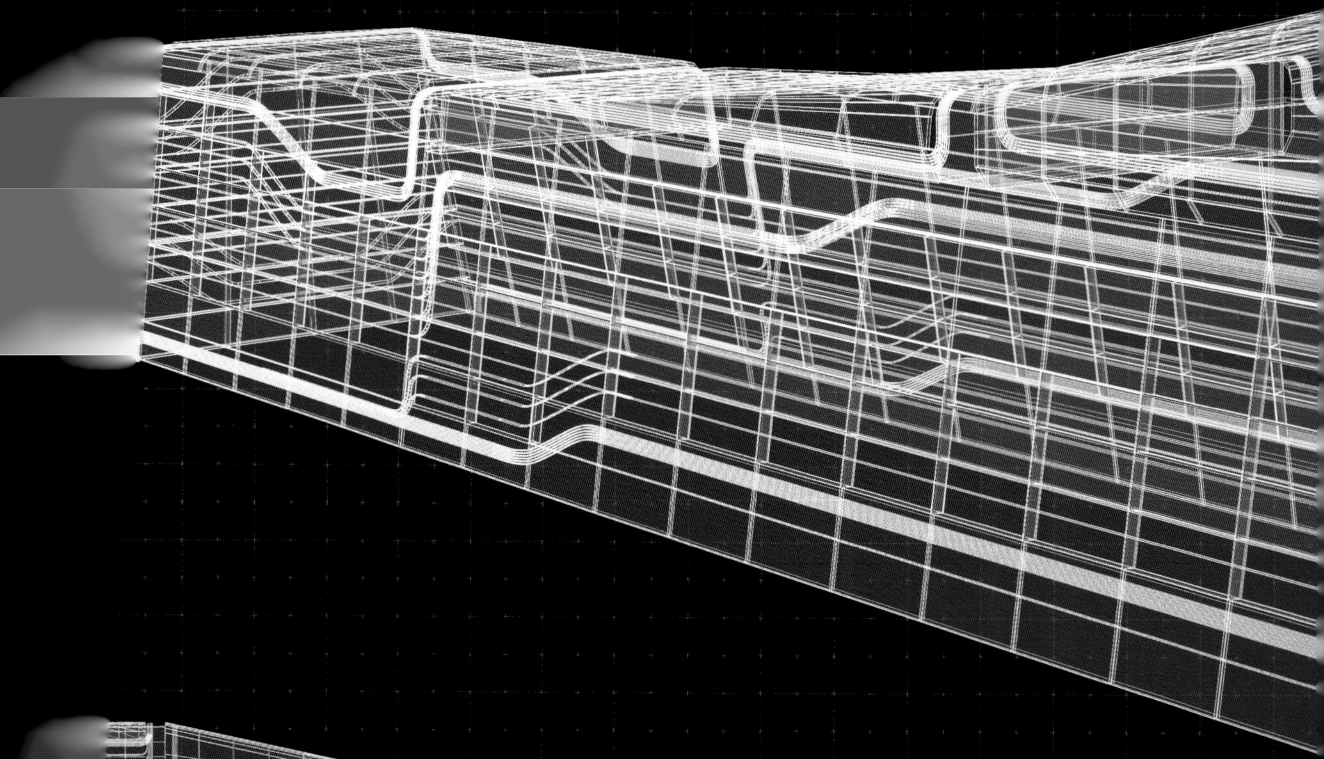

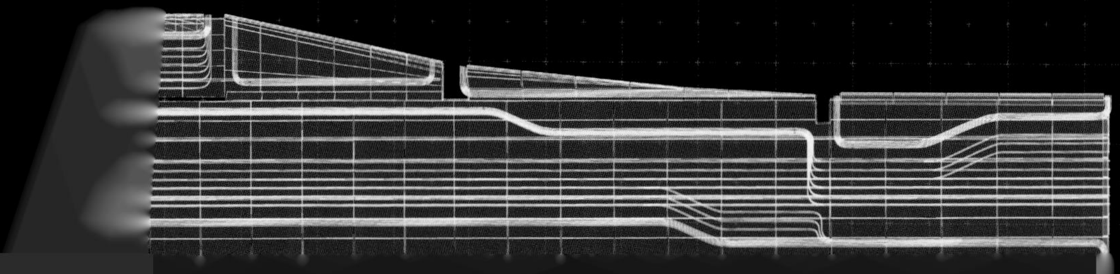

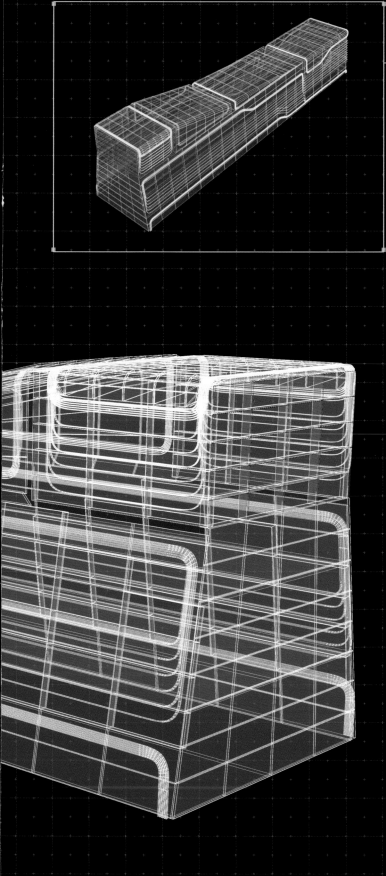

newtecnic

HOUSTON-TX

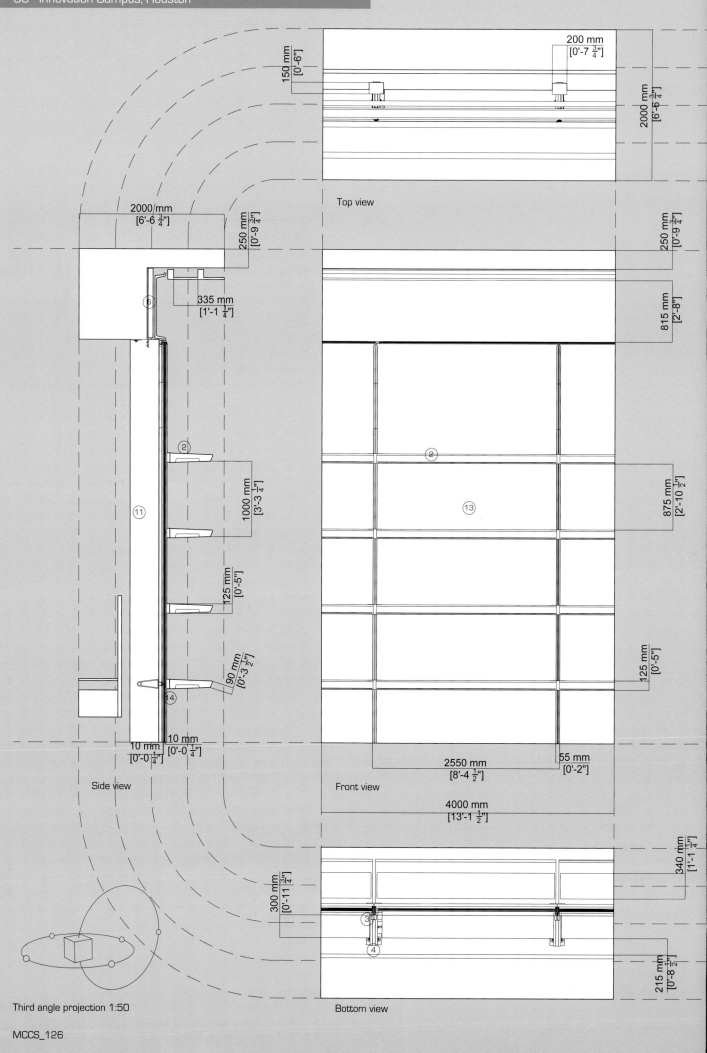

200 mm
[0'-7 ¾"]

150 mm
[0'-6"]

2000 mm
[6'-6 ¾"]

Top view

2000 mm
[6'-6 ¾"]

250 mm
[0'-9 ¾"]

2000 mm
[6'-6 ¾"]

250 mm
[0'-9 ¾"]

335 mm
[1'-1 ¼"]

815 mm
[2'-8"]

1000 mm
[3'-3 ¼"]

875 mm
[2'-10 ½"]

125 mm
[0'-5"]

90 mm
[0'-3 ½"]

125 mm
[0'-5"]

10 mm
[0'-0 ¼"]

10 mm
[0'-0 ¼"]

2550 mm
[8'-4 ½"]

55 mm
[0'-2"]

Side view

Front view

4000 mm
[13'-1 ½"]

340 mm
[1'-1 ¼"]

300 mm
[0'-11 ¾"]

215 mm
[0'-8 ½"]

Third angle projection 1:50

Bottom view

MCCS_126

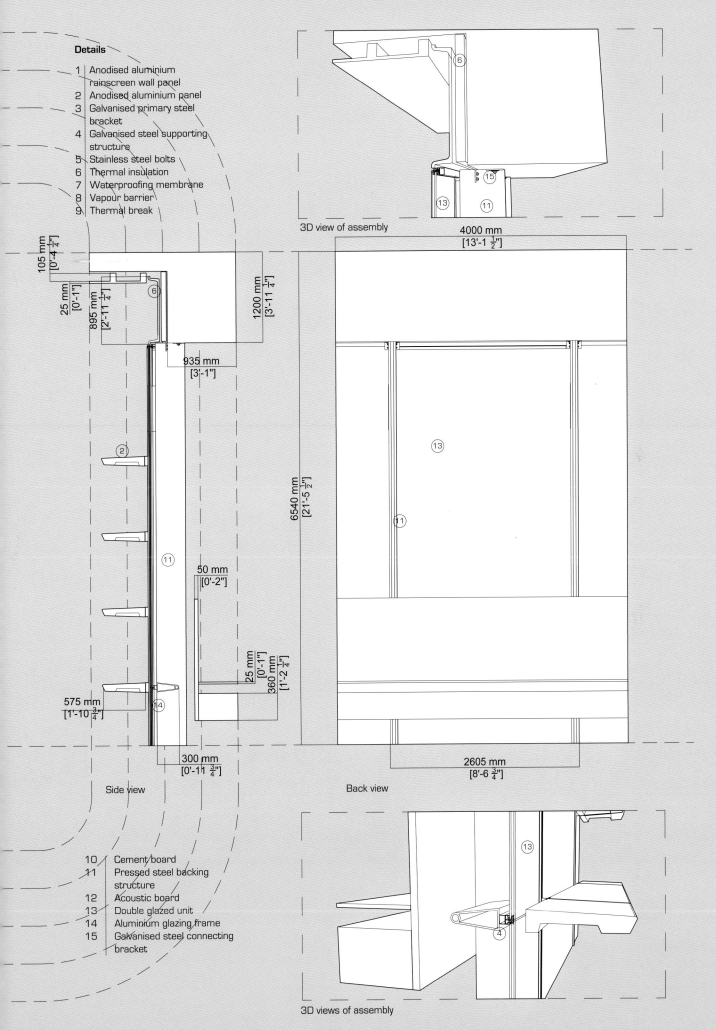

Details

1 | Anodised aluminium rainscreen wall panel
2 | Anodised aluminium panel
3 | Galvanised primary steel bracket
4 | Galvanised steel supporting structure
5 | Stainless steel bolts
6 | Thermal insulation
7 | Waterproofing membrane
8 | Vapour barrier
9 | Thermal break

3D view of assembly

105 mm
[0'-4 1/4"]

25 mm
[0'-1"]

895 mm
[2'-11 1/4"]

1200 mm
[3'-11 1/4"]

935 mm
[3'-1"]

50 mm
[0'-2"]

25 mm
[0'-1"]

360 mm
[1'-2 1/4"]

575 mm
[1'-10 3/4"]

300 mm
[0'-11 3/4"]

Side view

4000 mm
[13'-1 1/2"]

6540 mm
[21'-5 1/2"]

2605 mm
[8'-6 3/4"]

Back view

10 | Cement board
11 | Pressed steel backing structure
12 | Acoustic board
13 | Double glazed unit
14 | Aluminium glazing frame
15 | Galvanised steel connecting bracket

3D views of assembly

MCCS_127

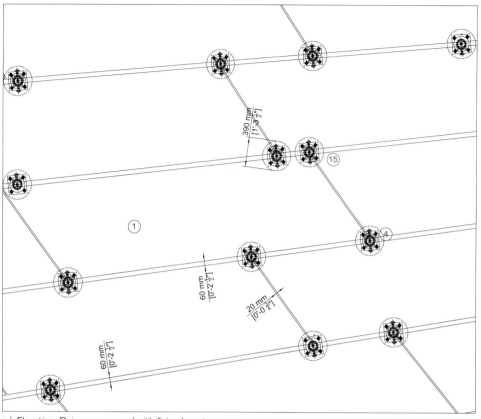

a | Elevation. Rainscreen panel with fixing layout

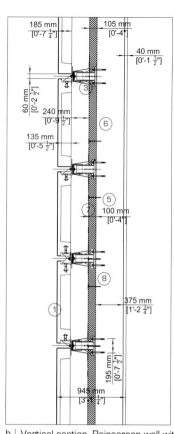

b | Vertical section. Rainscreen wall with
semi-interlocking horizontal joints

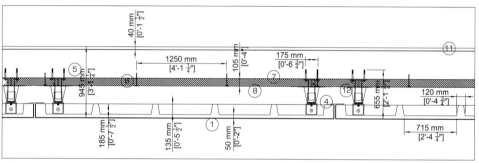

c | Horizontal section. Rainscreen wall with vertical joints

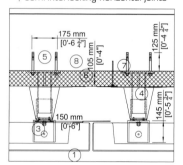

d | Horizontal section. Panel connection
detail with vertical joints

e | Exterior view

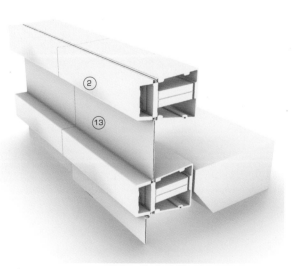

f | Typical bay. 3D view

1:25 scale

1:5 scale

| 1'-0 1/2" | 2'-1" | 3'-1 1/2" | 4'-2" |

2'-1/2" 5' 7'-1/2" 10'

| 250 | 500 | 750 | 1000 | 1250 | mm |

50 100 150 200 250 mm

1:25 scale

1:5 scale

Details

1	Anodised aluminium rainscreen wall panel	8	Vapour barrier
2	Anodised aluminium panel	9	Thermal break
3	Galvanised primary steel bracket	10	Cement board
		11	Pressed steel backing structure
4	Galvanised steel supporting structure	12	Acoustic board
5	Stainless steel bolts	13	Double glazed unit
6	Thermal insulation	14	Aluminium glazing frame
7	Waterproofing membrane	15	Galvanised steel connecting bracket

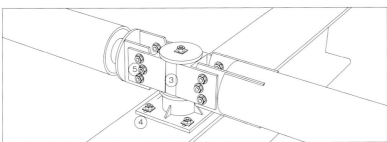

g | 3D view. Secondary steel tube section connecting to primary steel I beam

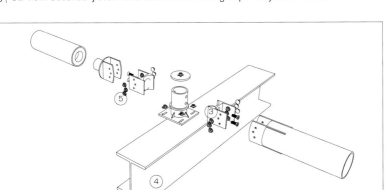

h | 3D view. Exploded detail showing connection between secondary and primary structure

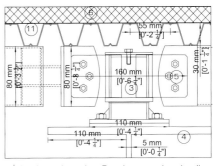

j | Horizontal section. Panel connection detail

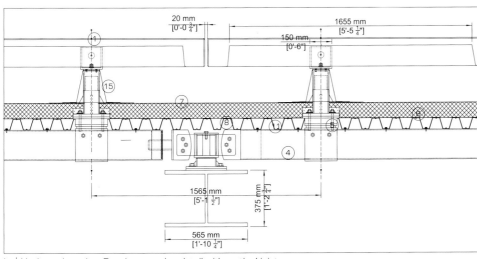

k | Horizontal section. Panel connection detail with vertical joints

m | Vertical section. Steel connection

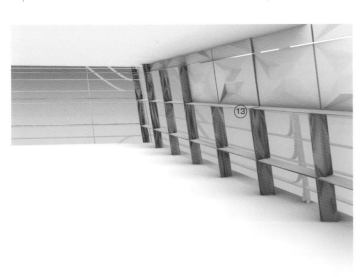

n | Interior view

p | Typical bay. 3D view

q | Typical bay. 3D view

MCCS_129

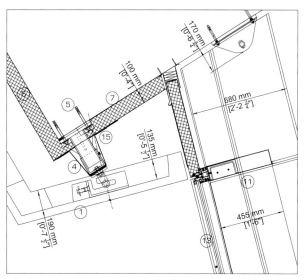

a | Vertical section. Corner junction of unitized glazing unit and opaque panel

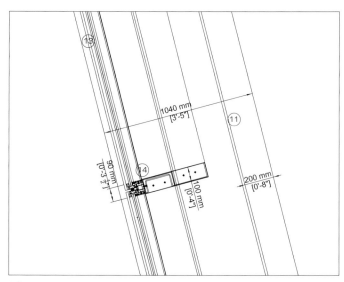

b | Vertical section. Junction between double glazed units

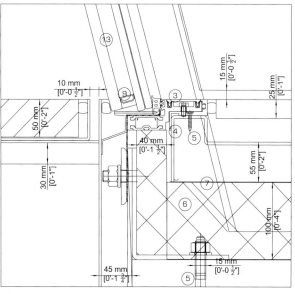

c | Vertical section. Inclined double glazed unit connecting to slab edge

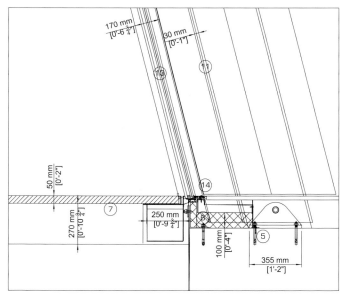

d | Vertical section. Inclined double glazed unit connection at slab edge

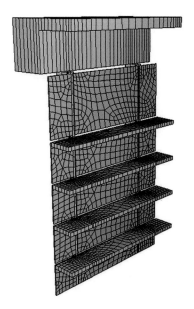

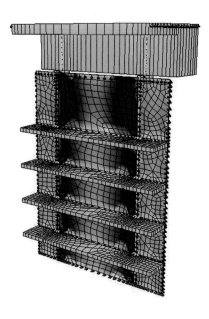

e | Finite element model of a typical bay   f | Utilization distribution within quadrilateral elements

Compression
-0.57

Tension
0.57

Facade system	Metal rainscreen with unitized glazing units
Facade zone	500mm
Primary structure type	Steel moment frame
Secondary structure type	Cold formed steel sections
Weight of secondary structure (kN/m²)	0.13
Facade bracket type	Cast aluminium brackets, bolted through unitised joints
Number of components in fixing system	6
Weight of facade, including secondary structure (kN/m²)	0.74

1:25 scale
1:5 scale
1:25 scale
1:5 scale

e | Horizontal section. Louvre fixed to glazing frame

Details

1 | Anodised aluminium rainscreen wall panel
2 | Anodised aluminium panel
3 | Galvanised primary steel bracket
4 | Galvanised steel supporting structure
5 | Stainless steel bolts
6 | Thermal insulation
7 | Waterproofing membrane
8 | Vapour barrier
9 | Thermal break
10 | Cement board
11 | Pressed steel backing structure
12 | Acoustic board
13 | Double glazed unit
14 | Aluminium glazing frame
15 | Galvanised steel connecting bracket

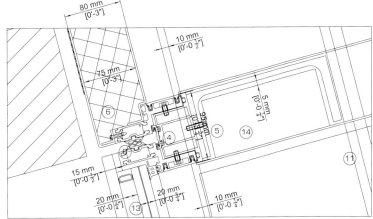

f | Vertical section. Junction between double glazed unit and insulated metal panel

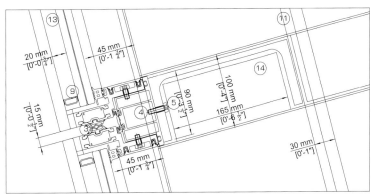

g | Vertical section. Double glazed units fixed to supporting frame with toggle connection and silicone sealed

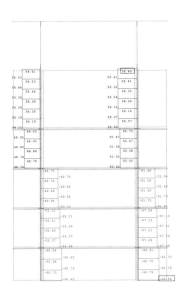

n | Axial force distribution in steel frame [kN]

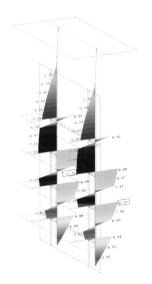

p | Bending moment distribution in aluminium frame [kNm]

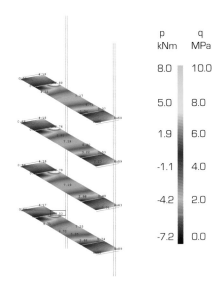

q | Principal tension stress distribution in aluminium louvres [MPa]

MCCS_131

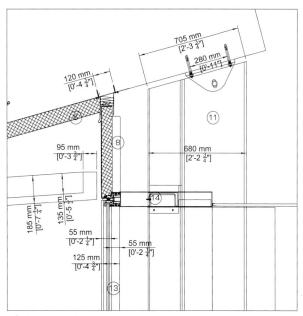

a | Vertical section. Junction with window

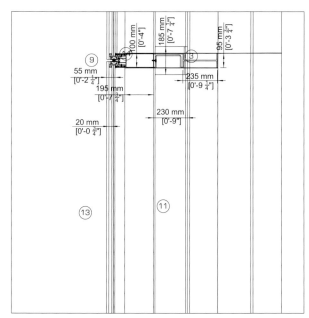

b | Vertical section. Curtain wall connection to secondary structure

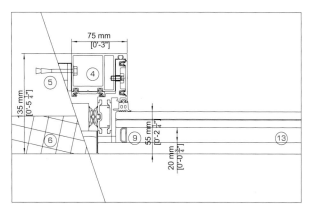

c | Horizontal section. Junction between double glazed unit and insulated metal panel

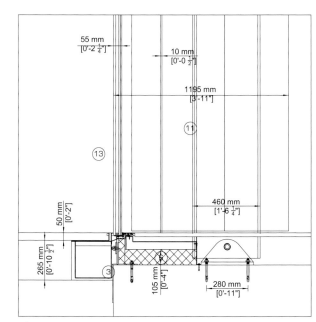

d | Vertical section. Curtain wall connection at slab edge

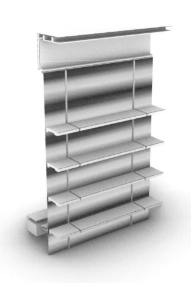

kWh/m²

800
667
533
400
267
133

Period	1 year
With shading	12.8 MWh
Without shading	22.4 MWh
Solar reduction	43%

e | Annual cumulative solar radiation analysis on glazed facade with shading system

f | Annual cumulative solar radiation analysis on glazed facade without shading system

1:25 scale

1:5 scale

250 500 750 1000 1250 mm

1:25 scale

50 100 150 200 250 mm

1:5 scale

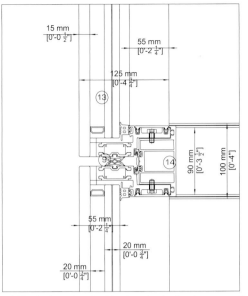

15 mm [0'-0 ½"]
55 mm [0'-2 ¼"]
125 mm [0'-4 ⅞"]
(13)
90 mm [0'-3 ½"]
100 mm [0'-4"]
(14)
55 mm [0'-2 ¼"]
20 mm [0'-0 ¾"]
20 mm [0'-0 ¾"]

Details

1 | Anodised aluminium rainscreen wall panel
2 | Anodised aluminium panel
3 | Galvanised primary steel bracket
4 | Galvanised steel supporting structure
5 | Stainless steel bolts
6 | Thermal insulation
7 | Waterproofing membrane
8 | Vapour barrier
9 | Thermal break
10 | Cement board
11 | Pressed steel backing structure
12 | Acoustic board
13 | Double glazed unit
14 | Aluminium glazing frame
15 | Galvanised steel connecting bracket

g | Vertical section. Double glazed units fixed to supporting frame with toggle connection and silicone sealed

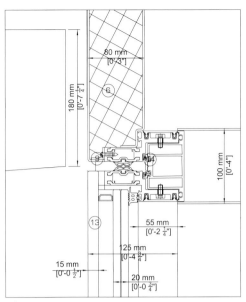

80 mm [0'-3"]
(6)
180 mm [0'-7 ¼"]
100 mm [0'-4"]
(13)
55 mm [0'-2 ¼"]
125 mm [0'-4 ⅞"]
15 mm [0'-0 ½"]
20 mm [0'-0 ¾"]

h | Vertical section. Junction between double glazed unit and insulated metal panel

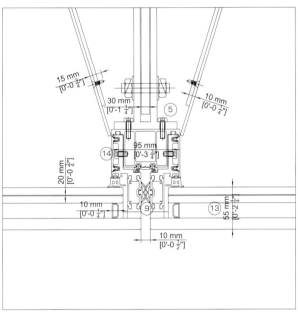

15 mm [0'-0 ¾"]
30 mm [0'-1 ¼"]
10 mm [0'-0 ¼"]
(5)
(14)
95 mm [0'-3 ¾"]
20 mm [0'-0 ¾"]
10 mm [0'-0 ¼"]
(9)
55 mm [0'-2 ¼"]
(13)
10 mm [0'-0 ½"]

j | Horizontal section. Connection to external louvre

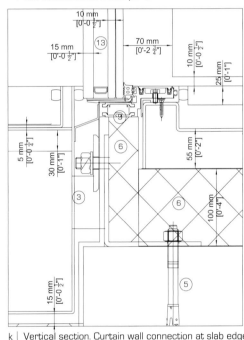

10 mm [0'-0 ½"]
15 mm [0'-0 ½"]
(13)
70 mm [0'-2 ¾"]
10 mm [0'-0 ½"]
25 mm [0'-1"]
5 mm [0'-0 ¼"]
30 mm [0'-1"]
(9)
(6)
55 mm [0'-2"]
(3)
(6)
100 mm [0'-4"]
15 mm [0'-0 ½"]
(5)

k | Vertical section. Curtain wall connection at slab edge

EXT: 40°C

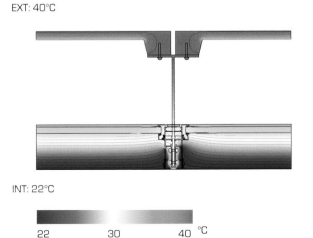

INT: 22°C

22   30   40 °C

m | Thermal performance analysis of a rainscreen cladding connection Isotherms showing temperature distribution across assembly

EXT: 0°C

INT: 22°C

0   10   22 °C

n | Thermal performance analysis of a rainscreen cladding connection Isotherms showing temperature distribution across assembly

MCCS_133

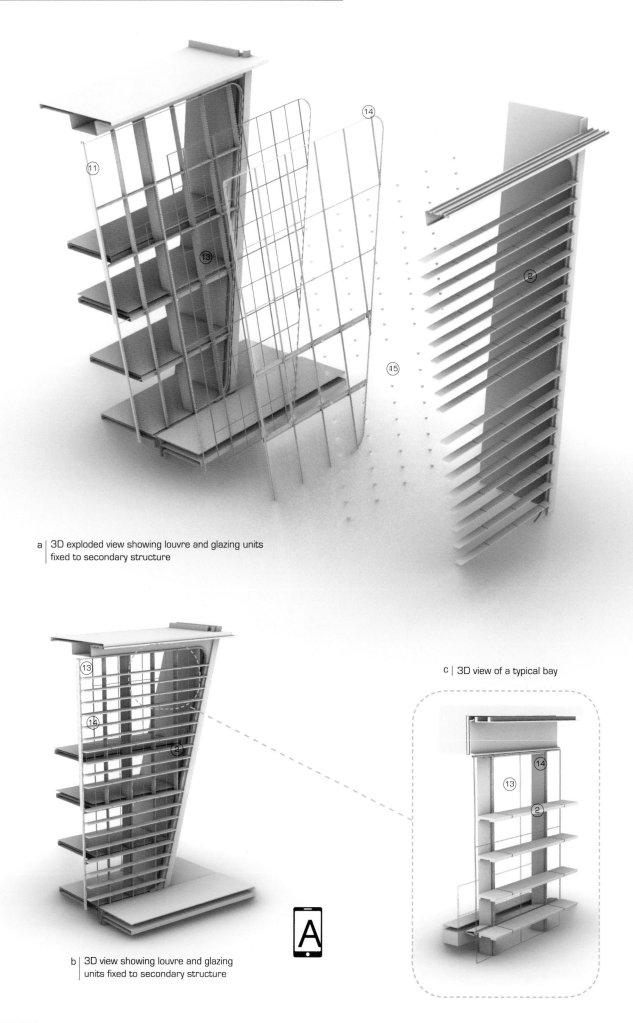

a | 3D exploded view showing louvre and glazing units
fixed to secondary structure

c | 3D view of a typical bay

b | 3D view showing louvre and glazing
units fixed to secondary structure

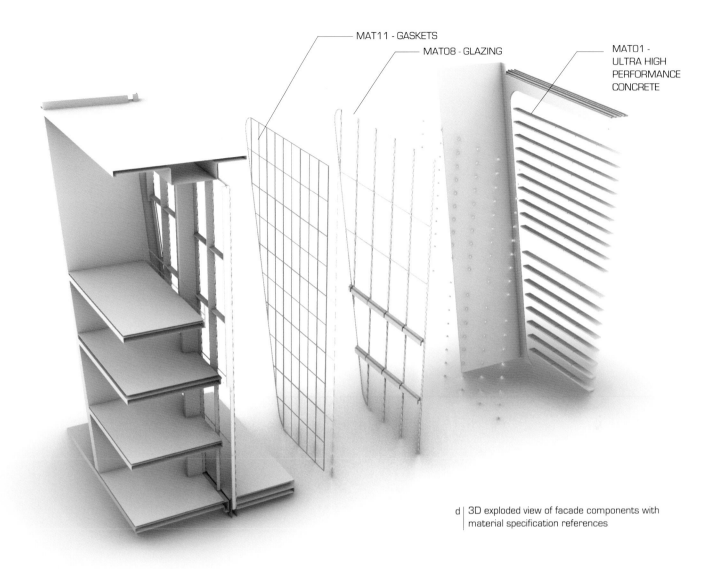

MAT11 - GASKETS

MAT08 - GLAZING

MAT01 -
ULTRA HIGH
PERFORMANCE
CONCRETE

d | 3D exploded view of facade components with
material specification references

Details

1 | Anodised aluminium
rainscreen wall panel
2 | Anodised aluminium panel
3 | Galvanised primary steel
bracket
4 | Galvanised steel supporting
structure
5 | Stainless steel bolts
6 | Thermal insulation
7 | Waterproofing membrane
8 | Vapour barrier
9 | Thermal break
10 | Cement board
11 | Pressed steel backing
structure
12 | Acoustic board
13 | Double glazed unit
14 | Aluminium glazing frame
15 | Galvanised steel connecting
bracket

e | 3D view showing louvre and glazing
units fixed to secondary structure

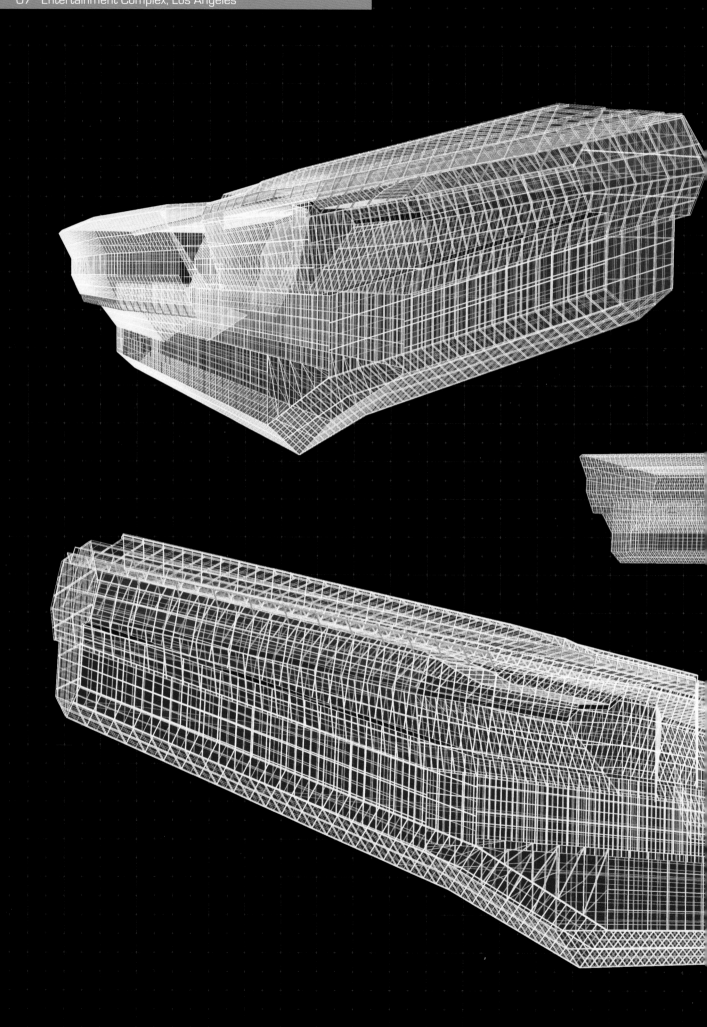

ENTERTAINMENT COMPLEX

LOS ANGELES, CA, USA

34°3'8.0460"   N
118°14'37.2588"   W

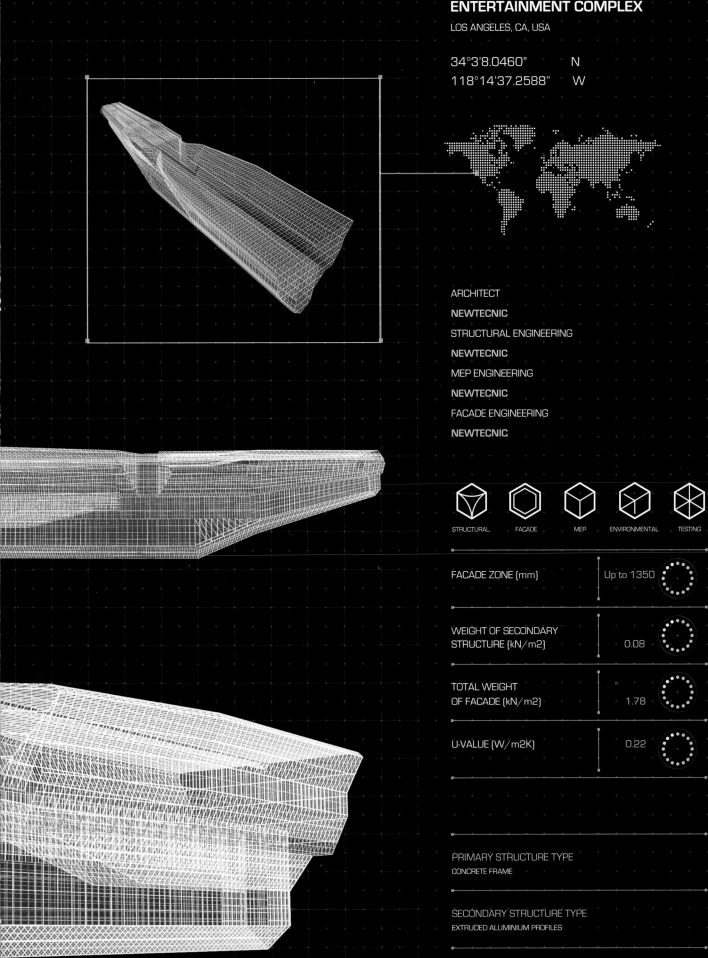

ARCHITECT
NEWTECNIC
STRUCTURAL ENGINEERING
NEWTECNIC
MEP ENGINEERING
NEWTECNIC
FACADE ENGINEERING
NEWTECNIC

STRUCTURAL   FACADE   MEP   ENVIRONMENTAL   TESTING

FACADE ZONE (mm)	Up to 1350	
WEIGHT OF SECONDARY STRUCTURE (kN/m2)	0.08	
TOTAL WEIGHT OF FACADE (kN/m2)	1.78	
U-VALUE (W/m2K)	0.22	

PRIMARY STRUCTURE TYPE
CONCRETE FRAME

SECONDARY STRUCTURE TYPE
EXTRUDED ALUMINIUM PROFILES

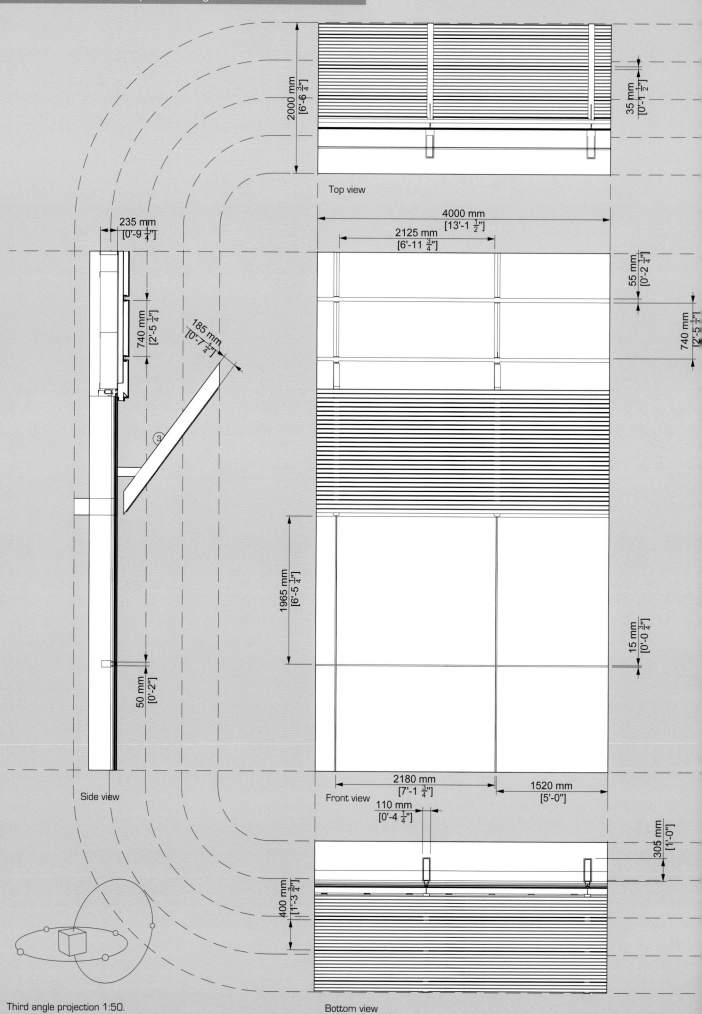

Top view

235 mm
[0'-9 ¼"]

2000 mm
[6'-6 ¾"]

35 mm
[0'-1 ½"]

4000 mm
[13'-1 ½"]

2125 mm
[6'-11 ¾"]

55 mm
[0'-2 ¼"]

740 mm
[2'-5 ¼"]

185 mm
[0'-7 ¼"]

740 mm
[2'-5 ¼"]

1965 mm
[6'-5 ¼"]

15 mm
[0'-0 ¾"]

50 mm
[0'-2"]

2180 mm
[7'-1 ¾"]

1520 mm
[5'-0"]

110 mm
[0'-4 ¼"]

305 mm
[1'-0"]

400 mm
[1'-3 ¾"]

Side view

Front view

Bottom view

Third angle projection 1:50.

MCCS_140

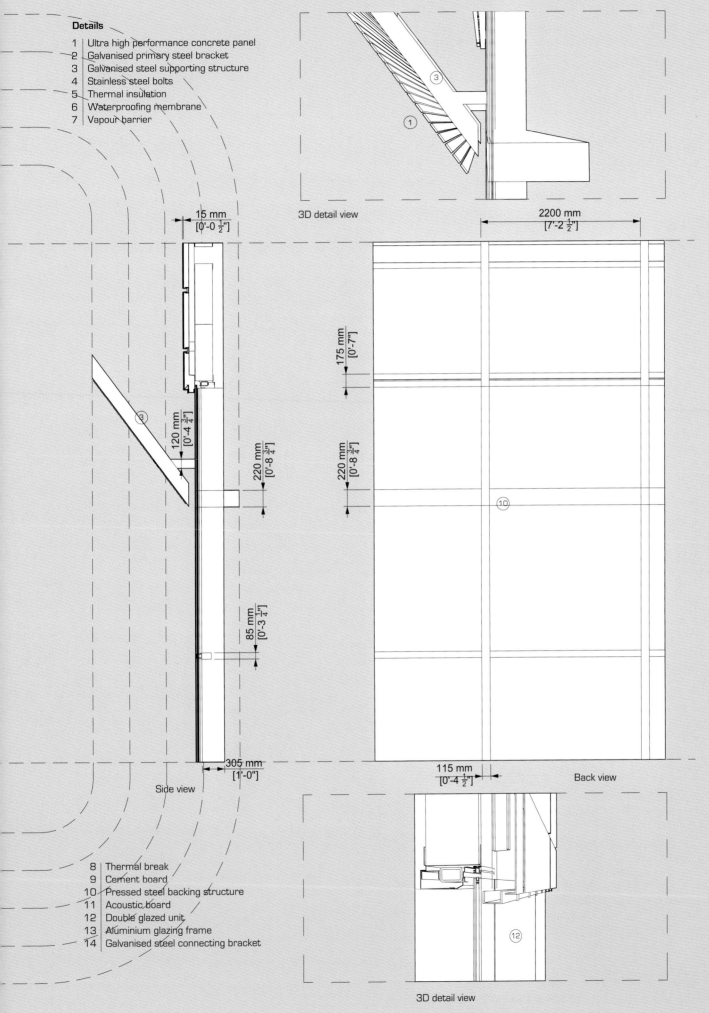

Details

1 | Ultra high performance concrete panel
2 | Galvanised primary steel bracket
3 | Galvanised steel supporting structure
4 | Stainless steel bolts
5 | Thermal insulation
6 | Waterproofing membrane
7 | Vapour barrier

3D detail view

15 mm
[0'-0 ½"]

2200 mm
[7'-2 ½"]

175 mm
[0'-7"]

120 mm
[0'-4 ¾"]

220 mm
[0'-8 ¾"]

220 mm
[0'-8 ¾"]

85 mm
[0'-3 ¼"]

305 mm
[1'-0"]

Side view

115 mm
[0'-4 ½"]

Back view

8 | Thermal break
9 | Cement board
10 | Pressed steel backing structure
11 | Acoustic board
12 | Double glazed unit
13 | Aluminium glazing frame
14 | Galvanised steel connecting bracket

3D detail view

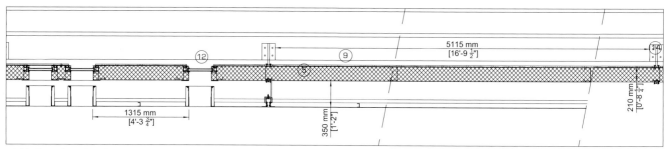

a | Horizontal section. Panel connection with primary structure

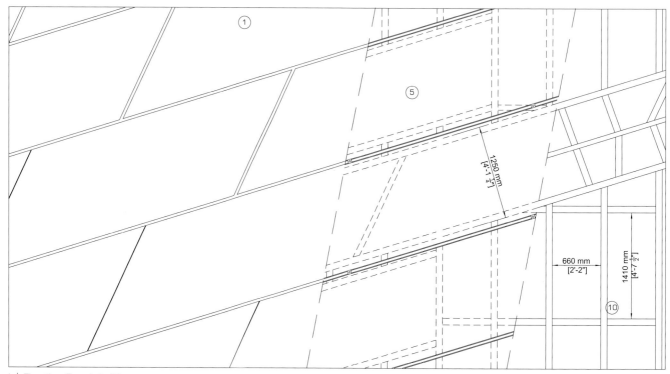

b | Elevation. Facade buildup

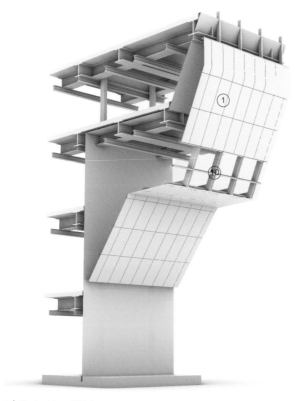

c | Typical bay. 3D view

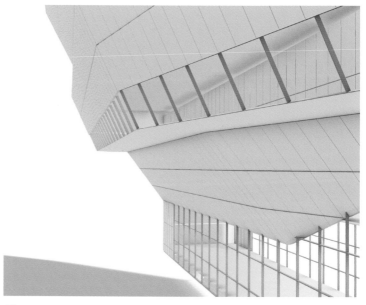

d | Exterior view

1:50 scale
1:10 scale

1:50 scale
1:10 scale

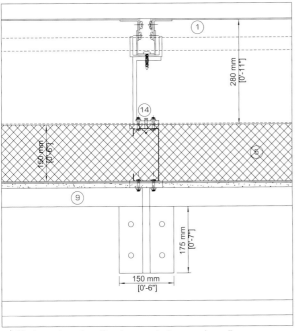

e | Horizontal section. Panel supported on carrier rail

f | Horizontal section. Junction between double glazed unit and opaque panel

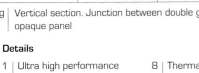

g | Vertical section. Junction between double glazed unit and opaque panel

Details

1	Ultra high performance concrete panel	8	Thermal break
		9	Cement board
2	Galvanised primary steel bracket	10	Pressed steel backing structure
3	Galvanised steel supporting structure	11	Acoustic board
4	Stainless steel bolts	12	Double glazed unit
5	Thermal insulation	13	Aluminium glazing frame
6	Waterproofing membrane	14	Galvanised steel connecting bracket
7	Vapour barrier		

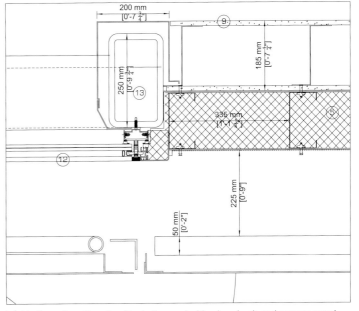

h | Horizontal section. Junction between double glazed unit and opaque panel

j | Interior view

k | Typical bay. 3D view

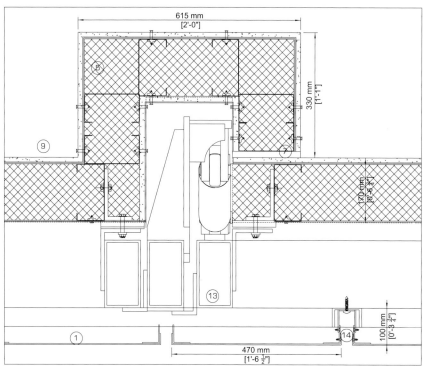

a | Horizontal section. Rainscreen panel supported by backing wall

b | Horizontal section. Internal corner

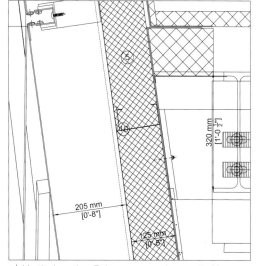

c | Vertical section. Rainscreen panel supported by backing wall

Details

1 | Ultra high performance concrete panel
2 | Galvanised primary steel bracket
3 | Galvanised steel supporting structure
4 | Stainless steel bolts
5 | Thermal insulation
6 | Waterproofing membrane
7 | Vapour barrier
8 | Thermal break
9 | Cement board
10 | Pressed steel backing structure
11 | Acoustic board
12 | Double glazed unit
13 | Aluminium glazing frame
14 | Galvanised steel connecting bracket

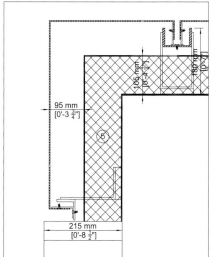

d | Horizontal section. External corner

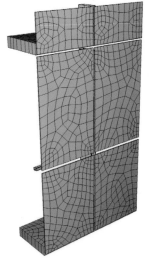

e | Finite element model of a typical bay   f | Utilization distribution within quadrilateral elements

Compression
-0.31

Tension
0.31

Facade system	UHPC open-joint rainscreen with full height stick glazing
Facade zone	Up to 1350mm
Primary structure type	Concrete frame
Secondary structure type	Extruded aluminium profiles
Weight of secondary structure (kN/m²)	0.08
Facade bracket type	Serrated plates; post drilled anchorages
Number of components in fixing system	8
Weight of facade, including secondary structure (kN/m²)	1.78

1:50 scale

2' - 1" 4' - 2" 6' - 3" 8' - 4"

5" 10" 1'-3" 1'-8"

1:10 scale

500 1000 1500 2000 2500 mm

100 200 300 400 500 mm

1:50 scale

1:10 scale

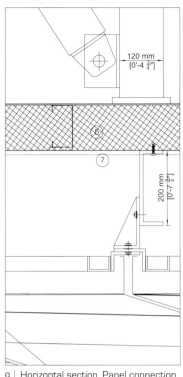

g | Horizontal section. Panel connection

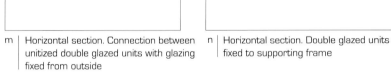

h | Horizontal section. Double glazed unit connection

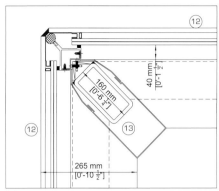

j | Horizontal section. External corner

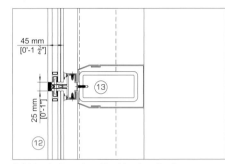

k | Vertical section. Double glazed units

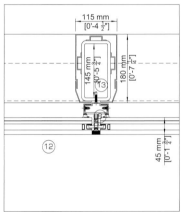

m | Horizontal section. Connection between unitized double glazed units with glazing fixed from outside

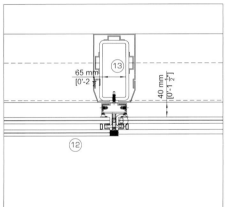

n | Horizontal section. Double glazed units fixed to supporting frame

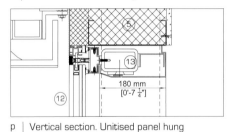

p | Vertical section. Unitised panel hung from top of slab

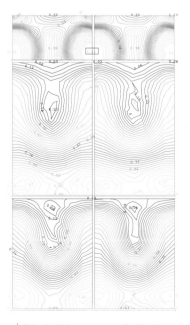

q | Principal shear stress distribution in glazing panels (MPa)

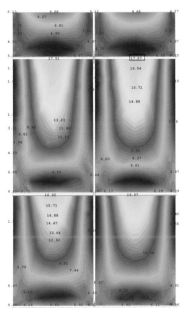

r | Principal tension stress distribution in glazing panels (MPa)

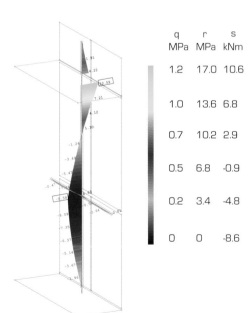

s | Bending moment distribution in aluminium frame (kNm)

q MPa	r MPa	s kNm
1.2	17.0	10.6
1.0	13.6	6.8
0.7	10.2	2.9
0.5	6.8	-0.9
0.2	3.4	-4.8
0	0	-8.6

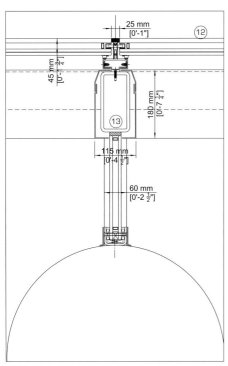

a | Horizontal section. Double glazed units fixed to supporting frame

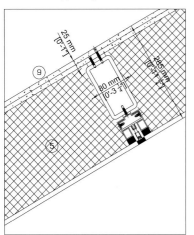

c | Horizontal section. Panel supported by secondary structure

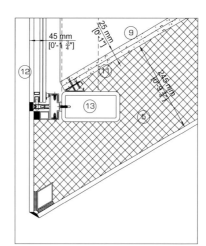

b | Horizontal section. External corner

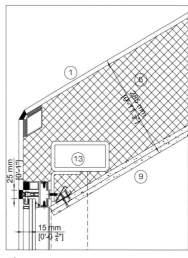

d | Horizontal section. Double glazed unit connection at external corner

Details

1 | Ultra high performance concrete panel
2 | Galvanised primary steel bracket
3 | Galvanised steel supporting structure
4 | Stainless steel bolts
5 | Thermal insulation
6 | Waterproofing membrane
7 | Vapour barrier

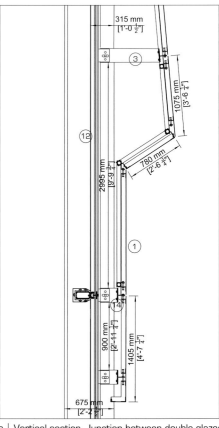

e | Vertical section. Junction between double glazed unit and opaque panel

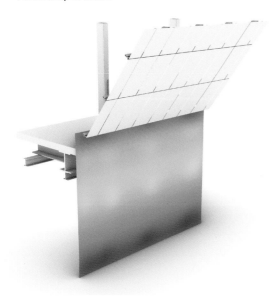

f | Annual cumulative solar radiation analysis on glazed facade with shading system

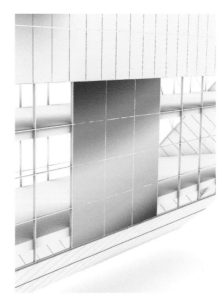

g | Annual cumulative solar radiation analysis on glazed facade without shading system

kWh/m²

1400
1167
933
700
467
233

Period	1 year
With shading	19.4 MWh
Without shading	39.2 MWh
Solar reduction	51%

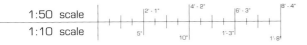

1:50 scale

1:10 scale

1:50 scale

1:10 scale

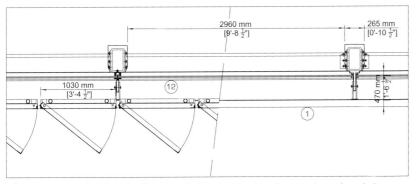

2960 mm
[9'-8 ½"]

265 mm
[0'-10 ½"]

1030 mm
[3'-4 ½"]

470 mm
[1'-6 ½"]

12

1

8 | Thermal break
9 | Cement board
10 | Pressed steel backing structure
11 | Acoustic board
12 | Double glazed unit
13 | Aluminium glazing frame
14 | Galvanised steel connecting bracket

h | Horizontal section. Junction between double glazed unit and outward opening window

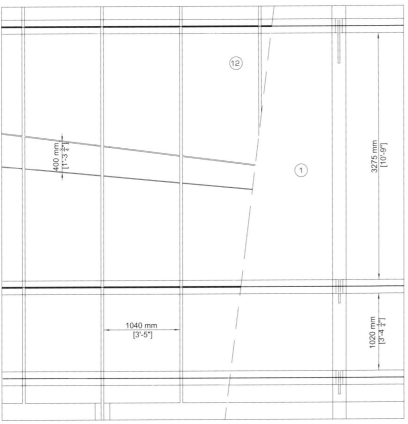

12

1

400 mm
[1'-3 ¾"]

3275 mm
[10'-9"]

1040 mm
[3'-5"]

1020 mm
[3'-4 ¼"]

130 mm
[0'-5"]

675 mm
[2'-2 ½"]

125 mm
[0'-5"]

1

12

1655 mm
[5'-5 ¼"]

350 mm
[1'-1 ¼"]

14

185 mm
[0'-7 ¼"]

205 mm
[0'-8 ¼"]

j | Elevation. Rainscreen facade buildup

k | Vertical section. Junction between double glazed unit and opaque panel

EXT: 40°C   INT: 22°C

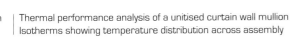

22   30   40 °C

m | Thermal performance analysis of a unitised curtain wall mullion
  | Isotherms showing temperature distribution across assembly

EXT: 0°C   INT: 22°C

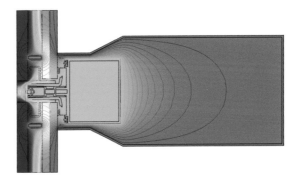

0   10   22 °C

n | Thermal performance analysis of a unitised curtain wall mullion
  | Isotherms showing temperature distribution across assembly

MCCS_147

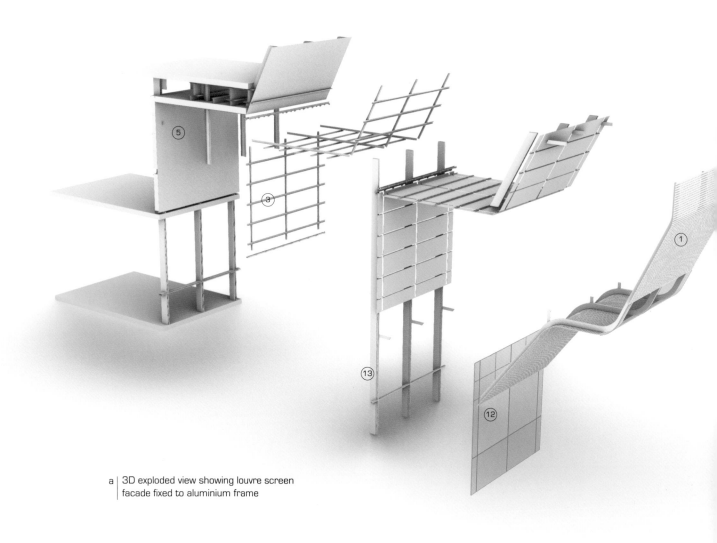

a | 3D exploded view showing louvre screen
    facade fixed to aluminium frame

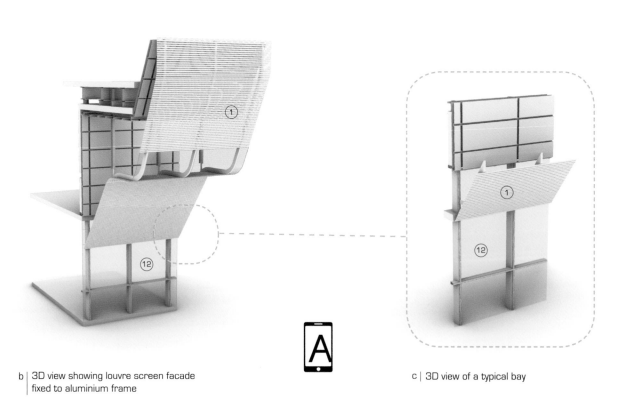

b | 3D view showing louvre screen facade
    fixed to aluminium frame

c | 3D view of a typical bay

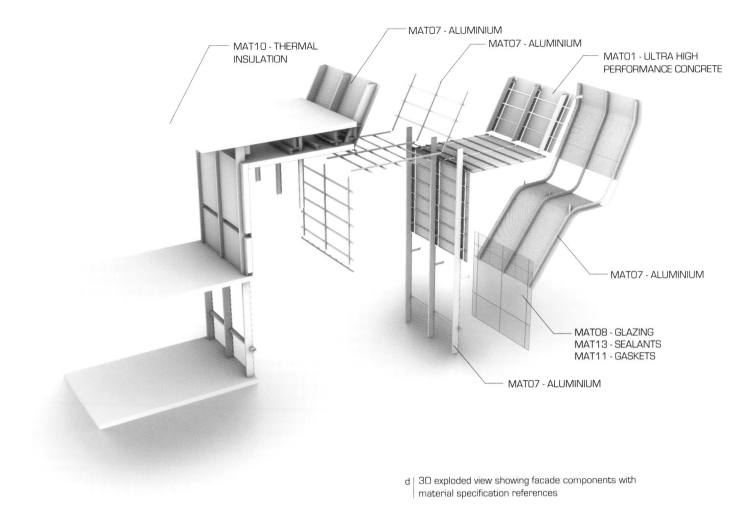

MAT10 - THERMAL
INSULATION

MAT07 - ALUMINIUM

MAT07 - ALUMINIUM

MAT01 - ULTRA HIGH
PERFORMANCE CONCRETE

MAT07 - ALUMINIUM

MAT08 - GLAZING
MAT13 - SEALANTS
MAT11 - GASKETS

MAT07 - ALUMINIUM

d | 3D exploded view showing facade components with
material specification references

Details

1	Ultra high performance concrete panel
2	Galvanised primary steel bracket
3	Galvanised steel supporting structure
4	Stainless steel bolts
5	Thermal insulation
6	Waterproofing membrane
7	Vapour barrier
8	Thermal break
9	Cement board
10	Pressed steel backing structure
11	Acoustic board
12	Double glazed unit
13	Aluminium glazing frame
14	Galvanised steel connecting bracket

e | 3D view showing louvre screen facade
fixed to aluminium frame

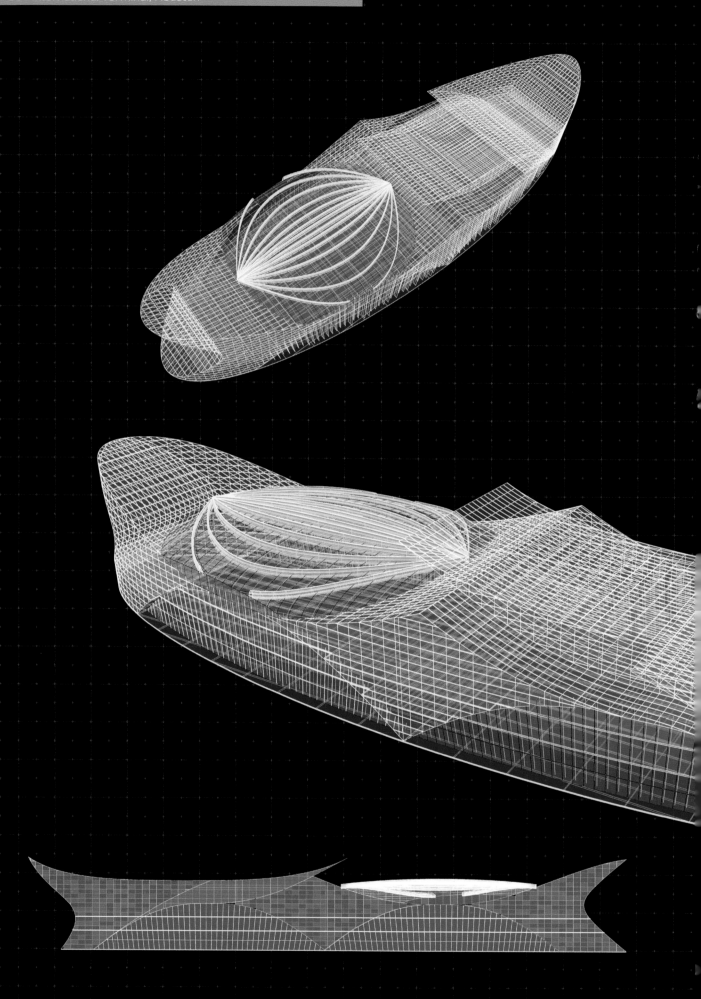

INTERNATIONAL TERMINAL

HOUSTON, TX, USA

29°44'59.6652"   N
95°21'30.3156"   W

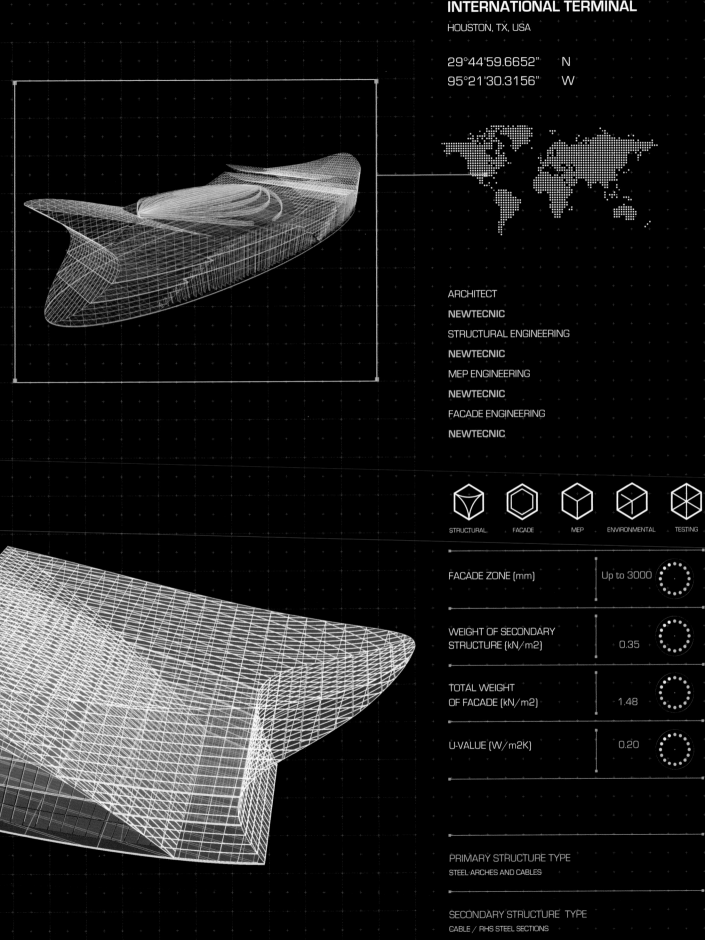

ARCHITECT
NEWTECNIC
STRUCTURAL ENGINEERING
NEWTECNIC
MEP ENGINEERING
NEWTECNIC
FACADE ENGINEERING
NEWTECNIC

STRUCTURAL	FACADE	MEP	ENVIRONMENTAL	TESTING

FACADE ZONE (mm)	Up to 3000	
WEIGHT OF SECONDARY STRUCTURE (kN/m2)	0.35	
TOTAL WEIGHT OF FACADE (kN/m2)	1.48	
U-VALUE (W/m2K)	0.20	

PRIMARY STRUCTURE TYPE
STEEL ARCHES AND CABLES

SECONDARY STRUCTURE TYPE
CABLE / RHS STEEL SECTIONS

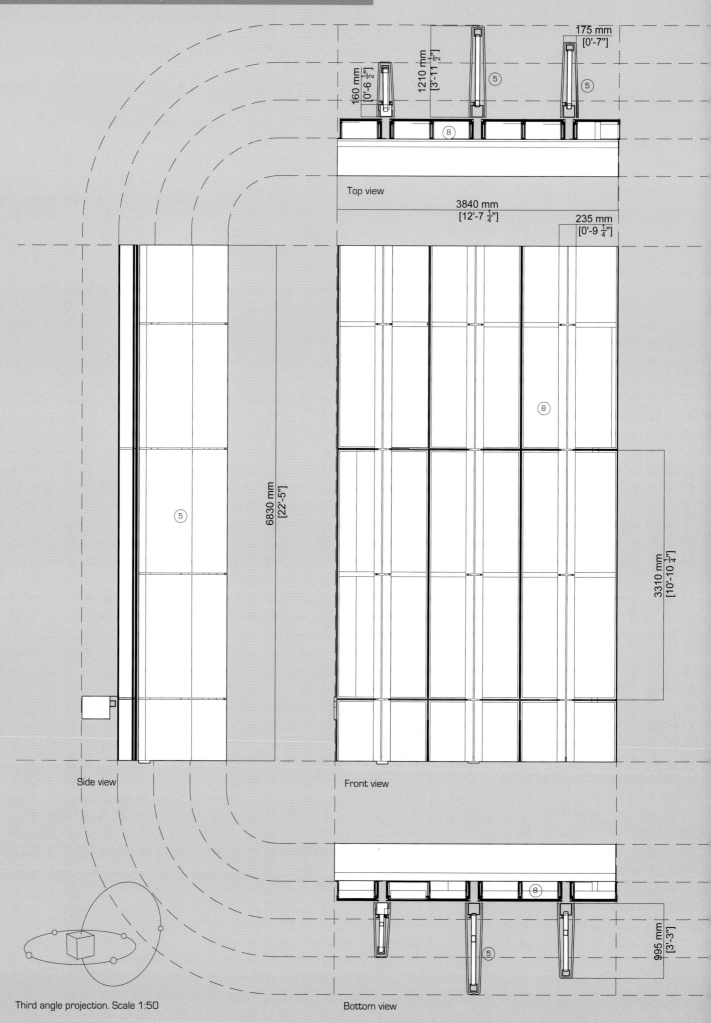

160 mm
[0'-6 1/2"]

1210 mm
[3'-11 1/2"]

175 mm
[0'-7"]

5

5

8

Top view

3840 mm
[12'-7 1/4"]

235 mm
[0'-9 1/4"]

6830 mm
[22'-5"]

5

8

3310 mm
[10'-10 1/4"]

Side view

Front view

8

995 mm
[3'-3"]

5

Third angle projection. Scale 1:50

Bottom view

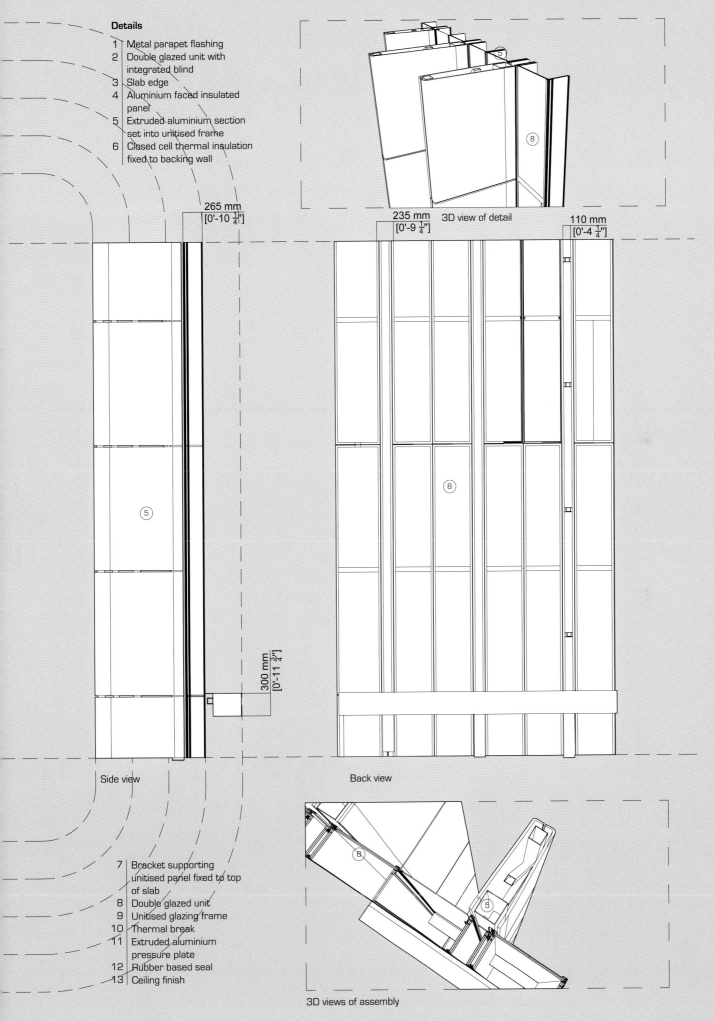

Details

1 | Metal parapet flashing
2 | Double glazed unit with integrated blind
3 | Slab edge
4 | Aluminium faced insulated panel
5 | Extruded aluminium section set into unitised frame
6 | Closed cell thermal insulation fixed to backing wall

265 mm
[0'-10 $\frac{1}{4}$"]

300 mm
[0'-11 $\frac{3}{4}$"]

3D view of detail

235 mm
[0'-9 $\frac{1}{4}$"]

110 mm
[0'-4 $\frac{1}{4}$"]

Side view

Back view

7 | Bracket supporting unitised panel fixed to top of slab
8 | Double glazed unit
9 | Unitised glazing frame
10 | Thermal break
11 | Extruded aluminium pressure plate
12 | Rubber based seal
13 | Ceiling finish

3D views of assembly

MCCS_155

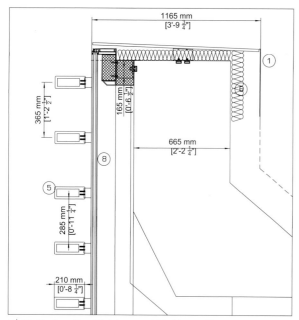

a | Vertical section. Metal parapet flashing and louvre

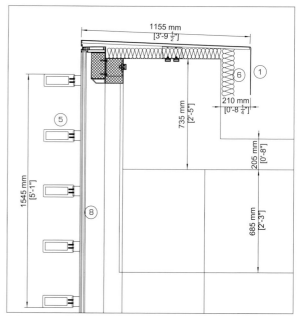

b | Vertical section. Metal parapet flashing and louvre

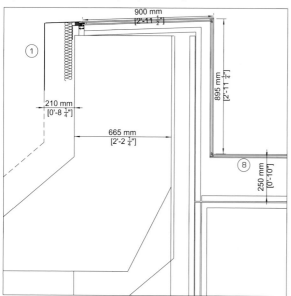

c | Vertical section. Parapet

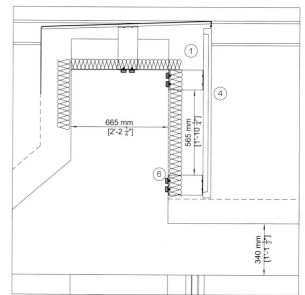

d | Vertical section. Parapet

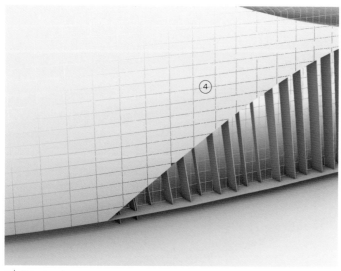

e | Exterior view

f | Interior view

1:25 scale

1:5 scale

1:25 scale

1:5 scale

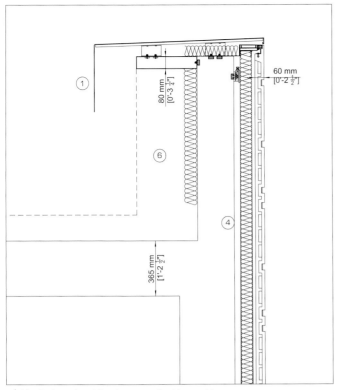

g | Vertical section. Metal parapet flashing and louvre

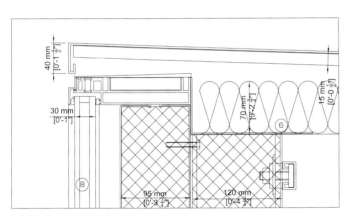

j | Vertical section. Metal parapet flashing

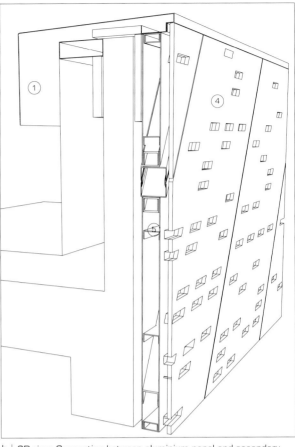

h | 3D view. Connection between aluminium panel and secondary structure

Details

1	Metal parapet flashing	7	Bracket supporting
2	Double glazed unit with		unitised panel fixed to top
	integrated blind		of slab
3	Slab edge	8	Double glazed unit
4	Aluminium faced insulated	9	Unitised glazing frame
	panel	10	Thermal break
5	Extruded aluminium section	11	Extruded aluminium
	set into unitised frame		pressure plate
6	Closed cell thermal insulation	12	Rubber based seal
	fixed to backing wall	13	Ceiling finish

k | Typical bay. 3D view

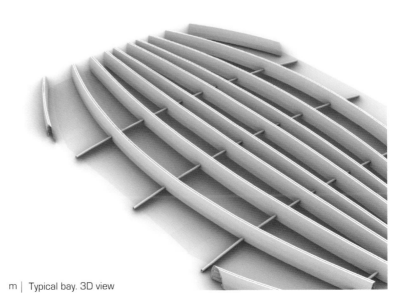

m | Typical bay. 3D view

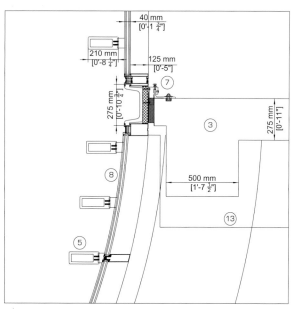

a | Vertical section. Facade profile at floor slab level

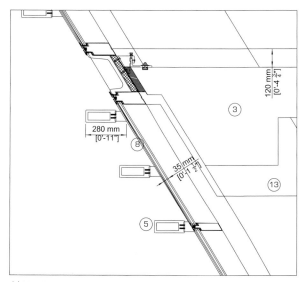

b | Vertical section. Facade profile at floor slab level

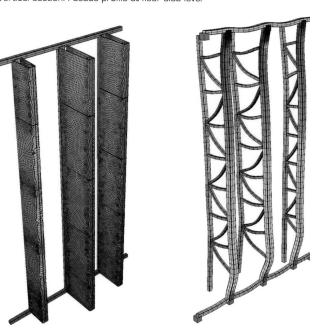

c | Vertical section. Facade profile at floor slab level

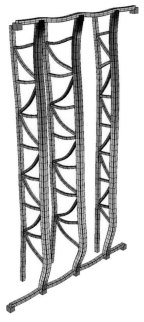

d | Vertical section. Facade profile at floor slab level

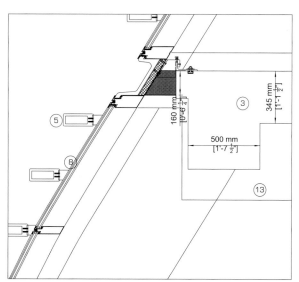

e | Finite element model of a typical bay

f | Utilization distribution within quadrilateral elements

Compression
-0.67

Tension
0.67

Facade system	UHPC rainscreen with glazing unitized panels
Facade zone	Up to 3000mm
Primary structure type	Steel arches and cables
Secondary structure type	RHS steel sections
Weight of secondary structure [kN/m²]	0.15
Facade bracket type	Serrated plates; welded and bolted
Number of components in fixing system	5
Weight of facade, including secondary structure [kN/m²]	1.48

1:25 scale

1:5 scale

1' 0 1/2"   2'-1"   3'-1 1/2"   4'-2"

2'-1/2"   5"   7'-1/2"   10"

250   500   750   1000   1250 mm

50   100   150   200   250 mm

1:25 scale

1:5 scale

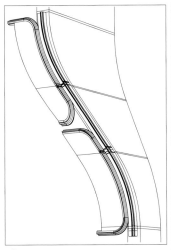

g | 3D view. Rainscreen cladding

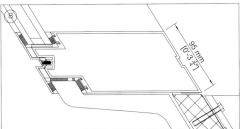

h | Vertical section. Extruded aluminium section set into unitised frame

95 mm [0'-3 3/4"]

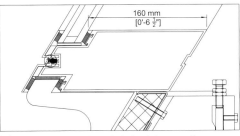

j | Vertical section. Extruded aluminium section set into unitised frame

160 mm [0'-6 1/2"]

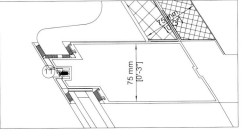

k | Vertical section. Extruded aluminium section set into unitised frame

75 mm [0'-3"]

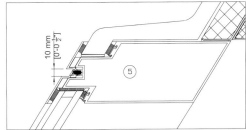

m | Vertical section. Extruded aluminium section set into unitised frame

10 mm [0'-0 1/2"]

Details

1 | Metal parapet flashing
2 | Double glazed unit with integrated blind
3 | Slab edge
4 | Aluminium faced insulated panel
5 | Extruded aluminium section set into unitised frame
6 | Closed cell thermal insulation fixed to backing wall
7 | Bracket supporting unitised panel fixed to top of slab
8 | Double glazed unit
9 | Unitised glazing frame
10 | Thermal break
11 | Extruded aluminium pressure plate
12 | Rubber based seal
13 | Ceiling finish

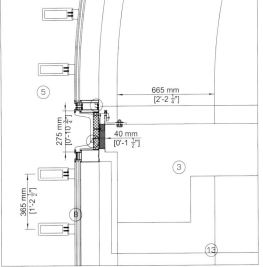

665 mm [2'-2 1/4"]

275 mm [0'-10 3/4"]

40 mm [0'-1 1/2"]

365 mm [1'-2 1/2"]

n | Vertical section. Facade profile at floor slab level

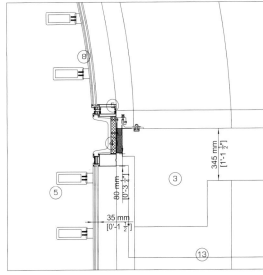

345 mm [1'-1 1/2"]

80 mm [0'-3 1/4"]

35 mm [0'-1 1/2"]

p | Vertical section. Facade profile at floor slab level

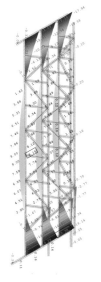

q | Bending moment distribution in steel frame (kNm)

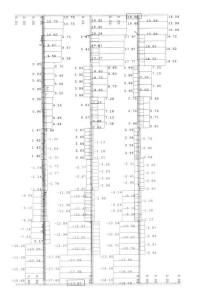

r | Axial force distribution in steel frame (kN)

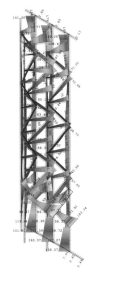

s | Von Mises stress distribution in steel frame (MPa)

q kNm	s MPa
8.1	226.4
2.6	182.3
-2.9	138.1
-8.4	94.0
-13.9	50.0
-19.4	5.7

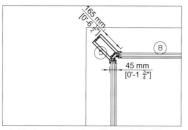

a | Horizontal section. Unitised double glazed panels assembly

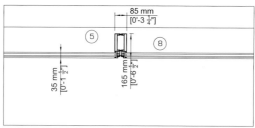

b | Horizontal section. Unitised double glazed panels assembly

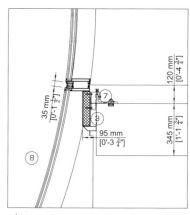

c | Vertical section. Unitised double glazed at floor slab

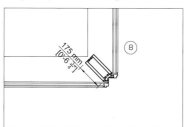

d | Horizontal section. Unitised double glazed panels assembly

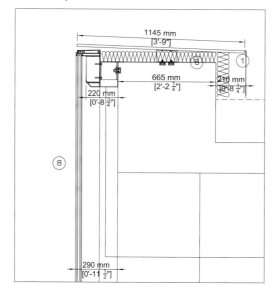

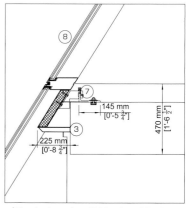

e | Vertical section. Unitised double glazed at floor slab

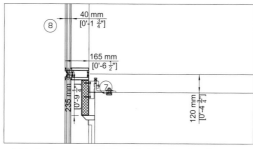

g | Vertical sections. Unitised double glazed at floor slab and parapet level

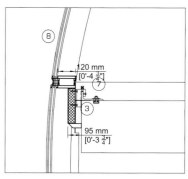

h | Vertical section. Unitised double glazed at floor slab

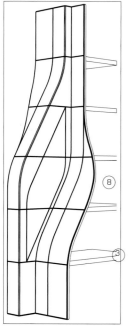

f | 3D view. Curved and folded glass corner detail

j | Annual cumulative solar radiation analysis on glazed facade with shading system

k | Annual cumulative solar radiation analysis on glazed facade without shading system

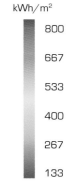

kWh/m²

800
667
533
400
267
133

Period	1 year
With shading	12.6 MWh
Without shading	22.4 MWh
Solar reduction	44 %

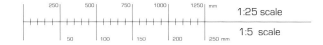

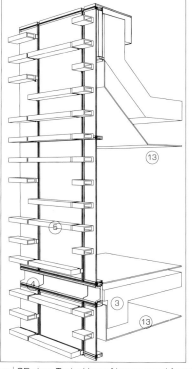

m | 3D view. Typical bay of louvre panel facade

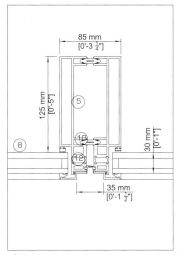

n | Horizontal section. Unitised double glazed

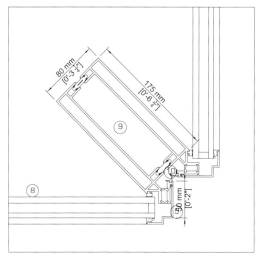

p | Horizontal section. Unitised double glazed

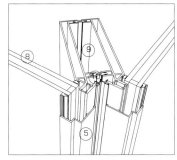

q | 3D view. Glazing mullion detail

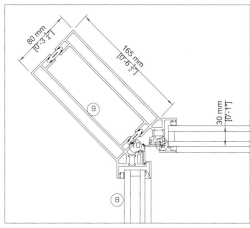

r | Horizontal section. Unitised double glazed

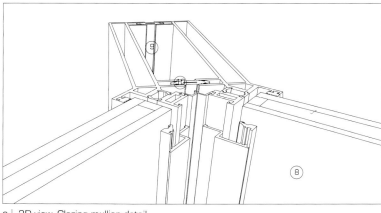

s | 3D view. Glazing mullion detail

Details

1	Metal parapet flashing	7	Bracket supporting unitised panel fixed to top of slab
2	Double glazed unit with integrated blind		
3	Slab edge	8	Double glazed unit
4	Aluminium faced insulated panel	9	Unitised glazing frame
		10	Thermal break
5	Extruded aluminium section set into unitised frame	11	Extruded aluminium pressure plate
6	Closed cell thermal insulation fixed to backing wall	12	Rubber based seal
		13	Ceiling finish

EXT: 40°C

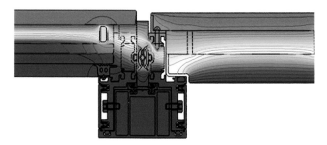

INT: 22°C

22   30   40 °C

t | Thermal performance analysis of a unitised curtain wall mullion
| Isotherms showing temperature distribution across assembly

EXT: 0°C

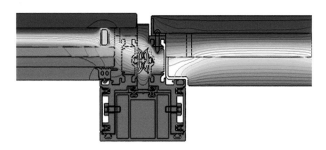

INT: 22°C

0   10   22 °C

u | Thermal performance analysis of a unitised curtain wall mullion
| Isotherms showing temperature distribution across assembly

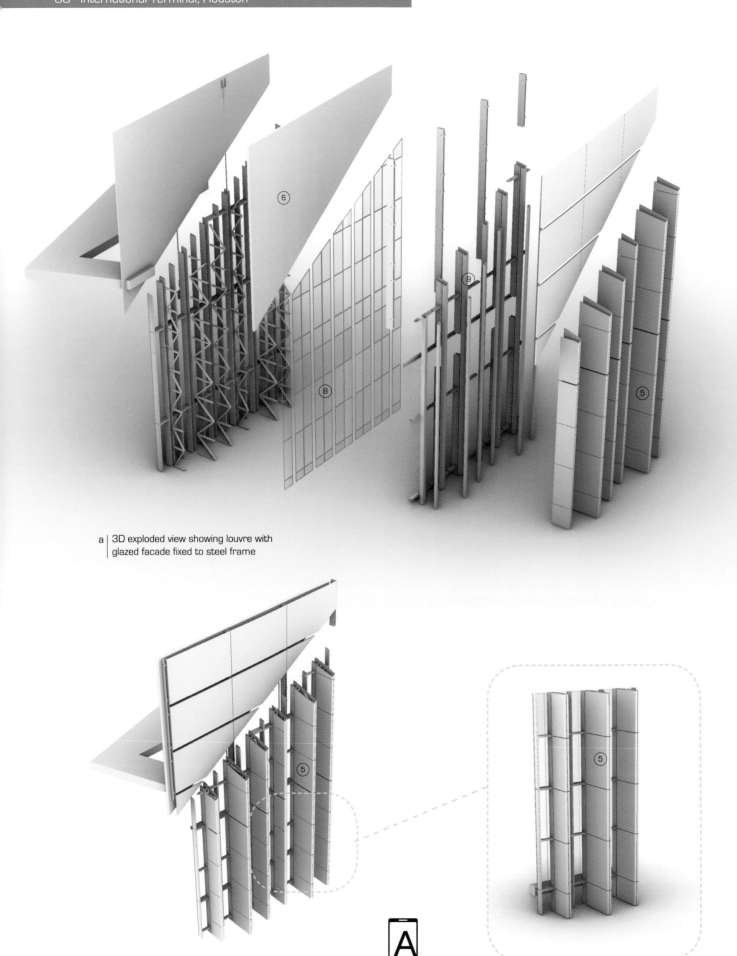

a | 3D exploded view showing louvre with
glazed facade fixed to steel frame

b | 3D view showing louvre with glazed facade
fixed to steel frame

c | 3D view of a typical bay

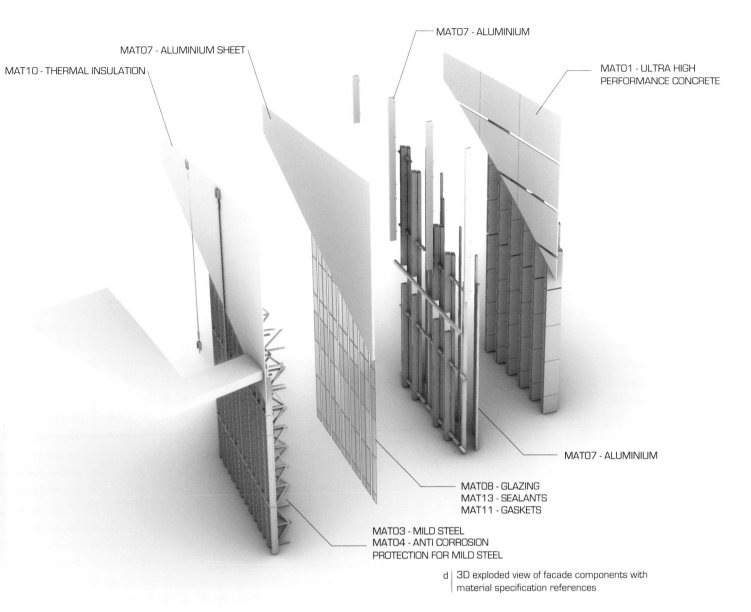

MAT10 - THERMAL INSULATION

MAT07 - ALUMINIUM SHEET

MAT07 - ALUMINIUM

MAT01 - ULTRA HIGH
PERFORMANCE CONCRETE

MAT07 - ALUMINIUM

MAT08 - GLAZING
MAT13 - SEALANTS
MAT11 - GASKETS

MAT03 - MILD STEEL
MAT04 - ANTI CORROSION
PROTECTION FOR MILD STEEL

d | 3D exploded view of facade components with
material specification references

e | 3D view showing louvre with glazed
facade fixed to steel frame

Details

1 | Metal parapet flashing
2 | Double glazed unit with
integrated blind
3 | Slab edge
4 | Aluminium faced insulated panel
5 | Extruded aluminium section set
into unitised frame
6 | Closed cell thermal insulation
fixed to backing wall
7 | Bracket supporting unitised
panel fixed to top of slab
8 | Double glazed unit
9 | Unitised glazing frame
10 | Thermal break
11 | Extruded aluminium pressure
plate
12 | Rubber based seal
13 | Ceiling finish

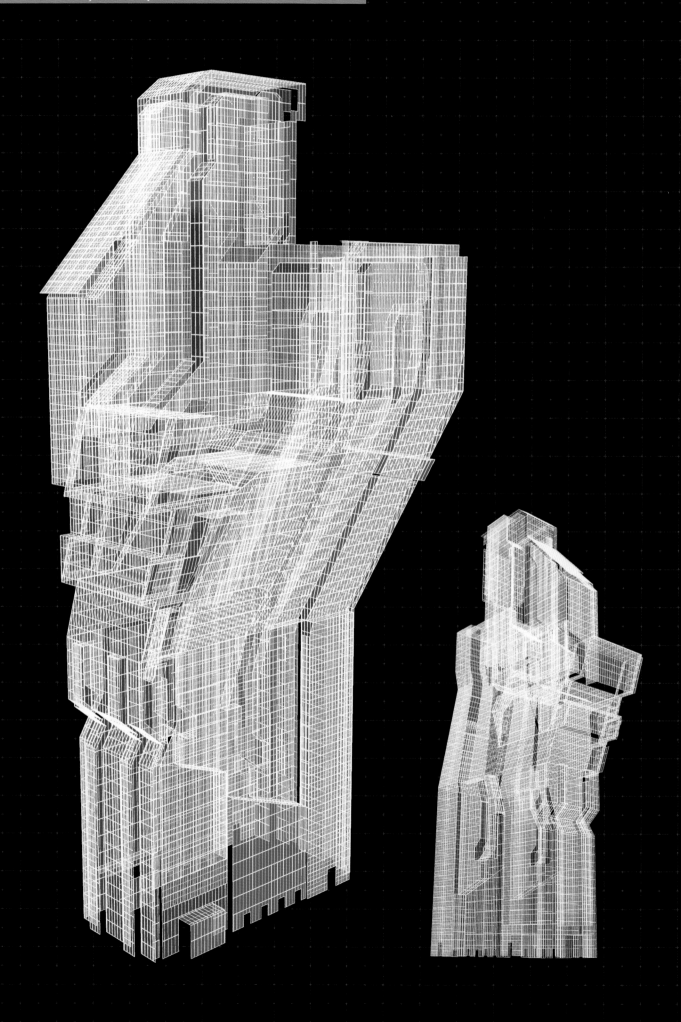

LABORATORY TOWER

RIYADH, KSA

24°46'27.3540"   N
46°44'18.9096"   E

ARCHITECT
NEWTECNIC

STRUCTURAL ENGINEERING
NEWTECNIC

MEP ENGINEERING
NEWTECNIC

FACADE ENGINEERING
NEWTECNIC

STRUCTURAL   FACADE   MEP   ENVIRONMENTAL   TESTING

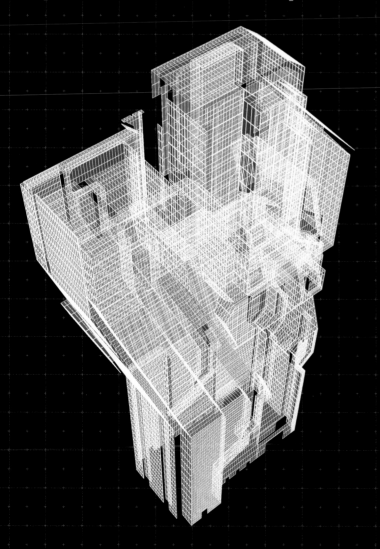

FACADE ZONE (mm)	850	
WEIGHT OF SECONDARY STRUCTURE (kN/m2)	0.35	
TOTAL WEIGHT OF FACADE (kN/m2)	1.89	
U-VALUE (W/m2K)	0.32	

PRIMARY STRUCTURE TYPE
BUNDLED TUBE

SECONDARY STRUCTURE TYPE
RHS STEEL SECTIONS

FACADE BRACKET TYPE
SPIDER BRACKET WITH TWO ADJUSTABLE ARMS

MCCS_167

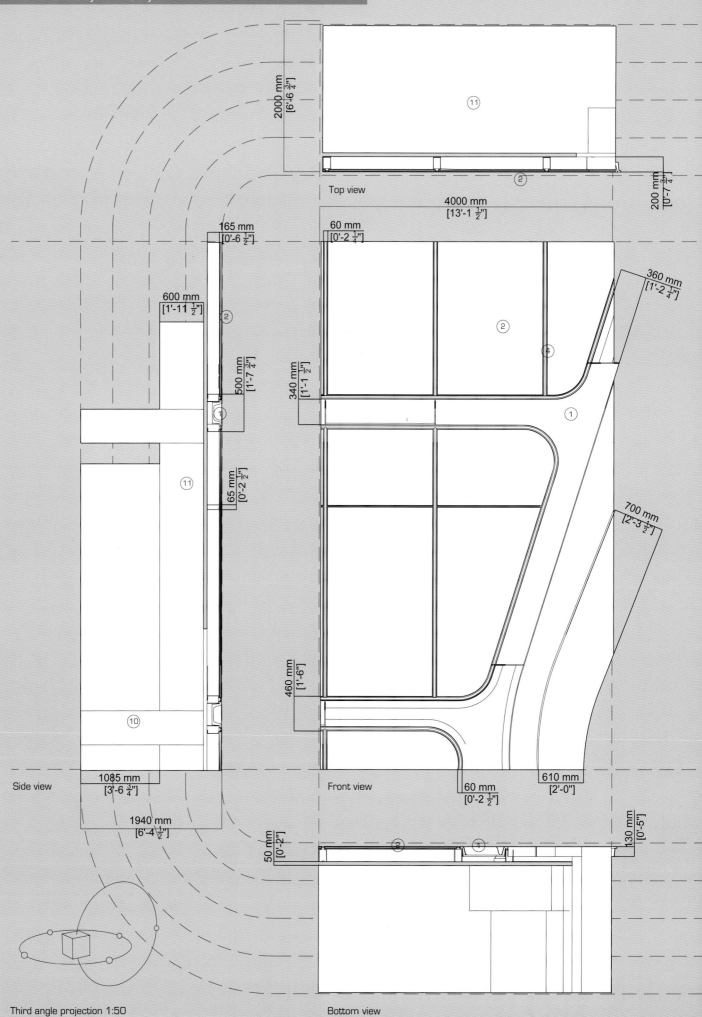

Top view

2000 mm
[6'-6 3/4"]

②

200 mm
[0'-7 3/4"]

165 mm
[0'-6 1/2"]

600 mm
[1'-11 1/2"]

②

500 mm
[1'-7 3/4"]

①

65 mm
[0'-2 1/2"]

⑪

⑩

4000 mm
[13'-1 1/2"]

60 mm
[0'-2 1/4"]

②

360 mm
[1'-2 1/4"]

④

②

①

340 mm
[1'-1 1/2"]

460 mm
[1'-6"]

700 mm
[2'-3 1/2"]

Side view

1085 mm
[3'-6 3/4"]

1940 mm
[6'-4 1/2"]

Front view

60 mm
[0'-2 1/2"]

610 mm
[2'-0"]

50 mm
[0'-2"]

②

①

130 mm
[0'-5"]

Third angle projection 1:50

Bottom view

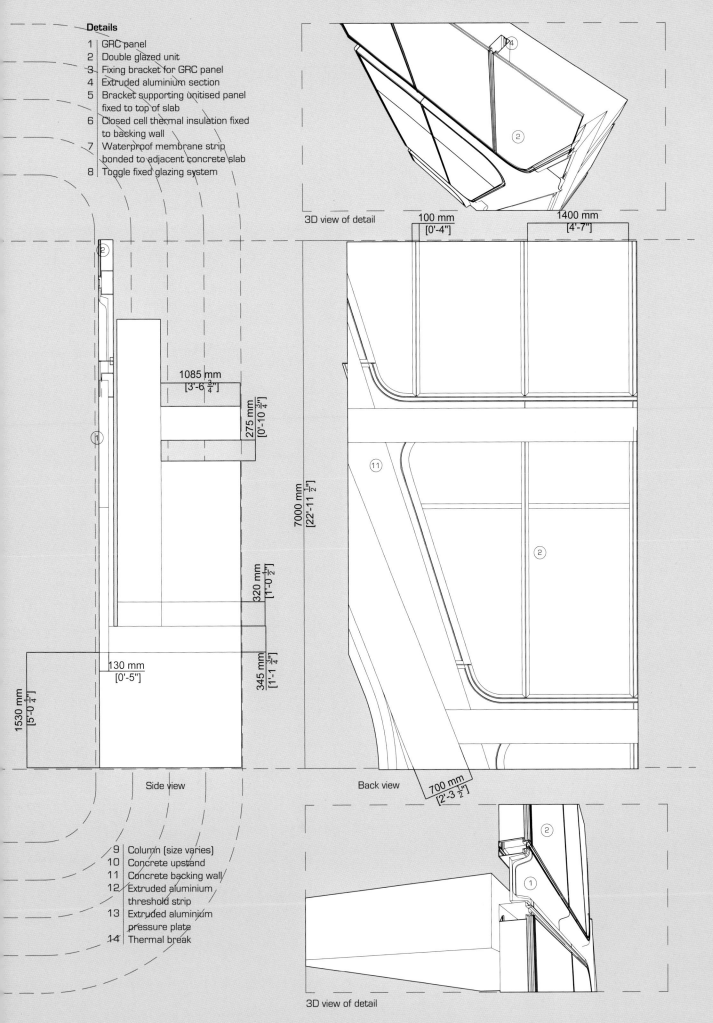

Details

1 | GRC panel
2 | Double glazed unit
3 | Fixing bracket for GRC panel
4 | Extruded aluminium section
5 | Bracket supporting unitised panel
fixed to top of slab
6 | Closed cell thermal insulation fixed
to backing wall
7 | Waterproof membrane strip
bonded to adjacent concrete slab
8 | Toggle fixed glazing system

3D view of detail

100 mm
[0'-4"]

1400 mm
[4'-7"]

1085 mm
[3'-6 3/4"]

275 mm
[0'-10 3/4"]

7000 mm
[22'-11 1/2"]

320 mm
[1'-0 1/2"]

130 mm
[0'-5"]

345 mm
[1'-1 3/4"]

1530 mm
[5'-0 1/4"]

Side view

Back view

700 mm
[2'-3 1/2"]

9 | Column (size varies)
10 | Concrete upstand
11 | Concrete backing wall
12 | Extruded aluminium
threshold strip
13 | Extruded aluminium
pressure plate
14 | Thermal break

3D view of detail

MCCS_169

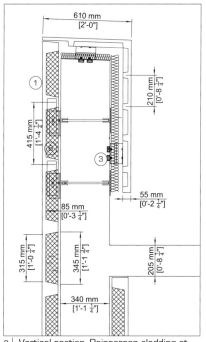

a | Vertical section. Rainscreen cladding at parapet level

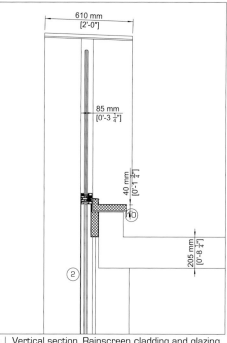

b | Vertical section. Rainscreen cladding and glazing system parapet level

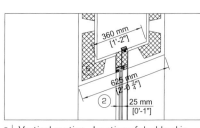

c | Vertical section. Junction of double skin glazing

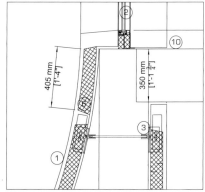

d | Vertical section. Rainscreen cladding at floor slab details

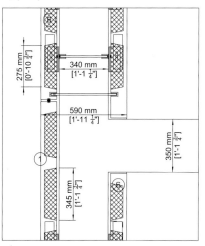

e | Vertical section. Rainscreen cladding at floor slab level

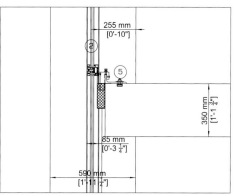

f | Vertical section. Double glazed unit connecting to slab edge

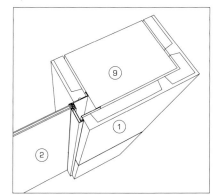

g | 3D views. Double glazed unit

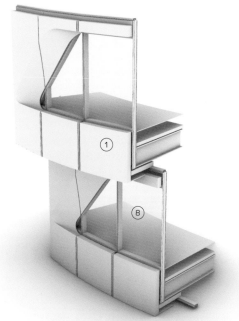

h | Typical bay: 3D view

j | Typical bay: 3D view

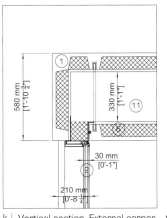

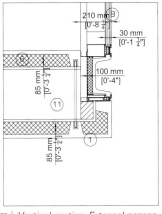

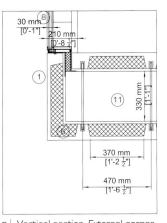

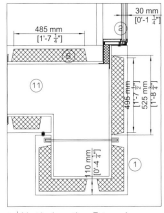

k | Vertical section. External corner

m | Vertical section. External corner

n | Vertical section. External corner

p | Vertical section. External corner

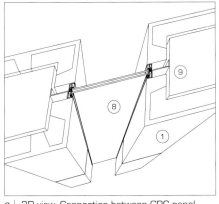

Details

1 | GRC panel
2 | Double glazed unit
3 | Fixing bracket for GRC panel
4 | Extruded aluminium section
5 | Bracket supporting unitised panel fixed to top of slab
6 | Closed cell thermal insulation fixed to backing wall
7 | Waterproof membrane strip bonded to adjacent concrete slab
8 | Toggle fixed glazing system

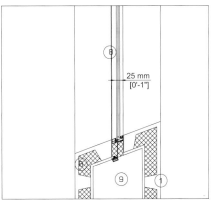

q | 3D view. Connection between GRC panel and insert window

r | Vertical section. Connection between GRC panel and double glazed unit

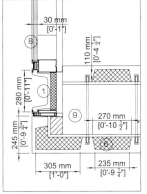

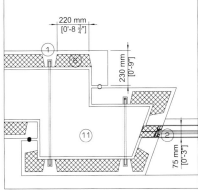

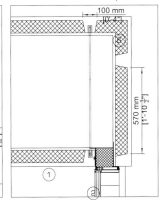

9 | Column (size varies)
10 | Concrete upstand
11 | Concrete backing wall
12 | Extruded aluminium threshold strip
13 | Extruded aluminium pressure plate
14 | Thermal break

s | Horizontal section. External corner

t | Horizontal section. Junction between glazed units and GRC panel

u | Vertical section. External corner

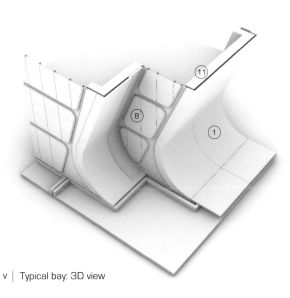

v | Typical bay: 3D view

w | Interior view

MCCS_171

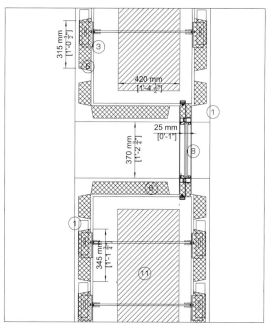

a | Vertical section. Assembly of double glazed unit

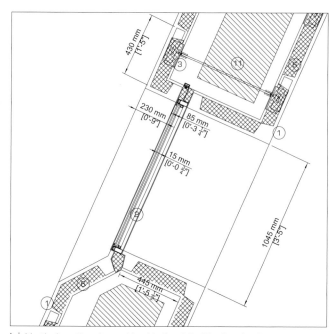

b | Vertical section. Assembly of inclined double glazed unit

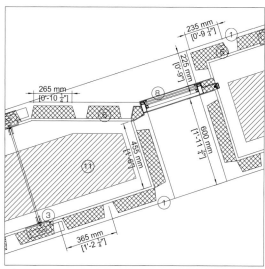

c | Horizontal section. Assembly of double glazed unit

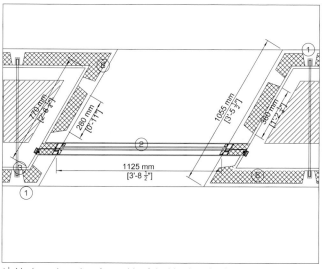

d | Horizontal section. Assembly of double glazed unit

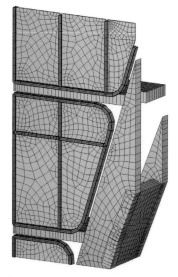

Facade system	FRP open-joint rain-screen with double skin façade
Facade zone	850 mm
Primary structure type	Bundled tube
Secondary structure type	RHS steel sections
Weight of secondary structure (kN/m²)	0.35
Facade bracket type	Spider bracket with two adjustable arms
Number of components in fixing system	10
Weight of facade, including secondary structure (kN/m²)	1.89

e | Finite element model of a typical bay

Compression
-0.57

Tension
0.57

f | Utilization distribution within quadrilateral elements

1:25 scale

1:5 scale

250 500 750 1000 1250 mm

1:25 scale

1:5 scale

50 100 150 200 250 mm

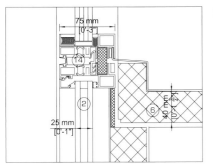

75 mm [0'-3"]

25 mm [0'-1"]

40 mm

(14)

(2)

(6)

g | Vertical section. Double glazed unit

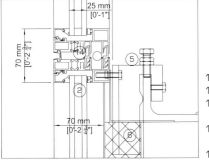

25 mm [0'-1"]

70 mm [0'-2 ¾"]

70 mm [0'-2 ¾"]

(2)

(5)

(6)

h | Vertical section. Double glazed unit

Details

1 | GRC panel
2 | Double glazed unit
3 | Fixing bracket for GRC panel
4 | Extruded aluminium section
5 | Bracket supporting unitised panel fixed to top of slab
6 | Closed cell thermal insulation fixed to backing wall
7 | Waterproof membrane strip bonded to adjacent concrete slab
8 | Toggle fixed glazing system
9 | Column (size varies)
10 | Concrete upstand
11 | Concrete backing wall
12 | Extruded aluminium threshold strip
13 | Extruded aluminium pressure plate
14 | Thermal break

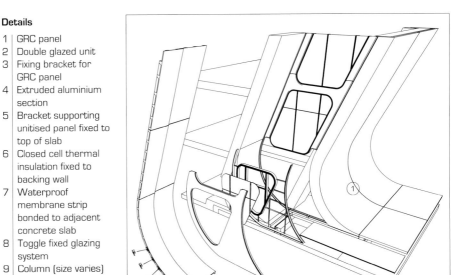

j | 3D view. Exploded view of facade system

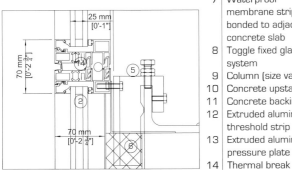

415 mm [1'-4 ½"]

25 mm [0'-1"]

1125 mm [3'-8 ½"]

645 mm [2'-1 ½"]

465 mm [1'-6 ¼"]

k | Horizontal section. Connection between GRC and double glazed unit

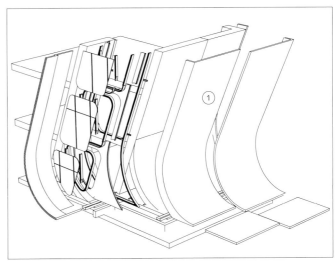

m | 3D view. Exploded view of facade system

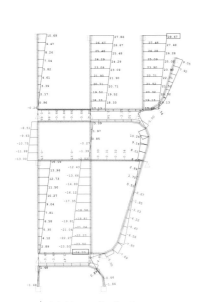

n | Axial force distribution in steel frame [kN]

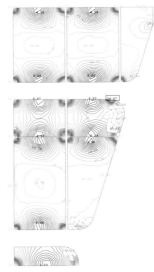

p | Principal shear stress distribution in glazing panels [MPa]

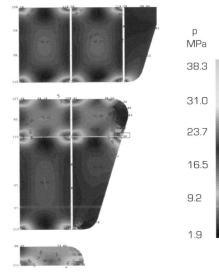

q | Principal tension stress distribution in glazing panels [MPa]

p MPa	q MPa
38.3	65.5
31.0	57.5
23.7	49.5
16.5	41.5
9.2	33.5
1.9	25.5

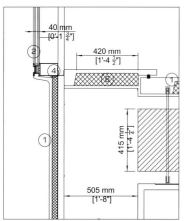

a | Horizontal section. Junction of double glazed unit and GRC panel

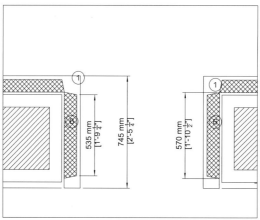

b | Horizontal section. GRC panel

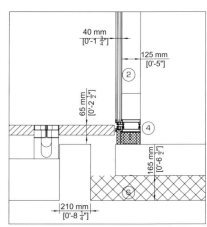

c | Vertical section. Double glazed units at ground level

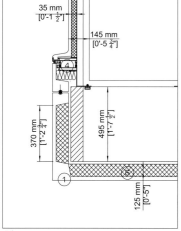

d | Horizontal section. External corner

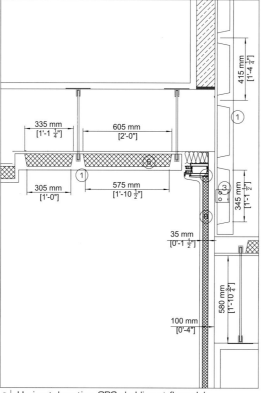

e | Horizontal section. GRC cladding at floor slab

Details

1 | GRC panel
2 | Double glazed unit
3 | Fixing bracket for GRC panel
4 | Extruded aluminium section
5 | Bracket supporting unitised panel fixed to top of slab
6 | Closed cell thermal insulation fixed to backing wall
7 | Waterproof membrane strip bonded to adjacent concrete slab
8 | Toggle fixed glazing system
9 | Column (size varies)
10 | Concrete upstand
11 | Concrete backing wall
12 | Extruded aluminium threshold strip
13 | Extruded aluminium pressure plate
14 | Thermal break

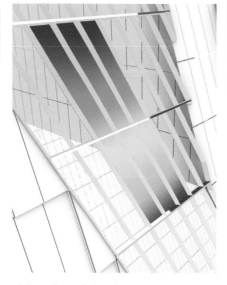

f | Annual cumulative solar radiation analysis on glazed facade with shading system

g | Annual cumulative solar radiation analysis on glazed facade without shading system

Period	1 year
With shading	21.8 MWh
Without shading	36.4MWh
Solar reduction	40%

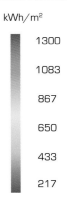

kWh/m²

1300
1083
867
650
433
217

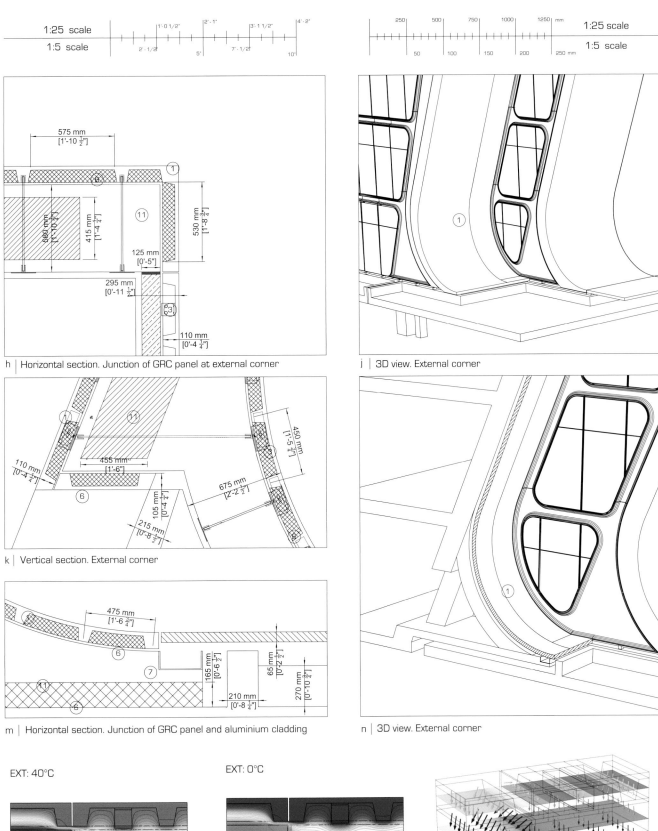

1:25 scale

1:5 scale

1'·0 1/2"   2'·1"   3'·1 1/2"   4'·2"

2'·1/2"   5'   7'·1/2"   10'

250   500   750   1000   1250 mm

50   100   150   200   250

1:25 scale

1:5 scale

575 mm
[1'-10 1/2"]

680 mm
[2'-2 3/4"]

415 mm
[1'-4 1/4"]

530 mm
[1'-8 3/4"]

125 mm
[0'-5"]

295 mm
[0'-11 1/2"]

110 mm
[0'-4 1/4"]

h | Horizontal section. Junction of GRC panel at external corner

j | 3D view. External corner

110 mm
[0'-4 1/4"]

455 mm
[1'-6"]

450 mm
[1'-5 3/4"]

675 mm
[2'-2 1/2"]

105 mm
[0'-4 1/4"]

215 mm
[0'-8 1/2"]

k | Vertical section. External corner

475 mm
[1'-6 3/4"]

165 mm
[0'-6 1/2"]

65 mm
[0'-2 1/2"]

270 mm
[0'-10 3/4"]

210 mm
[0'-8 1/4"]

m | Horizontal section. Junction of GRC panel and aluminium cladding

n | 3D view. External corner

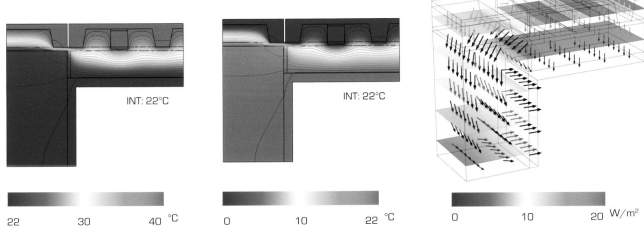

EXT: 40°C

EXT: 0°C

INT: 22°C

INT: 22°C

22   30   40 °C

0   10   22 °C

0   10   20 W/m²

p | Thermal performance analysis of UHPC panels supported by concrete
Isotherms showing temperature distribution across assembly

q | Thermal performance analysis of panels supported by
concrete. Total energy flux across assembly varies

a | 3D exploded view showing glazing panel fixed to
aluminium frame

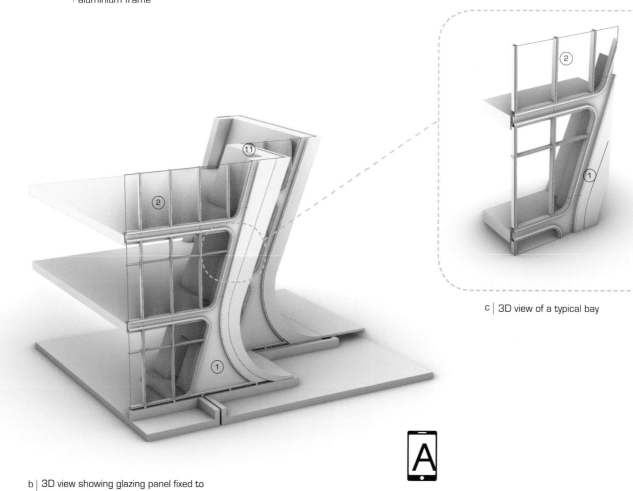

c | 3D view of a typical bay

b | 3D view showing glazing panel fixed to
aluminium frame

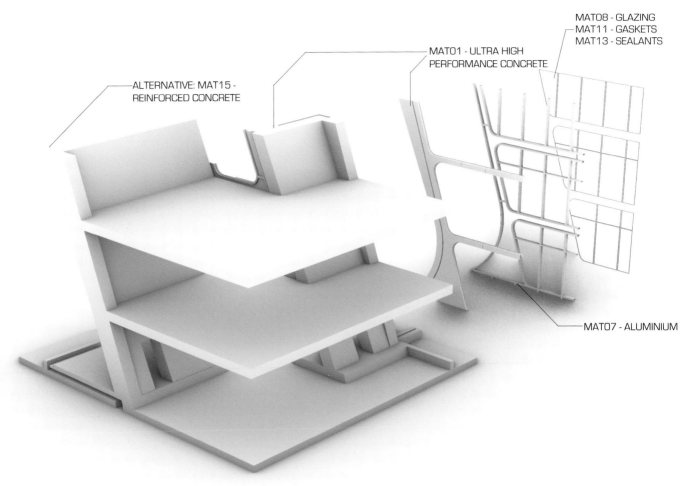

ALTERNATIVE: MAT15 -
REINFORCED CONCRETE

MAT01 - ULTRA HIGH
PERFORMANCE CONCRETE

MAT08 - GLAZING
MAT11 - GASKETS
MAT13 - SEALANTS

MAT07 - ALUMINIUM

d | 3D exploded view of facade components with
material specification references

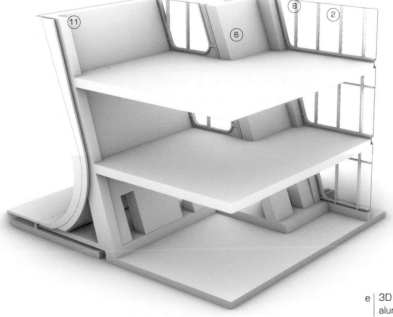

Details

1 | GRC panel
2 | Double glazed unit
3 | Fixing bracket for GRC panel
4 | Extruded aluminium section
5 | Bracket supporting unitised panel
fixed to top of slab
6 | Closed cell thermal insulation fixed
to backing wall
7 | Waterproof membrane strip
bonded to adjacent concrete slab
8 | Toggle fixed glazing system
9 | Column (size varies)
10 | Concrete upstand
11 | Concrete backing wall
12 | Extruded aluminium threshold strip
13 | Extruded aluminium pressure plate
14 | Thermal break

e | 3D view showing glazing panel fixed to
aluminium frame

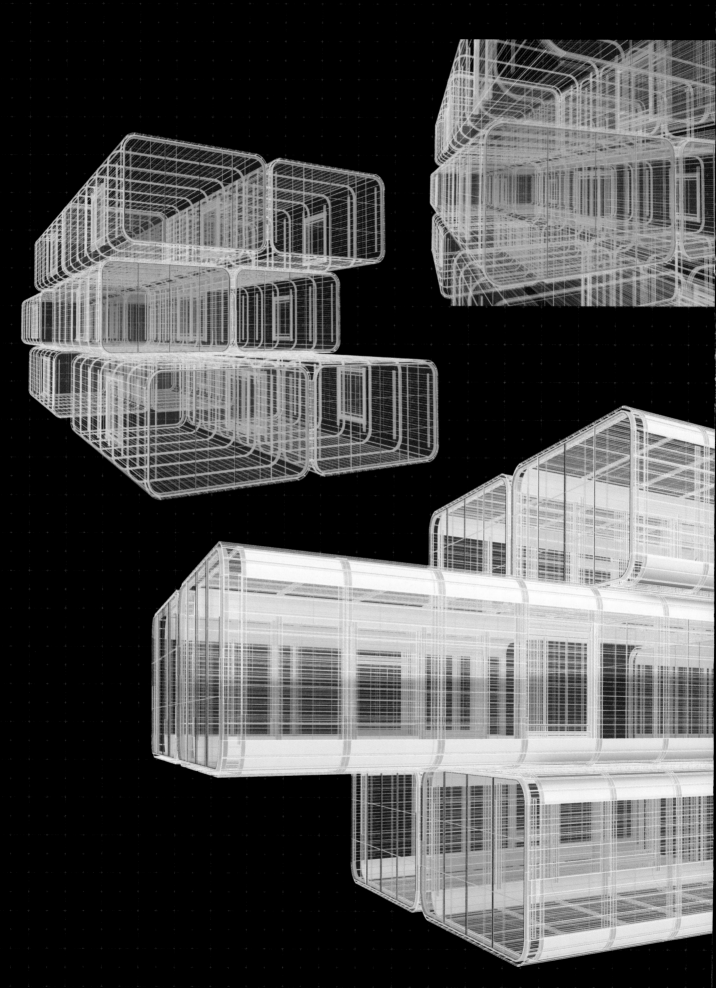

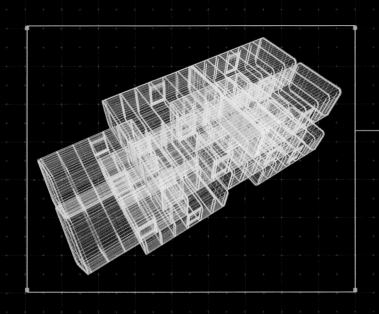

MIXED-USE DESIGN DISTRICT

HONG KONG

22°18'9.7596"   N
114°10'37.9776"   E

ARCHITECT
NEWTECNIC

STRUCTURAL ENGINEERING
NEWTECNIC

MEP ENGINEERING
NEWTECNIC

FACADE ENGINEERING
NEWTECNIC

STRUCTURAL   FACADE   MEP   ENVIRONMENTAL   TESTING

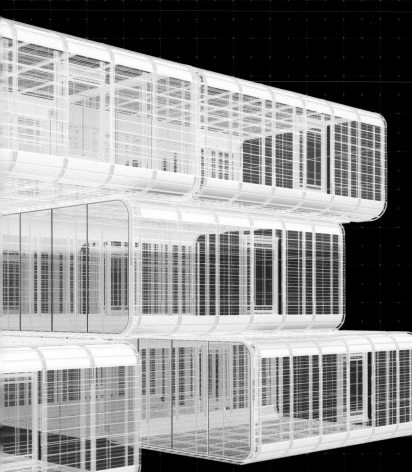

FACADE ZONE (mm)	270	
WEIGHT OF SECONDARY STRUCTURE (kN/m2)	0.04	
TOTAL WEIGHT OF FACADE (kN/m2)	0.35	
U-VALUE (W/m2K)	0.38	

PRIMARY STRUCTURE TYPE
STRUCTURAL TIMBER FRAME

SECONDARY STRUCTURE TYPE
TIMBER BATTENS

FACADE BRACKET TYPE
SERRATED PLATES

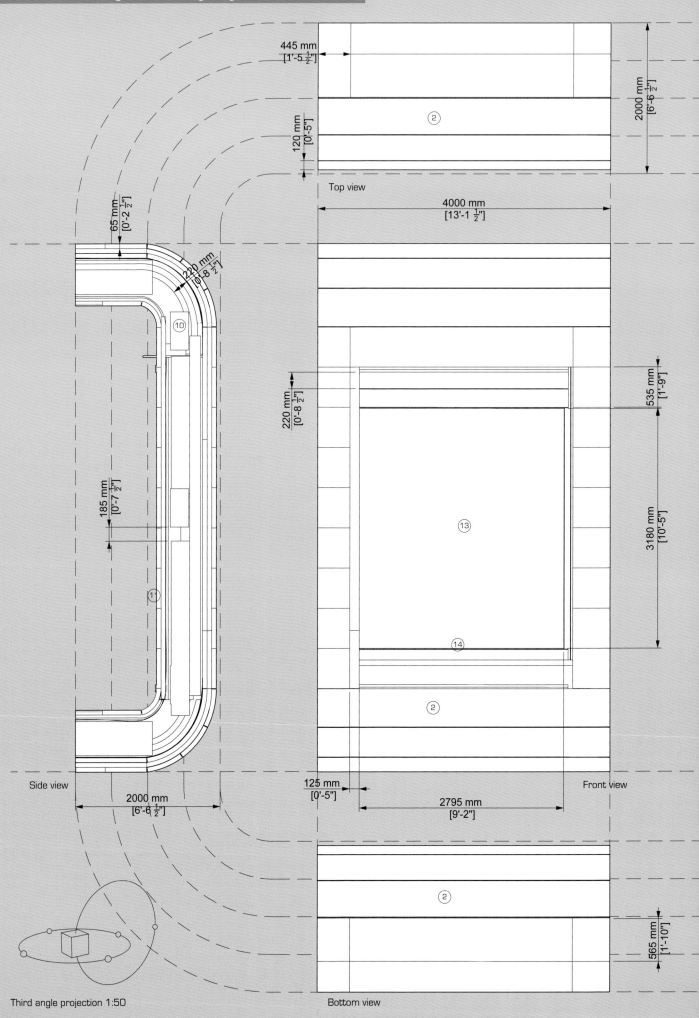

445 mm
[1'-5 ½"]

2000 mm
[6'-6 ½"]

120 mm
[0'-5"]

Top view

4000 mm
[13'-1 ½"]

65 mm
[0'-2 ½"]

220 mm
[0'-8 ½"]

220 mm
[0'-8 ½"]

535 mm
[1'-9"]

185 mm
[0'-7 ½"]

3180 mm
[10'-5"]

Side view

2000 mm
[6'-6 ½"]

125 mm
[0'-5"]

2795 mm
[9'-2"]

Front view

565 mm
[1'-10"]

Bottom view

Third angle projection 1:50

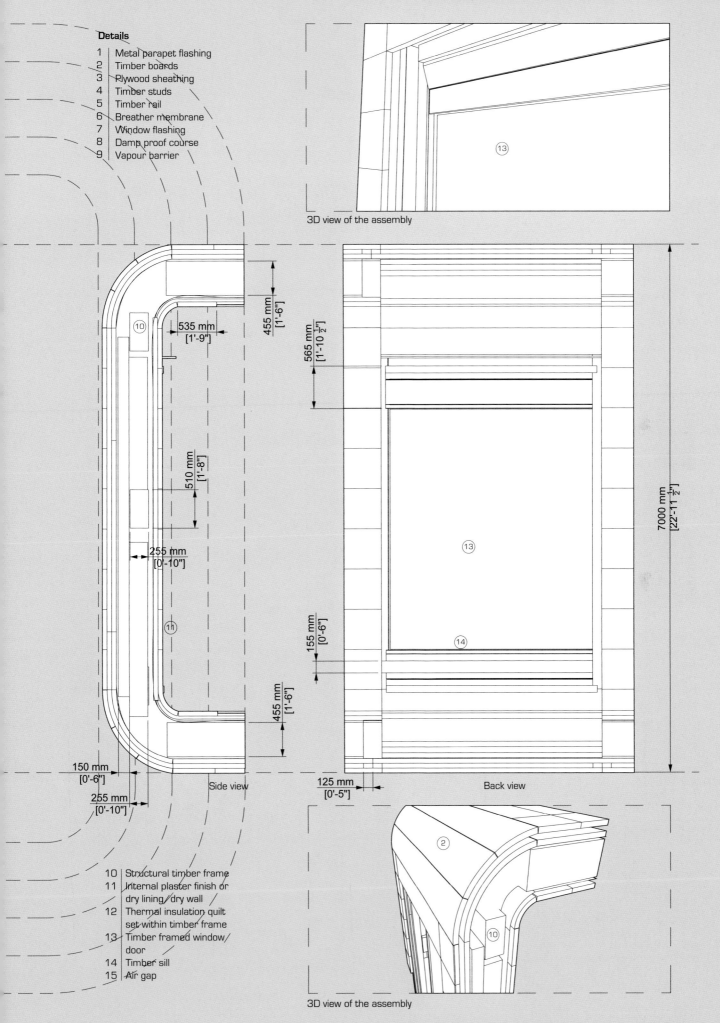

Details

1	Metal parapet flashing
2	Timber boards
3	Plywood sheathing
4	Timber studs
5	Timber rail
6	Breather membrane
7	Window flashing
8	Damp proof course
9	Vapour barrier

455 mm
[1'-6"]

535 mm
[1'-9"]

565 mm
[1'-10 $\frac{1}{2}$"]

510 mm
[1'-8"]

255 mm
[0'-10"]

7000 mm
[22'-11 $\frac{1}{2}$"]

155 mm
[0'-6"]

455 mm
[1'-6"]

150 mm
[0'-6"]

Side view

255 mm
[0'-10"]

125 mm
[0'-5"]

Back view

10	Structural timber frame
11	Internal plaster finish or dry lining / dry wall
12	Thermal insulation quilt set within timber frame
13	Timber framed window / door
14	Timber sill
15	Air gap

3D view of the assembly

3D view of the assembly

MCCS_183

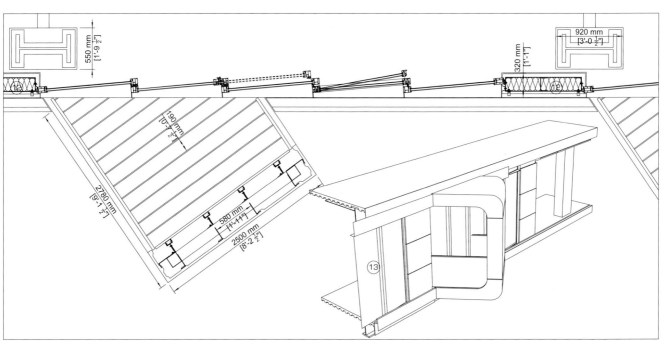

a │ Horizontal section and 3D view. Connection between glazing and primary structure

Details

1	Metal parapet flashing
2	Timber boards
3	Plywood sheathing
4	Timber studs
5	Timber rail
6	Breather membrane
7	Window flashing
8	Damp proof course
9	Vapour barrier
10	Structural timber frame
11	Internal plaster finish or dry lining/dry wall
12	Thermal insulation quilt set within timber frame
13	Timber framed window/door
14	Timber sill
15	Air gap

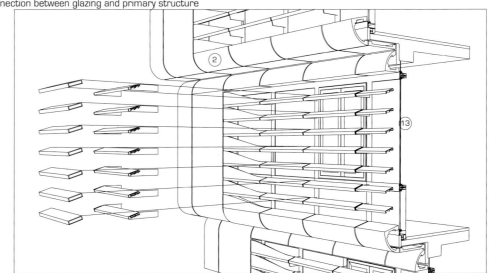

b │ 3D view. Exploded view showing louvre and supporting system

c │ Interior view

d │ Typical bay. 3D view

1:50 scale

1:10 scale

2'- 1"   4'- 2"   6'- 3"   8'- 4"

5"   10"   1'- 3"   1'- 8"

500   1000   1500   2000   2500 mm

100   200   300   400   500 mm

1:50 scale

1:10 scale

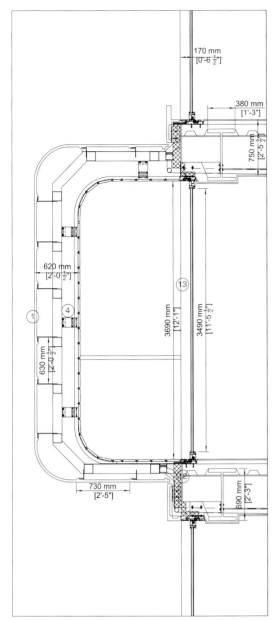

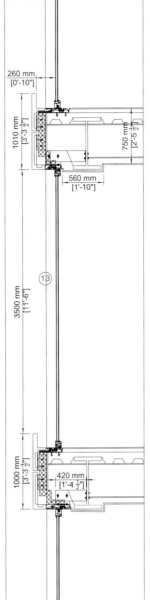

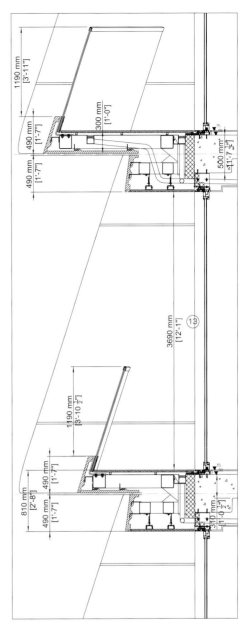

e | Vertical section. Rainscreen assembly   f | Vertical section. Glazing system   g | Vertical section. Glazing and panel at floor slab

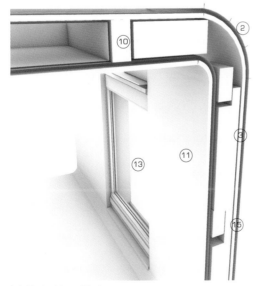

h | Typical bay. 3D view

j | Exterior view

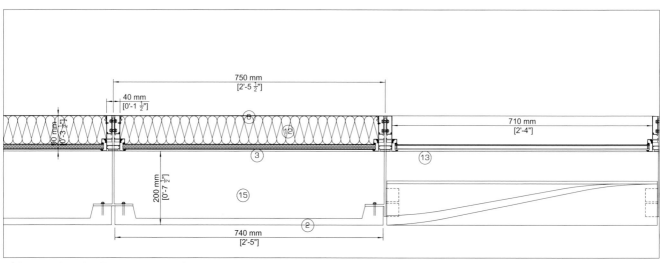

a | Horizontal section. Facade assembly of panel and glazing system

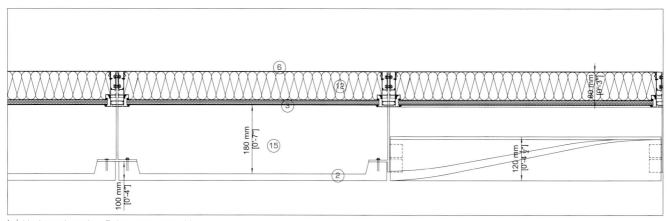

b | Horizontal section. Rainscreen assembly

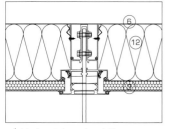

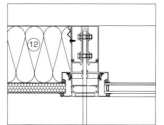

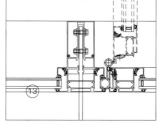

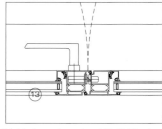

c | Horizontal section 1:5. Connection between insulated panels

d | Horizontal section 1:5. Connection between panel and glazing

e | Horizontal section 1:5. Unitised double glazed unit

f | Horizontal section 1:5. Unitised double glazed unit

Facade system	Timber boards with stick glazing
Facade zone	270mm
Primary structure type	Structural timber frame
Secondary structure type	Timber battens
Weight of secondary structure (kN/m²)	0.04
Facade bracket type	Serrated plates
Number of components in fixing system	2
Weight of facade, including secondary structure (kN/m²)	0.35

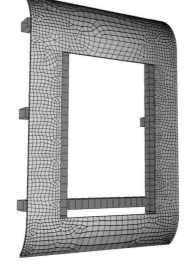

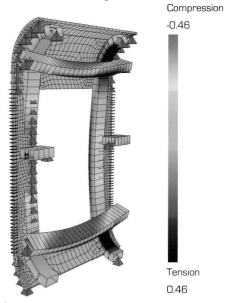

Compression

-0.46

Tension

0.46

g | Finite element model of a typical bay

h | Utilization distribution within quadrilateral elements

Details

1 | Metal parapet flashing
2 | Timber boards
3 | Plywood sheathing
4 | Timber studs
5 | Timber rail
6 | Breather membrane

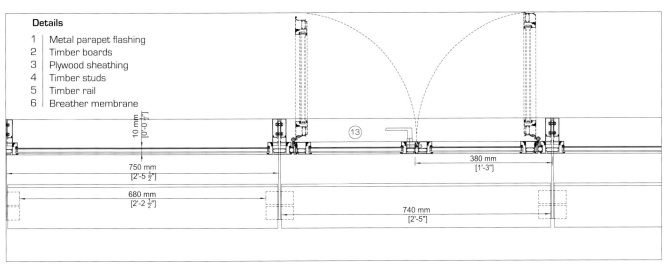

j | Horizontal section. Rainscreen assembly of cladding and window system

7 | Window flashing
8 | Damp proof course
9 | Vapour barrier
10 | Structural timber frame
11 | Internal plaster finish or dry lining/dry wall

12 | Thermal insulation quilt set within timber frame
13 | Timber framed window/door
14 | Timber sill
15 | Air gap

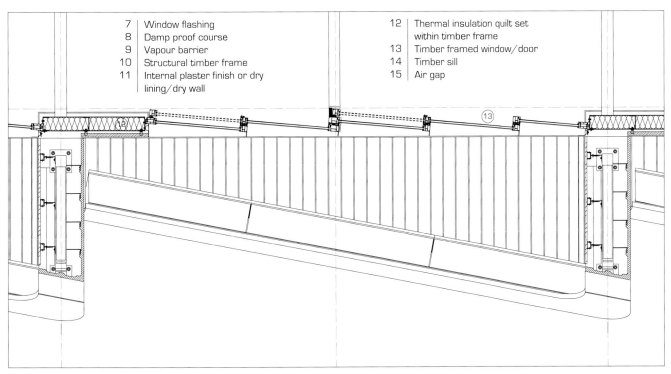

k | Horizontal section. Rainscreen assembly of cladding and glazing system

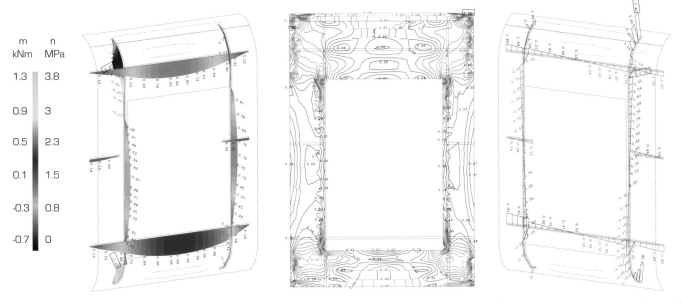

m | Bending moment distribution in timber frame [kNm]   n | Shear stress distribution in cladding [MPa]   p | Shear force distribution in timber frame [kN]

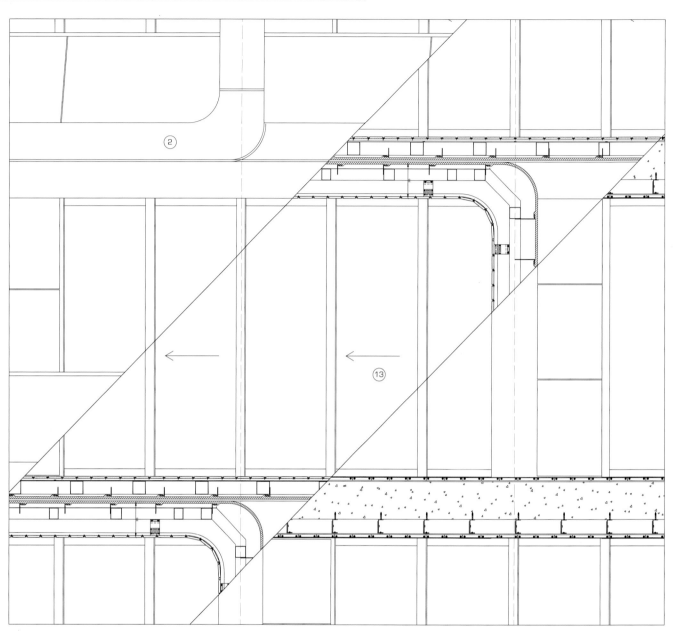

a │ Elevation view of facade buildup

Period	With shading	Without shading	Solar reduction
1 year	14.8 MWh	16.8 MWh	12%

kWh/m²

600

500

400

300

200

100

b │ Top left: Annual cumulative solar radiation analysis on glazed facade with shading system

c │ Top right: Annual cumulative solar radiation analysis on glazed facade without shading system

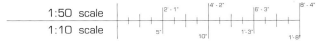

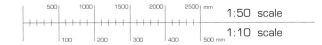

Details

1	Metal parapet flashing
2	Timber boards
3	Plywood sheathing
4	Timber studs
5	Timber rail
6	Breather membrane
7	Window flashing
8	Damp proof course
9	Vapour barrier
10	Structural timber frame
11	Internal plaster finish or dry lining/dry wall
12	Thermal insulation quilt set within timber frame
13	Timber framed window/door
14	Timber sill
15	Air gap

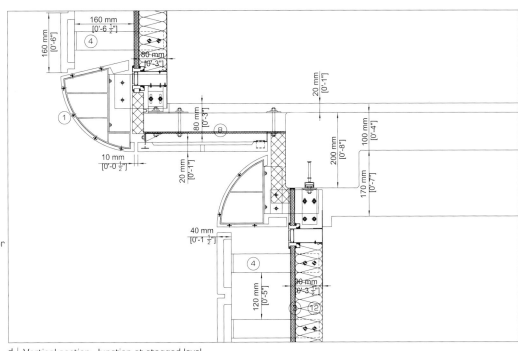

d | Vertical section. Junction at stagged level

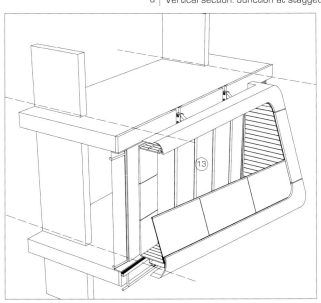

e | 3D view. External view of balcony

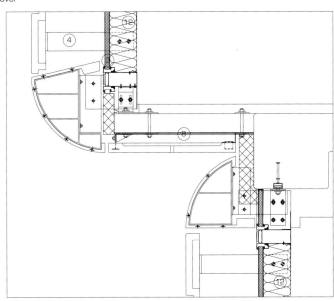

f | Vertical section. Junction at stagged level

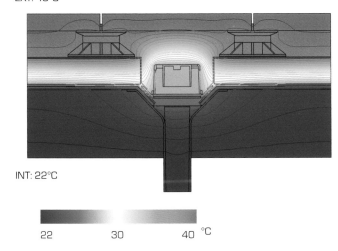

EXT: 40°C

INT: 22°C

g | Thermal performance analysis of a timber panel fixing system
Isotherms showing temperature distribution across assembly

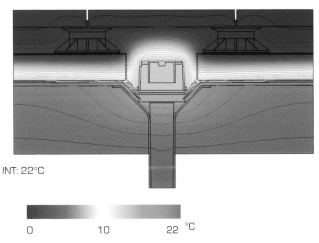

EXT: 0°C

INT: 22°C

h | Thermal performance analysis of a timber panel fixing system
Isotherms showing temperature distribution across assembly

a │ 3D exploded view showing rainscreen
cladding and window assembly

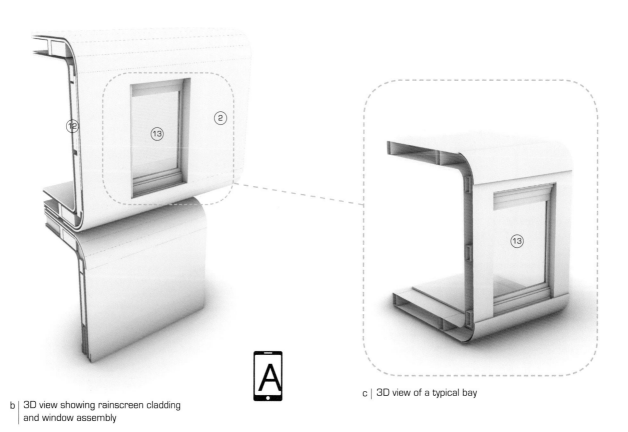

b │ 3D view showing rainscreen cladding
and window assembly

c │ 3D view of a typical bay

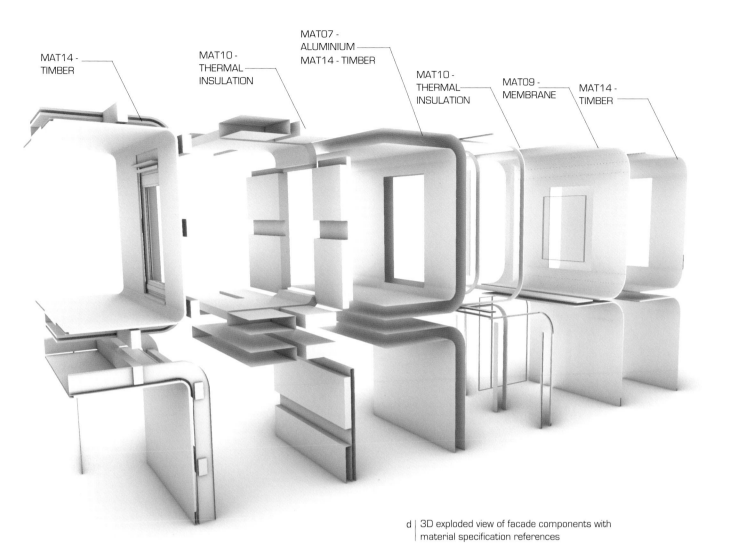

MAT14 -
TIMBER

MAT10 -
THERMAL
INSULATION

MAT07 -
ALUMINIUM
MAT14 - TIMBER

MAT10 -
THERMAL
INSULATION

MAT09 -
MEMBRANE

MAT14 -
TIMBER

d | 3D exploded view of facade components with
material specification references

e | 3D view showing rainscreen cladding
and window assembly

Details

1	Metal parapet flashing
2	Timber boards
3	Plywood sheathing
4	Timber studs
5	Timber rail
6	Breather membrane
7	Window flashing
8	Damp proof course
9	Vapour barrier
10	Structural timber frame
11	Internal plaster finish or dry lining/dry wall
12	Thermal insulation quilt set within timber frame
13	Timber framed window/door
14	Timber sill
15	Air gap

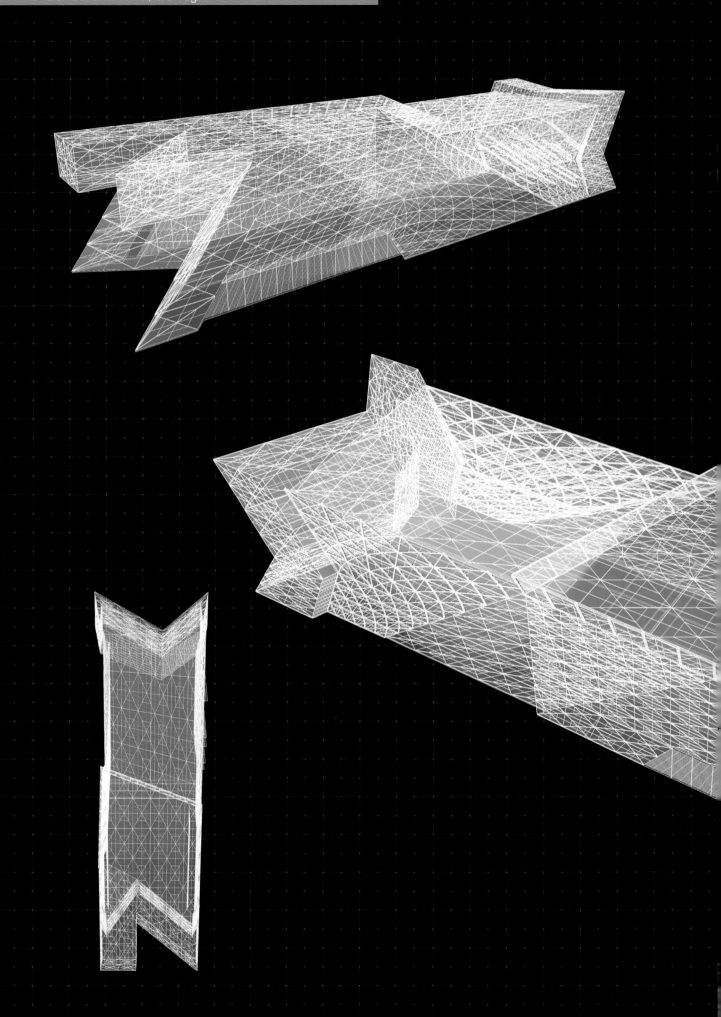

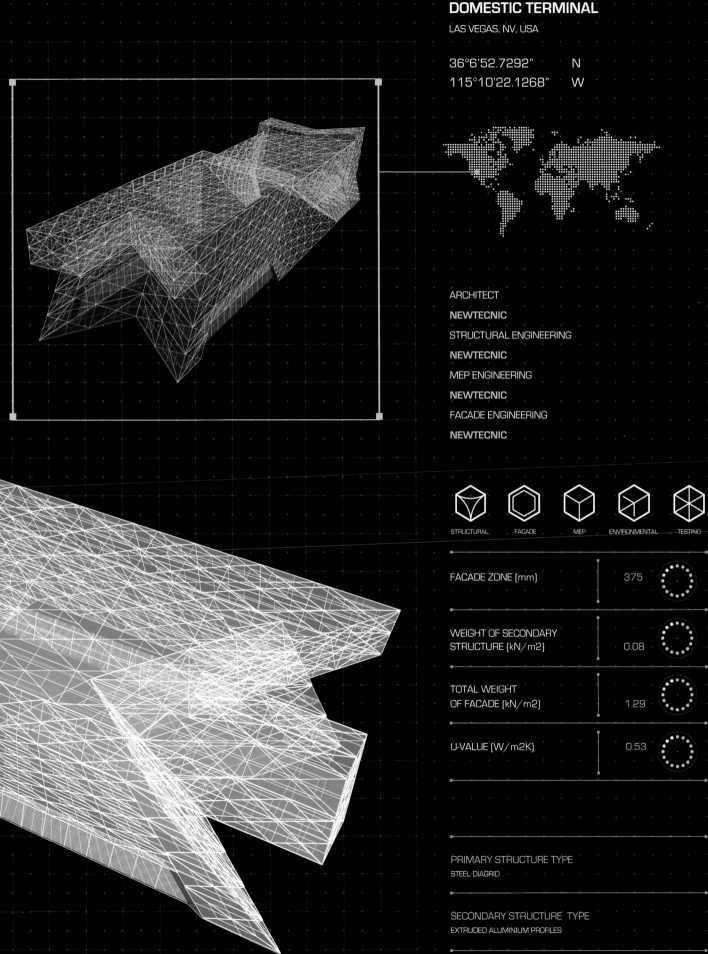

DOMESTIC TERMINAL

LAS VEGAS, NV, USA

36°6'52.7292"   N
115°10'22.1268"   W

ARCHITECT
NEWTECNIC
STRUCTURAL ENGINEERING
NEWTECNIC
MEP ENGINEERING
NEWTECNIC
FACADE ENGINEERING
NEWTECNIC

STRUCTURAL	FACADE	MEP	ENVIRONMENTAL	TESTING

FACADE ZONE (mm)	375	
WEIGHT OF SECONDARY STRUCTURE (kN/m2)	0.08	
TOTAL WEIGHT OF FACADE (kN/m2)	1.29	
U-VALUE (W/m2K)	0.53	

PRIMARY STRUCTURE TYPE
STEEL-DIAGRID

SECONDARY STRUCTURE TYPE
EXTRUDED ALUMINIUM PROFILES

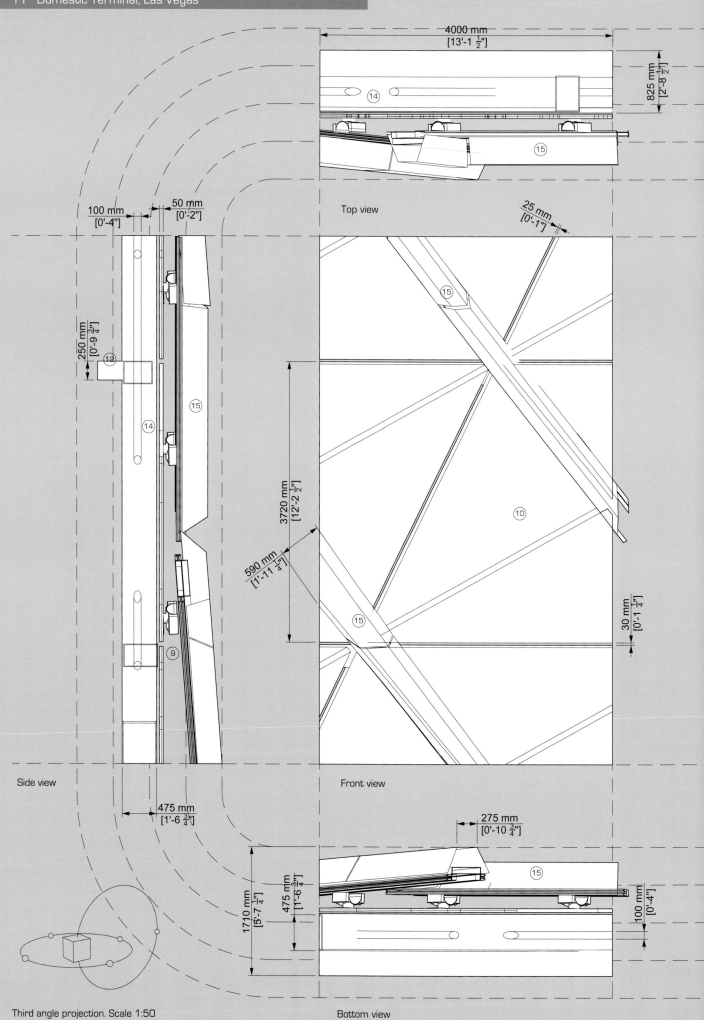

4000 mm
[13'-1 $\frac{1}{2}$"]

825 mm
[2'-8 $\frac{1}{2}$"]

14

15

Top view

25 mm
[0'-1"]

100 mm
[0'-4"]

50 mm
[0'-2"]

250 mm
[0'-9 $\frac{3}{4}$"]

12

15

14

9

15

3720 mm
[12'-2 $\frac{1}{2}$"]

590 mm
[1'-11 $\frac{1}{4}$"]

15

10

30 mm
[0'-1 $\frac{1}{4}$"]

Side view

Front view

475 mm
[1'-6 $\frac{3}{4}$"]

275 mm
[0'-10 $\frac{3}{4}$"]

15

1710 mm
[5'-7 $\frac{1}{4}$"]

475 mm
[1'-6 $\frac{3}{4}$"]

100 mm
[0'-4"]

Third angle projection. Scale 1:50

Bottom view

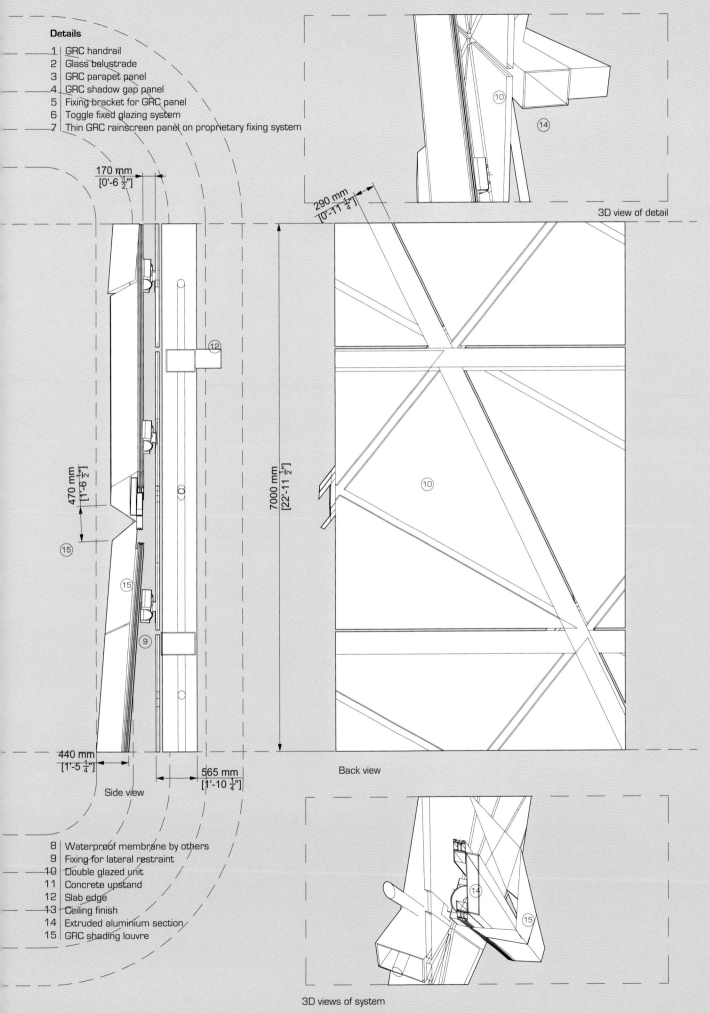

Details

1 GRC handrail
2 Glass balustrade
3 GRC parapet panel
4 GRC shadow gap panel
5 Fixing bracket for GRC panel
6 Toggle fixed glazing system
7 Thin GRC rainscreen panel on proprietary fixing system

170 mm
[0'-6 ½"]

290 mm
[0'-11 ¼"]

3D view of detail

470 mm
[1'-6 ½"]

7000 mm
[22'-11 ½"]

440 mm
[1'-5 ¼"]

565 mm
[1'-10 ¼"]

Side view

Back view

8 Waterproof membrane by others
9 Fixing for lateral restraint
10 Double glazed unit
11 Concrete upstand
12 Slab edge
13 Ceiling finish
14 Extruded aluminium section
15 GRC shading louvre

3D views of system

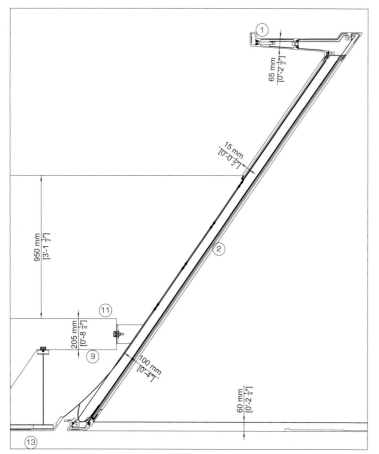

a | Vertical section. Glass balustrade connection to slab edge

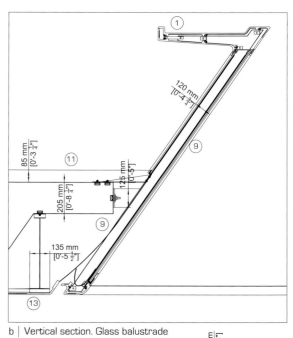

b | Vertical section. Glass balustrade

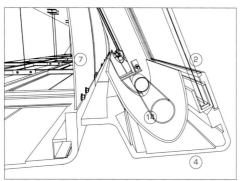

c | 3D view. Soffit detail of glass balustrade

d | Vertical section. Balustrade with thin GRC panels

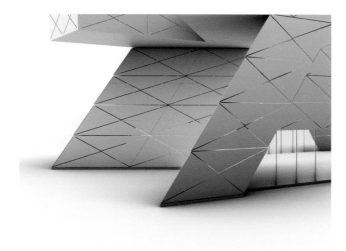

e | Exterior view

f | Interior view

1:25 scale

1:5 scale

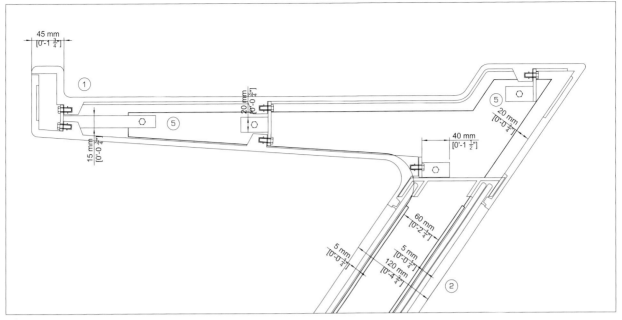

45 mm
[0'-1 ¾"]

20 mm
[0'-0 ¾"]

15 mm
[0'-0 ¾"]

40 mm
[0'-1 ½"]

20 mm
[0'-0 ¾"]

60 mm
[0'-2 ¼"]

5 mm
[0'-0 ¼"]

5 mm
[0'-0 ¼"]

120 mm
[0'-4 ¾"]

① ② ⑤

g | Vertical section. GRC handrail detail

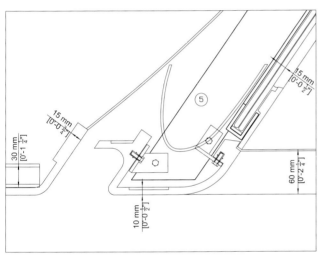

15 mm
[0'-0 ¾"]

15 mm
[0'-0 ¾"]

30 mm
[0'-1 ¼"]

60 mm
[0'-2 ¼"]

10 mm
[0'-0 ½"]

⑤

h | Vertical section. Soffit detail of glass balustrade

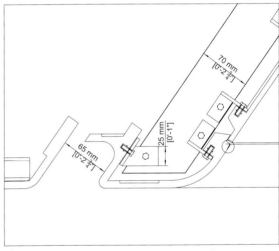

70 mm
[0'-2 ¾"]

65 mm
[0'-2 ¾"]

25 mm
[0'-1"]

⑦

j | Vertical section. Soffit detail of glass balustrade

④

k | Typical bay. 3D view

Details

1 | GRC handrail
2 | Glass balustrade
3 | GRC parapet panel
4 | GRC shadow gap panel
5 | Fixing bracket for GRC panel
6 | Toggle fixed glazing system
7 | Thin GRC rainscreen panel on proprietary fixing system
8 | Waterproof membrane by others
9 | Fixing for lateral restraint
10 | Double glazed unit
11 | Concrete upstand
12 | Slab edge
13 | Ceiling finish
14 | Extruded aluminium section
15 | GRC shading louvre

⑩

⑦

m | Typical bay. 3D view

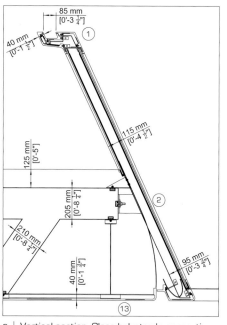

a | Vertical section. Glass balustrade connection to slab edge

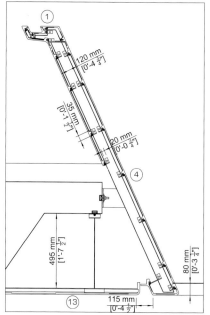

b | Vertical section. Balustrade with thin GRC panels

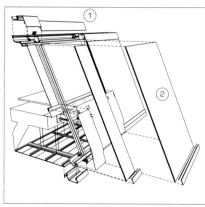

c | 3D view. Exploded components of glass balustrade

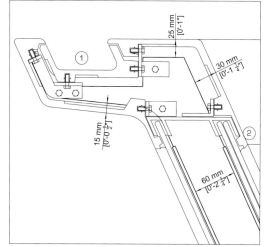

d | Vertical section. GRC handrail detail

e | Vertical section. GRC handrail detail

Details

1 | GRC handrail
2 | Glass balustrade
3 | GRC parapet panel
4 | GRC shadow gap panel
5 | Fixing bracket for GRC panel
6 | Toggle fixed glazing system
7 | Thin GRC rainscreen panel on proprietary fixing system
8 | Waterproof membrane by others
9 | Fixing for lateral restraint
10 | Double glazed unit
11 | Concrete upstand
12 | Slab edge
13 | Ceiling finish
14 | Extruded aluminium section
15 | GRC shading louvre

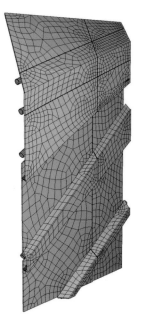

f | Finite element model of a typical bay

Facade system	Sprayed GRC used as permanent formwork
Facade zone	375mm
Primary structure type	Steel diagrid
Secondary structure type	Extruded aluminium profiles
Weight of secondary structure [kN/m²]	0.08
Facade bracket type	Spider bracket with four adjustable arms
Number of components in fixing system	8
Weight of facade, including secondary structure [kN/m²]	1.29

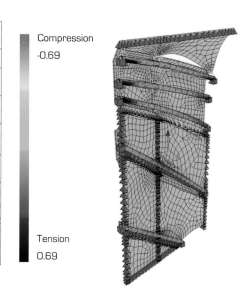

Compression
-0.69

Tension
0.69

g | Utilization distribution within quadrilateral elements

1:25 scale

1:5 scale

1:25 scale

1:5 scale

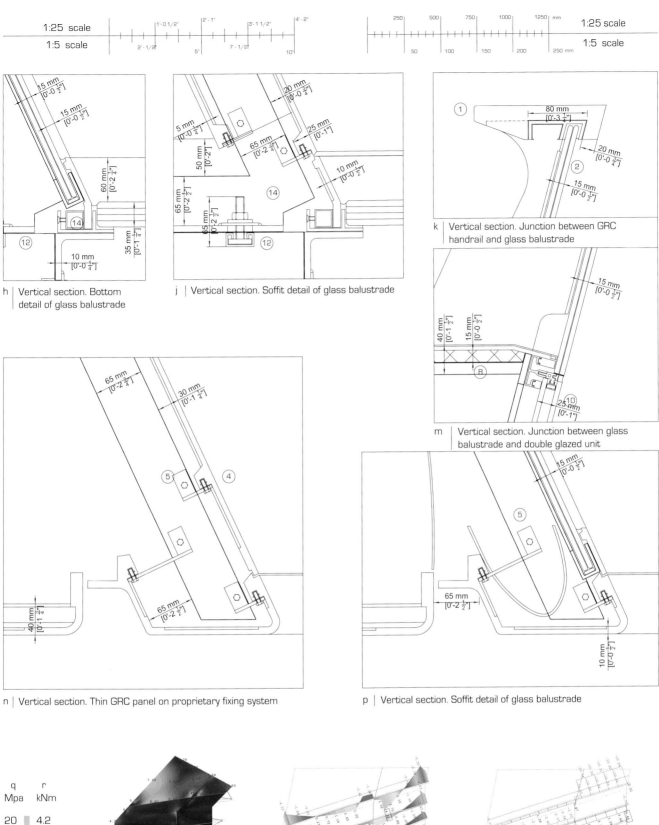

h | Vertical section. Bottom detail of glass balustrade

j | Vertical section. Soffit detail of glass balustrade

k | Vertical section. Junction between GRC handrail and glass balustrade

m | Vertical section. Junction between glass balustrade and double glazed unit

n | Vertical section. Thin GRC panel on proprietary fixing system

p | Vertical section. Soffit detail of glass balustrade

q | Principal tension stress distribution in glazing and opaque panels [MPa]

r | Bending moment distribution in Aluminum frame [kNm]

s | Axial force distribution in steel frame [kN]

q
Mpa

20
16
12
8
4
0

r
kNm

4.2
1.6
-0.6
-2.8
-5
-7.2

MCCS_201

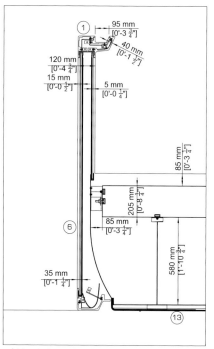

a | Vertical section. Glass balustrade

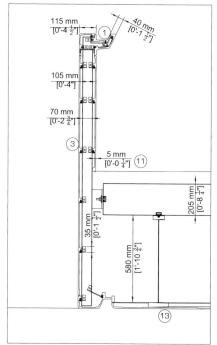

b | Vertical section. Glass balustrade

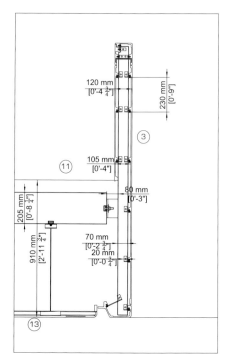

c | Vertical section. Parapet

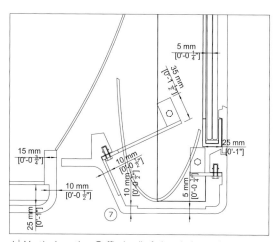

d | Vertical section. Soffit detail of glass balustrade

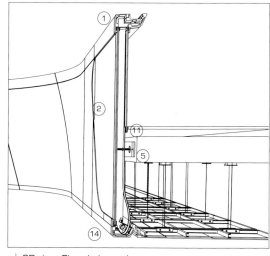

e | 3D view. Glass balustrade

f | Annual cumulative solar radiation analysis on glazed facade with shading system

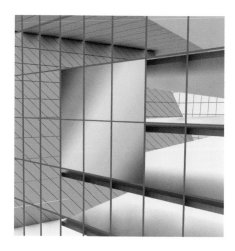

g | Annual cumulative solar radiation analysis on glazed facade without shading system

kWh/m²

1300
1083
867
650
433
217

Period	1 year
With shading	24.1 MWh
Without shading	36.4 MWh
Solar reduction	34%

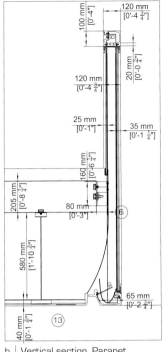

h | Vertical section. Parapet

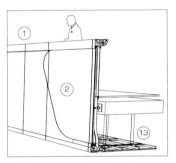

m | 3D view. Glass balustrade

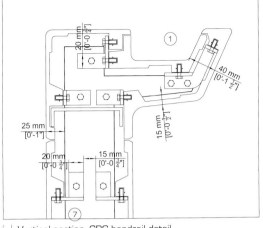

j | Vertical section. GRC handrail detail

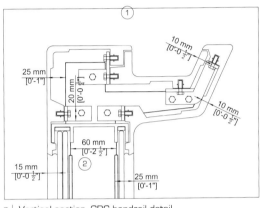

n | Vertical section. GRC handrail detail

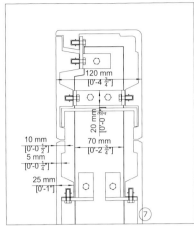

k | Vertical section. Thin GRC panel on proprietary fixing system

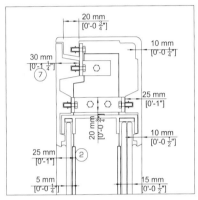

p | Vertical section. Thin GRC panel on proprietary fixing system

Details

1 | GRC handrail
2 | Glass balustrade
3 | GRC parapet panel
4 | GRC shadow gap panel
5 | Fixing bracket for GRC panel
6 | Toggle fixed glazing system
7 | Thin GRC rainscreen panel on proprietary fixing system
8 | Waterproof membrane by others
9 | Fixing for lateral restraint
10 | Double glazed unit
11 | Concrete upstand
12 | Slab edge
13 | Ceiling finish
14 | Extruded aluminium section
15 | GRC shading louvre

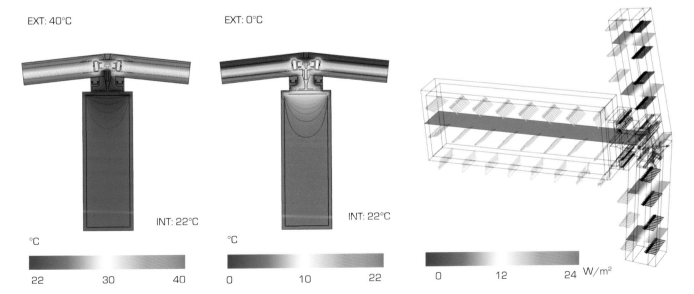

q | Thermal performance analysis of a unitised curtain wall mullion
| Isotherms showing temperature distribution across assembly

r | Thermal performance analysis of a unitised curtain wall mullion
| Total energy flux across assembly varies at different sections

MCCS_203

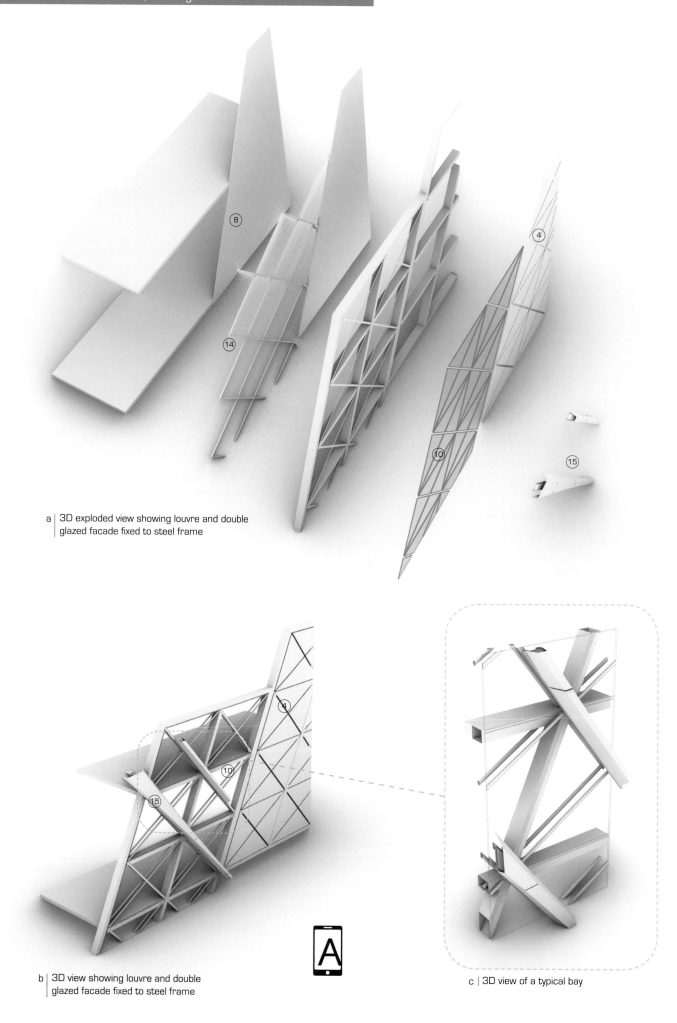

a | 3D exploded view showing louvre and double
glazed facade fixed to steel frame

b | 3D view showing louvre and double
glazed facade fixed to steel frame

c | 3D view of a typical bay

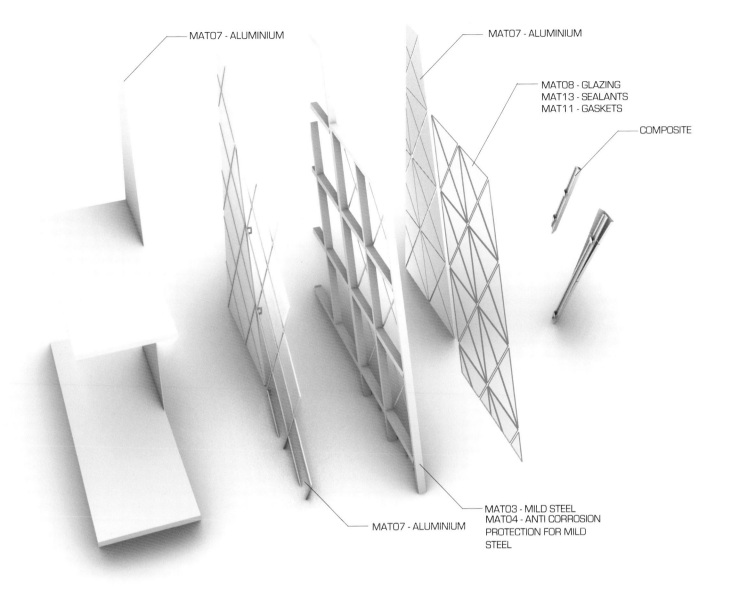

MAT07 - ALUMINIUM

MAT07 - ALUMINIUM

MAT08 - GLAZING
MAT13 - SEALANTS
MAT11 - GASKETS

COMPOSITE

MAT03 - MILD STEEL
MAT04 - ANTI CORROSION
PROTECTION FOR MILD
STEEL

MAT07 - ALUMINIUM

d | 3D exploded view showing facade components
  | with material specification references

Details

1 | GRC handrail
2 | Glass balustrade
3 | GRC parapet panel
4 | GRC shadow gap panel
5 | Fixing bracket for GRC panel
6 | Toggle fixed glazing system
7 | Thin GRC rainscreen panel on
  | proprietary fixing system
8 | Waterproof membrane by others
9 | Fixing for lateral restraint
10 | Double glazed unit
11 | Concrete upstand
12 | Slab edge
13 | Ceiling finish
14 | Extruded aluminium section
15 | GRC shading louvre

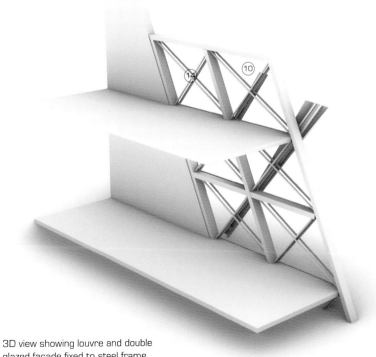

e | 3D view showing louvre and double
  | glazed facade fixed to steel frame

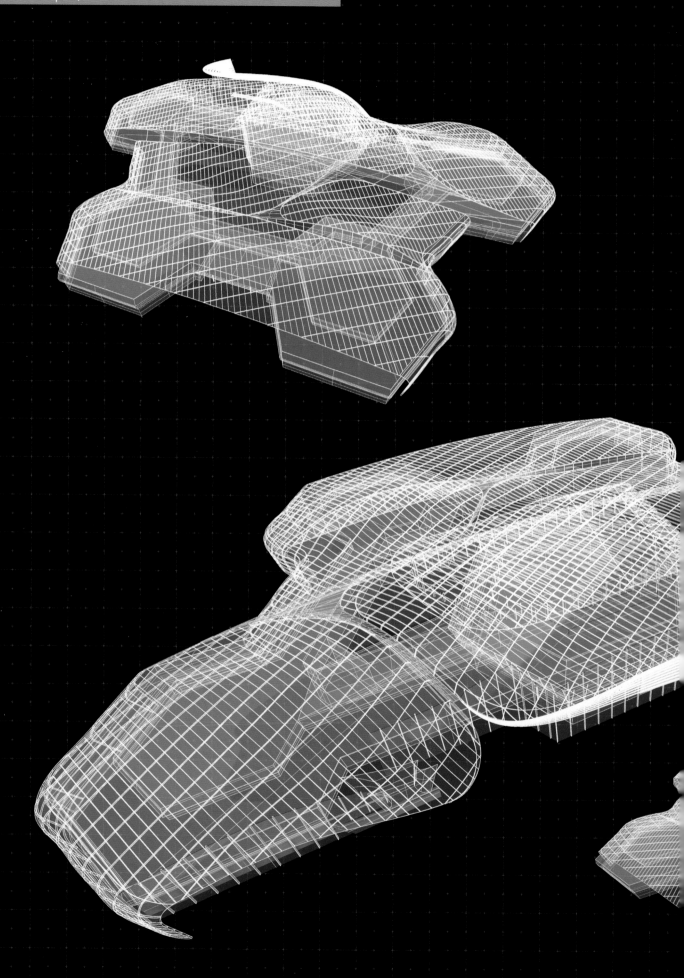

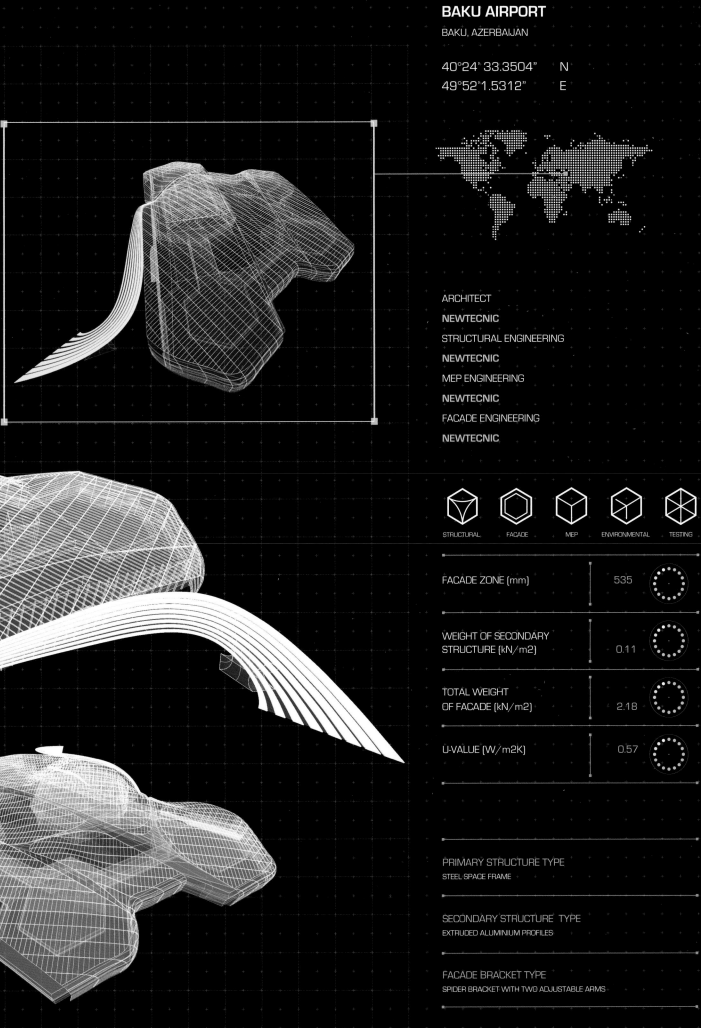

BAKU AIRPORT

BAKU, AZERBAIJAN

40°24' 33.3504"   N
49°52'1.5312"   E

ARCHITECT
NEWTECNIC
STRUCTURAL ENGINEERING
NEWTECNIC
MEP ENGINEERING
NEWTECNIC
FACADE ENGINEERING
NEWTECNIC

STRUCTURAL   FACADE   MEP   ENVIRONMENTAL   TESTING

FACADE ZONE [mm]	535	
WEIGHT OF SECONDARY STRUCTURE [kN/m2]	0.11	
TOTAL WEIGHT OF FACADE [kN/m2]	2.18	
U-VALUE [W/m2K]	0.57	

PRIMARY STRUCTURE TYPE
STEEL SPACE FRAME

SECONDARY STRUCTURE TYPE
EXTRUDED ALUMINIUM PROFILES

FACADE BRACKET TYPE
SPIDER BRACKET WITH TWO ADJUSTABLE ARMS

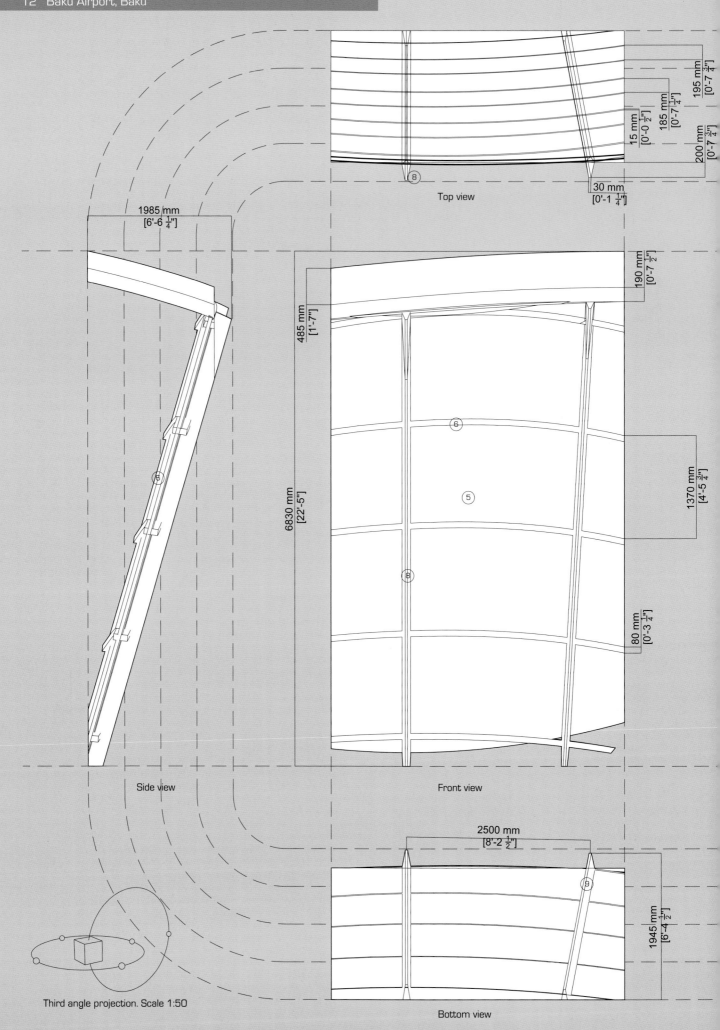

Top view

Side view

Front view

Bottom view

Third angle projection. Scale 1:50

1985 mm
[6'-6 1/4"]

15 mm
[0'-0 1/2"]

185 mm
[0'-7 1/4"]

195 mm
[0'-7 3/4"]

200 mm
[0'-7 3/4"]

30 mm
[0'-1 1/4"]

190 mm
[0'-7 1/2"]

485 mm
[1'-7"]

6830 mm
[22'-5"]

1370 mm
[4'-5 3/4"]

80 mm
[0'-3 1/4"]

2500 mm
[8'-2 1/2"]

1945 mm
[6'-4 1/2"]

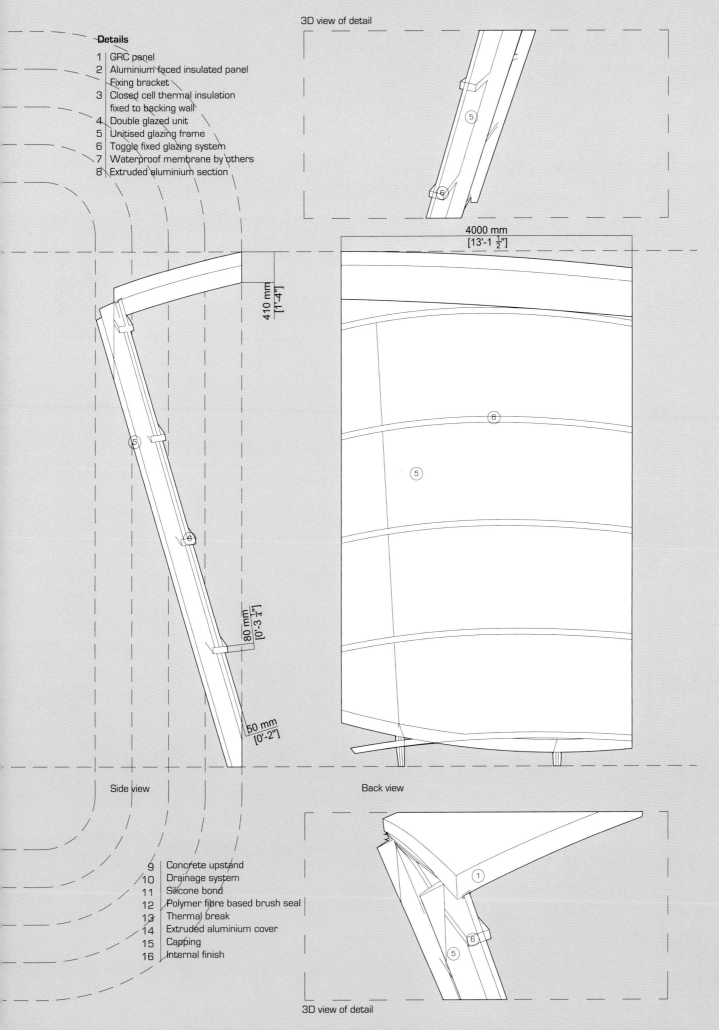

3D view of detail

Details

1 | GRC panel
2 | Aluminium faced insulated panel
Fixing bracket
3 | Closed cell thermal insulation fixed to backing wall
4 | Double glazed unit
5 | Unitised glazing frame
6 | Toggle fixed glazing system
7 | Waterproof membrane by others
8 | Extruded aluminium section

4000 mm
[13'-1 ½"]

410 mm
[1'-4"]

80 mm
[0'-3 ¼"]

50 mm
[0'-2"]

Side view

Back view

9 | Concrete upstand
10 | Drainage system
11 | Silicone bond
12 | Polymer fibre based brush seal
13 | Thermal break
14 | Extruded aluminium cover
15 | Capping
16 | Internal finish

3D view of detail

MCCS_211

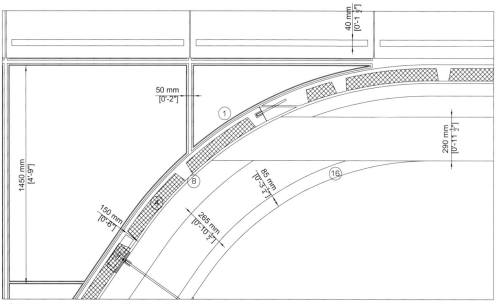

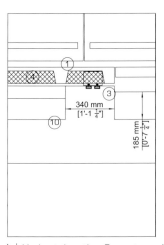

a | Horizontal section. Panel junction at corner

b | Horizontal section. Precast panel connecting to secondary steel

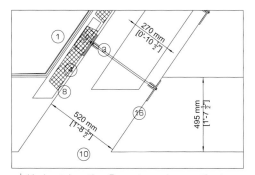

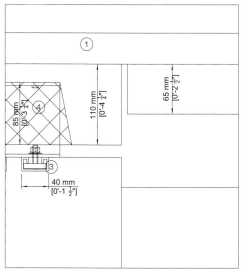

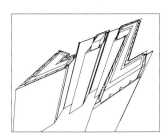

d | 3D view. Precast concrete panel with ribs

c | Horizontal section. Precast panel connecting to secondary steel

f | Vertical section. Panel connection detail

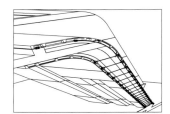

g | 3D view. Precast concrete panel with secondary structure

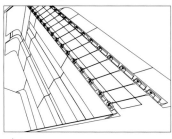

e | 3D view. Precast concrete panel with secondary structure

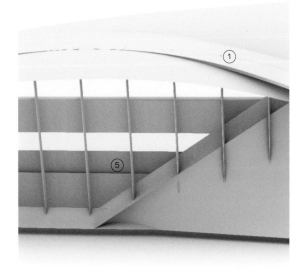

h | Typical bay. 3D view

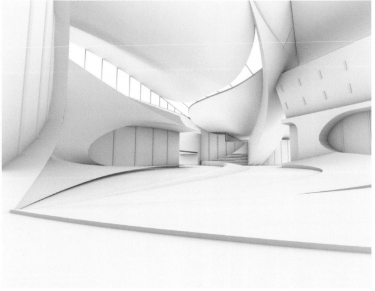

j | Interior view

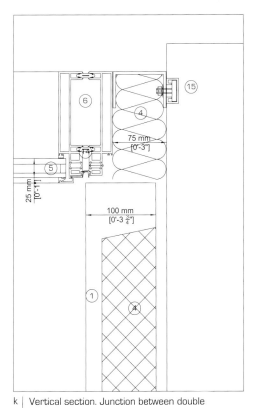

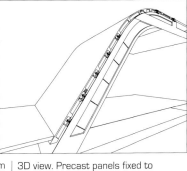

m | 3D view. Precast panels fixed to secondary structure

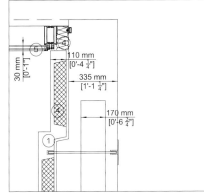

n | Horizontal section. Corner junction of double glazed unit with GRC cladding

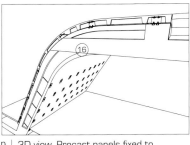

p | 3D view. Precast panels fixed to secondary structure

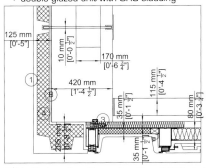

q | Vertical section. Corner junction of GRC cladding

k | Vertical section. Junction between double glazed unit and GRC panel

r | Horizontal section. Connection between GRC cladding and insulated metal panel

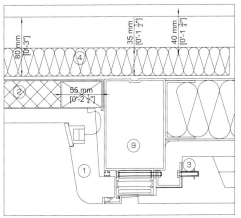

s | Horizontal section. Connection between GRC cladding and insulated metal panel

Details

1 | GRC panel
2 | Aluminium faced insulated panel
3 | Fixing bracket
4 | Closed cell thermal insulation fixed to backing wall
5 | Double glazed unit
6 | Unitised glazing frame
7 | Toggle fixed glazing system
8 | Waterproof membrane by others
9 | Extruded aluminium section
10 | Concrete upstand
11 | Drainage system
12 | Silicone bond
13 | Polymer fibre based brush seal
14 | Thermal break
15 | Extruded aluminium cover capping
16 | Internal finish

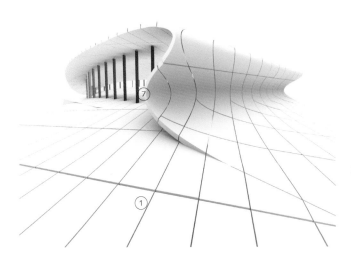

t | Exterior view

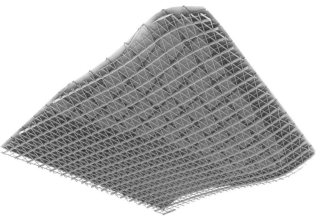

u | Typical bay. 3D view

MCCS_213

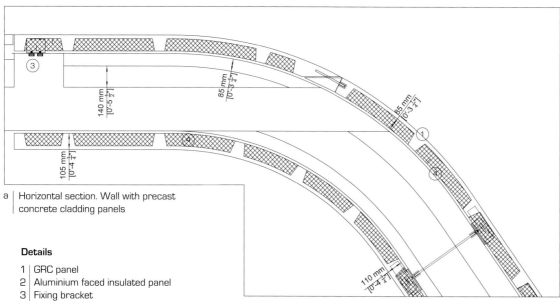

a | Horizontal section. Wall with precast
concrete cladding panels

Details

1 | GRC panel
2 | Aluminium faced insulated panel
3 | Fixing bracket
4 | Closed cell thermal insulation
fixed to backing wall
5 | Double glazed unit
6 | Unitised glazing frame
7 | Toggle fixed glazing system
8 | Waterproof membrane by others
9 | Extruded aluminium section

10 | Concrete upstand
11 | Drainage system
12 | Silicone bond
13 | Polymer fibre based brush seal
14 | Thermal break
15 | Extruded aluminium cover
capping
16 | Internal finish

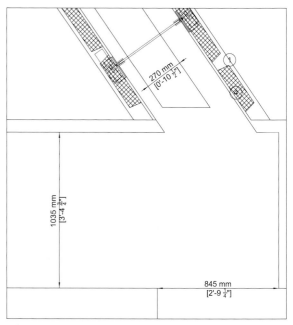

c | Horizontal section. Wall with precast concrete cladding panels

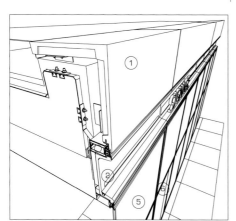

b | 3D view. Parapet

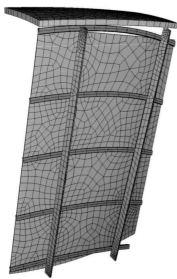

d | Finite element model of a typical bay

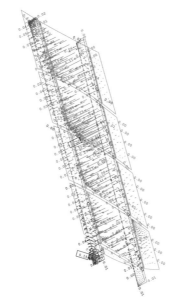

e | Nodal displacement distribution in glazing panels (mm)

Facade system	Precast GRC rainscreen with stick glazing
Facade zone	535 mm
Primary structure type	Steel space frame
Secondary structure type	Extruded aluminium profiles
Weight of secondary structure (kN/m²)	Spider bracket with two adjustable arms
Facade bracket type	0.11
Number of components in fixing system	22
Weight of facade, including secondary structure (kN/m²)	2.18

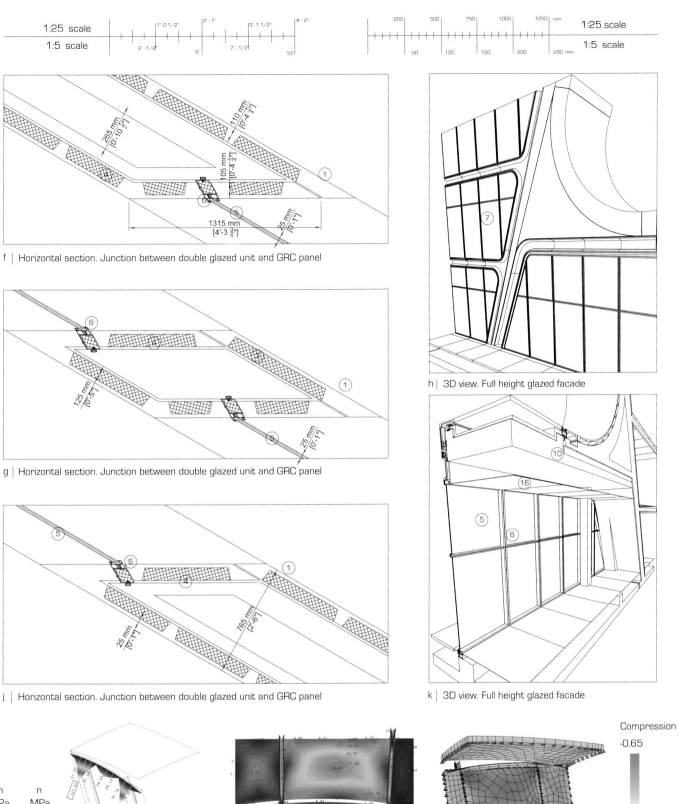

f | Horizontal section. Junction between double glazed unit and GRC panel

g | Horizontal section. Junction between double glazed unit and GRC panel

j | Horizontal section. Junction between double glazed unit and GRC panel

h | 3D view. Full height glazed facade

k | 3D view. Full height glazed facade

m | Von Mises stress distribution in steel frame [MPa]

n | Principal tension stress distribution [MPa]

p | Utilization distribution within quadrilateral elements

MCCS_215

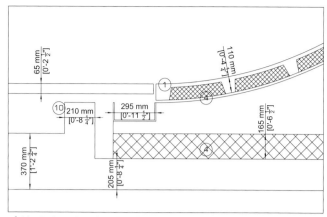

a | Vertical section. Junction of GRC panel at ground level

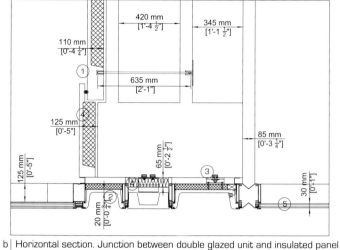

b | Horizontal section. Junction between double glazed unit and insulated panel

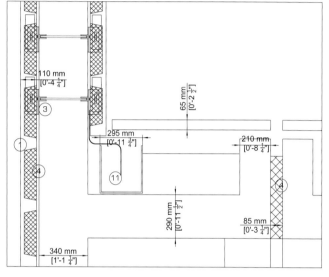

c | Vertical section. Concrete wall with GRC panel, junction with gutter

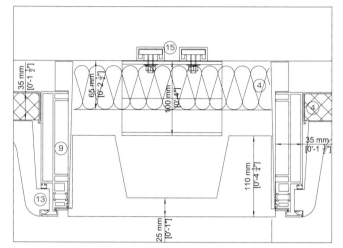

d | Horizontal section. Junction with shadow gap

Period	1 year
With shading	11.1 MWh
Without shading	14.0 MWh
Solar reduction	21 %

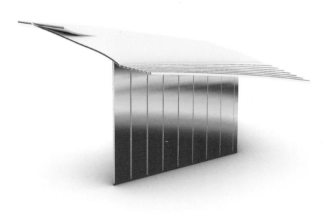

e | Annual cumulative solar radiation analysis
    on glazed facade with shading system

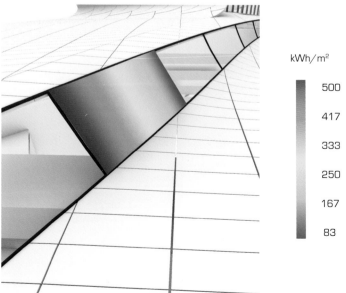

f | Annual cumulative solar radiation analysis
    on glazed facade without shading system

kWh/m²

500
417
333
250
167
83

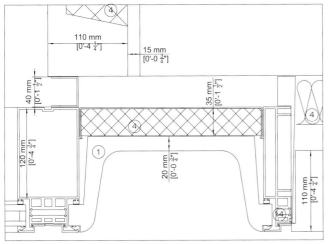

g | Horizontal section. Junction with shadow gap

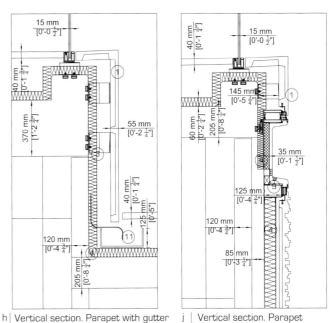

h | Vertical section. Parapet with gutter

j | Vertical section. Parapet

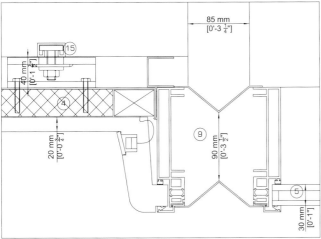

k | Horizontal section. Junction between double glazed unit and GRC panel

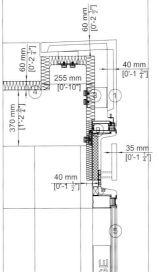

m | Vertical section. Parapet

n | Vertical section. Parapet

Details

1	GRC panel	10	Concrete upstand
2	Aluminium faced insulated panel	11	Drainage system
3	Fixing bracket	12	Silicone bond
4	Closed cell thermal insulation fixed to backing wall	13	Polymer fibre based brush seal
		14	Thermal break
5	Double glazed unit	15	Extruded aluminium cover capping
6	Unitised glazing frame		
7	Toggle fixed glazing system	16	Internal finish
8	Waterproof membrane by others		
9	Extruded aluminium section		

EXT: 40°C   INT: 22°C

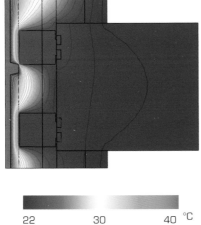

22   30   40 °C

p | Thermal performance analysis at connection with concrete slab
  | Isotherms showing temperature distribution across assembly

EXT: 0°C   INT: 22°C

0   10   22 °C

q | Thermal performance analysis at connection with concrete slab
  | Isotherms showing temperature distribution across assembly

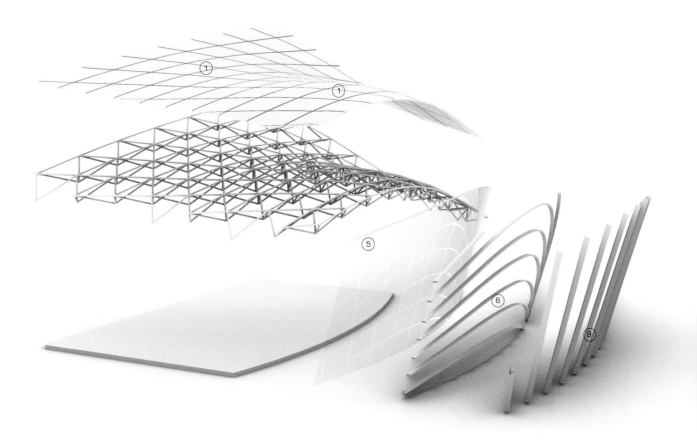

a | 3D exploded view showing floor to ceiling stick
    glazing with louvre

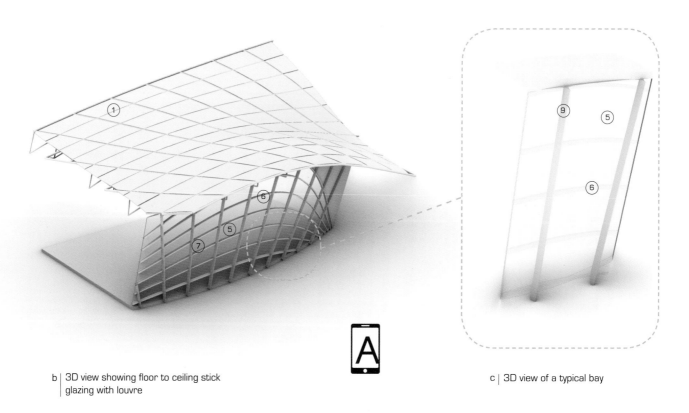

b | 3D view showing floor to ceiling stick
    glazing with louvre

c | 3D view of a typical bay

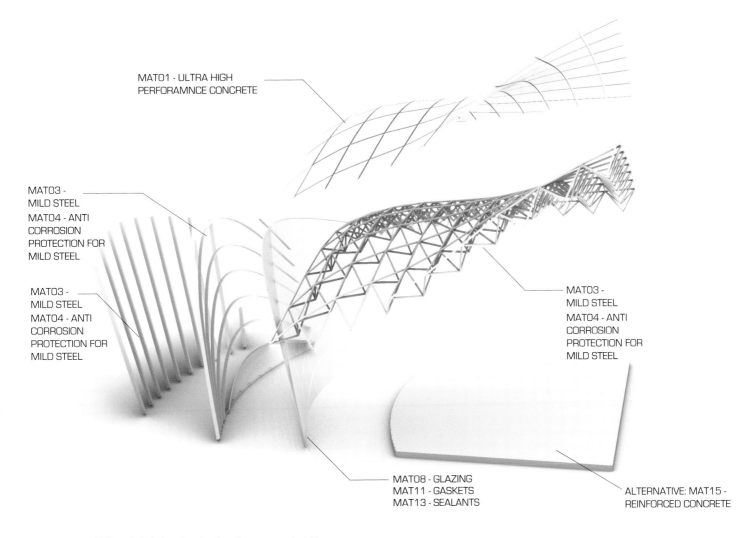

MAT01 - ULTRA HIGH
PERFORAMNCE CONCRETE

MAT03 -
MILD STEEL
MAT04 - ANTI
CORROSION
PROTECTION FOR
MILD STEEL

MAT03 -
MILD STEEL
MAT04 - ANTI
CORROSION
PROTECTION FOR
MILD STEEL

MAT03 -
MILD STEEL
MAT04 - ANTI
CORROSION
PROTECTION FOR
MILD STEEL

MAT08 - GLAZING
MAT11 - GASKETS
MAT13 - SEALANTS

ALTERNATIVE: MAT15 -
REINFORCED CONCRETE

d | 3D exploded view showing facade components with
material specification references

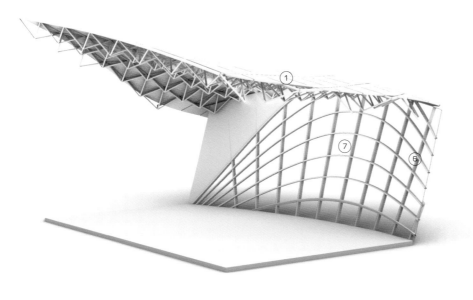

Details

1	GRC panel
2	Aluminium faced insulated panel
3	Fixing bracket
4	Closed cell thermal insulation fixed to backing wall
5	Double glazed unit
6	Unitised glazing frame
7	Toggle fixed glazing system
8	Waterproof membrane by others
9	Extruded aluminium section
10	Concrete upstand
11	Drainage system
12	Silicone bond
13	Polymer fibre based brush seal
14	Thermal break
15	Extruded aluminium cover capping
16	Internal finish

e | 3D view showing floor to ceiling stick
glazing with louvre

As an engineering design company ranked in the top three UK firms of the NCE 100 List, Newtecnic have produced a number of volumes on contemporary building technology which provide reference material for engineering and architecture students, and professionals around the world. The Modern Construction Series is published by Birkhäuser Verlag GmbH. In addition, the Facades Technical Review, from RIBA Publications was published in spring 2007.

All contents shown in this book, including photographs, have been created entirely by Newtecnic. Drawings and models were created and rendered by the Newtecnic team. The book was designed by Yasmin Watts. The text is by Andrew Watts. The text and overall content of the book was updated with contributions from Howard Tee, Ross Kunchev, Andrew Watts and Yasmin Watts.

David Marold is Acquisitions Editor at Birkhäuser Verlag GmbH in Vienna. He has driven this book from a set of basic layouts to a completed book. He has a passion for books and their design, ranging from their wider content to the quality of print paper, to the overall reader experience.

Newtecnic is an international world leader in the engineering design and architectural design of complex, highly ambitious construction projects and advanced building envelope systems. The company undertakes the engineering and architectural design of building structures, facades and MEP installations in partnership with leading international developers and large contractors.

Newtecnic is a building technology company that provides paths to construction to create a new generation of building forms and internal spaces. The company applies its own technologies using state-of-the-art project management practices, supported by high levels of innovation generated through cutting-edge research at leading universities. The company is a champion of near-future design, achieved through extensive rapid prototyping and in-depth construction simulations.

Founded in 2003, Newtecnic's design professionals team is completely and solely dedicated to the design and engineering of structures, facades and MEP. In partnership with the Engineering Departments of Cambridge University and the University of Houston. Newtecnic's R&D team analyses, develops, tests, validates and specifies new building products, technologies and methods. Newtecnic is certified for the ISO 9001 and ISO 27001 quality standards.

Newtecnic has offices in the US, the UK, Saudi Arabia, UAE and Hong Kong. The company is owned, directed and managed by long-established and experienced engineers and architects.

The building engineering design of Newtecnic is based on strong technical and visual concepts that are supported by analysis, modelling, geometry and coordination. Newtecnic's ability to develop design solutions iteratively within short time frames is crucial in delivering complex building projects on time and budget. Newtecnic's design work is based on an intensive use of the latest digital tools, such as Catia, Rhino, Revit, Maya, Sofistik, SAP2000, Comsol Multiphysics and Phoenics. The use of these tools links design to digital manufacturing as used by building contractors and fabricators.

Led by author Andrew Watts, Newtecnic is a world-leading firm of engineer-architects, with the Modern Construction series forming an essential part of their current work and research. The Newtecnic approach, based on research from first principles, allows the company to achieve design excellence for the complete building, from concept to production information, including engineering and architectural design for structure, facades and the internal environment. With 3D BIM, Newtecnic designs models that become highly evolved during the design process. Components of these BIM models, with accompanying text and images to illustrate design processes, form the basis of Modern Construction Envelopes. The engineering and architectural design skills of Newtecnic allows the firm to communicate, through the Modern Construction series, the key issues of 21st century building engineering and design. Newtecnic are holders of *The Queen's Award for Enterprise* and is ranked in the top three of *New Civil Engineer 100 Companies of the Year 2019*.

Newtecnic see the Modern Construction series of textbooks setting a legacy of technical expertise becoming available to the global engineering community.

Andrew Watts is the author of the Modern Construction series of textbooks. He is an engineer-architect who specialises in the engineering and architectural design of large-scale complex buildings. Andrew is a Fellow of three UK engineering institutions which represent his set of interests in engineering design: structures with the Institution of Civil Engineers; facades with the Institution of Engineering Designers; mechanical and electrical assemblies with the Institution of Engineering and Technology. He holds chartorships in the UK for engineering and for architecture from the Institution of Engineering Designers and the Royal Institute of British Architects. In the US, where he is based in Texas, Andrew is a member of the American Institute of Architects and the American Society of Civil Engineers.

Before establishing Newtecnic, Andrew and Yasmin Watts worked extensively both in the UK and abroad. During this time they were involved in a range of significant projects including Federation Square, Melbourne with LAB Architects, the Millennium Bridge, London, for Foster and Partners, Euralille and Institut du Monde Arabe, Paris for Jean Nouvel, and Cite Internationale, Lyon and the New Caledonia Cultural Centre for Renzo Piano Building Workshop. They have produced a number of volumes on contemporary building technology for students and professionals.

The following bibliography is suggested for further reading, based on the themes of the introductory essays.

Emerging technologies
Constructing Architecture: Materials, Processes, Structures; a Handbook by Andrea Deplazes
Birkhäuser, 2013

Facade Construction Manual
Thomas Herzog / Roland Krippner / Werner Lang
Birkhäuser, Edition Detail, 2012

Modern Construction Series by Andrew Watts: Modern Construction Handbook, Modern Construction Envelopes, Modern Construction Facades, Modern Construction Roofs,
Springer / Ambra / Birkhäuser, 2001–2016

Design method
Change by Design
Tim Brown
Harper Collins, 2009

Design Engineering: A Manual for Enhanced Creativity
W. Ernst Eder, Stanislav Hosnedl
CRC Press, 2008

Engineering Design: A Systematic Approach, Edition 3
Gerhard Pahl, W. Beitz, Jörg Feldhusen, Karl-Heinrich Grote
Springer, 2007

Handbook of Reliability, Availability, Maintainability and Safety in Engineering Design
Rudolph Frederick Stapelberg
Springer, 2009

The Future of Design Methodology
Herbert Birkhofer
Springer, 2011

The Ten Faces of Innovation
Tom Kelley
Profile Books, 2006

Project management
Agile Management: Leadership in an Agile Environment
Ángel Medinilla
Springer, 2012

Managing Agile
Alan Moran
Springer, 2015

Project Management for Environmental, Construction and Manufacturing Engineers
Nolberto Munier
Springer, 2013

Systems Engineering Agile Design Methodologies
James A. Crowder, Shelli A. Friess
Springer, 2013

When Professionals Have to Lead
Thomas J DeLong
Harvard Business School Press, 2007

Analysis and scientific foundations
Finite Element Analysis and Design of Metal Structures
Ehab Ellobody, Ran Feng, Ben Young
Elsevier, 2013

Introduction to Finite and Spectral Element Methods Using MATLAB, Second Edition: Edition 2
Constantine Pozrikidis
CRC Press, 2014

Introduction to Theoretical and Computational Fluid Dynamics: Edition 2
Constantine Pozrikidis
Oxford University Press, 2011

MATLAB Codes for Finite Element Analysis: Solids and Structures
A. J. M. Ferreira
Springer Science & Business Media, 2008

Multiphysics Modeling with Finite Element Methods
William B J Zimmerman
World Scientific, 2006

Design implementation and research method
Building Engineering and Systems Design
Frederick S Merritt, James Ambrose
Springer, 2012

Design Engineering Manual
Mike Tooley
Elsevier, 2010

Modern Construction, Lean Project Delivery and Integrated Practices
Lincoln H Forbes, Syed M Ahmed
Taylor and Francis, 2011

Project Quality Management, Critical Success Factors for Buildings
Sui Pheng Low, Joy Ong
Springer, 2014

Standards of Practice in Construction Specifying
Dennis J Hall, Nina M Giglio
Wiley, 2013

Sustainability in Engineering Design and Construction
J K Yates, Daniel Castro-Lacouture
Taylor and Francis, 2016

Author
Andrew Watts
London, England

Acquisitions Editor: David Marold, Birkhäuser Verlag, Vienna, Austria
Project and Production Editor: Angelika Heller, Birkhäuser Verlag, Vienna, Austria

Layout and Cover Design: Yasmin Watts, London, England
Cover image: Newtecnic Ltd
Proofreading: Alun Brown, Vienna, Austria
Printing and binding: Holzhausen Druck GmbH, Wolkersdorf, Austria

Library of Congress Control Number: 2018957755

Bibliographic information published by the German National Library
The German National Library lists this publication in the Deutsche Nationalbibliografie; detailed bibliographic data are available on the Internet at http://dnb.dnb.de

ISBN 978-3-0356-1771-9 Hardcover edition
ISBN 978-3-0356-1772-6 Softcover edition
e-ISBN 978-3-0356-1779-5

© 2019 Birkhäuser Verlag GmbH, Basel
P.O. Box 44, 4009 Basel, Switzerland
Part of Walter de Gruyter GmbH, Berlin/Boston

98765432   www.birkhauser.com

This book is augmented, so install the free Artivive app, and hold your smartphone over the marked 3D drawings within. Depending on your internet connection, you may be charged by your internet service provider.

1. Install the
Artivive app

2. Look for the Artivive images
marked with the icon

3. Hold your smartphone
over the image